Southern Literary Studies
Fred Hobson, Editor

The Evolving Self
in the Novels
of Gail Godwin

The Evolving Self
in the Novels
of Gail Godwin

Lihong Xie

Louisiana State University Press
Baton Rouge and London

Designer: Glynnis Phoebe
Typeface: Sabon
Typesetter: Moran Printing, Inc.
Printer and Binder: Thomson-Shore, Inc.

Library of Congress Cataloging-in-Publication Data

Xie, Lihong, date.
    The evolving self in the novels of Gail Godwin   /   Lihong Xie.
        p.   cm. — (Southern literary studies)
    Includes bibliographical references and index.
    ISBN 0-8071-1924-5 (cl)
    1. Godwin, Gail—Criticism and interpretation.   2. Feminism and
literature—Southern States—History—20th century.   3. Women and
literature—Southern States—History—20th century.   4. Self in
literature. I. Title. II. Series.
PS3557.O315Z97   1995
813'.54—dc20   94-30115
                                                  CIP

The author is grateful to Gail Godwin for permission to quote from her novels.
    Quotations from *The Perfectionists*, by Gail Godwin, copyright © 1970 by Gail
Godwin, are reprinted by permission of John Hawkins & Associates, Inc.
    Excerpts from *Glass People* by Gail Godwin, copyright © 1972 by Gail Godwin, are
reprinted by permission of Alfred A. Knopf, Inc. Excerpts from *The Odd Woman* by Gail
Godwin, copyright © 1974 by Gail Godwin, are reprinted by permission of Alfred A.
Knopf, Inc. Excerpts from *Violet Clay* by Gail Godwin, copyright © 1978 by Gail Godwin,
are reprinted by permission of Alfred A. Knopf, Inc.
    The author thanks Viking Penguin for permission to quote from the following works:
From *The Finishing School* by Gail Godwin. Copyright © 1984 by Gail Godwin. Used by
permission of Viking Penguin, a division of Penguin Books USA Inc. From *A Mother and
Two Daughters* by Gail Godwin. Copyright © 1982 by Gail Godwin. Used by permission of
Viking Penguin, a division of Penguin Books USA Inc.
    Excerpts from *A Southern Family*, © 1987, by Gail Godwin, and *Father Melancholy's
Daughter*, © 1991, by Gail Godwin, are reprinted by permission of William Morrow &
Company, Inc.
    Quotations from *Father Melancholy's Daughter*, by Gail Godwin, Penguin Books, 1992,
first published in the United Kingdom by André Deutsch, copyright © Gail Godwin, 1991,
are reproduced by permission of Penguin Books Ltd.

The paper in this book meets the guidelines for permanence and durability of the
Committee on Production Guidelines for Book Longevity of the Council on Library
Resources. ∞

To my beloved father and mother,
Xie Yun
and
Guo Lining

Contents

Preface

One of the most articulate writers on the contemporary literary scene to pursue the idea of the self, Gail Godwin (1937–) has developed, over the past two decades, a mature, dynamic vision of the self rendered with increasing artistic power. She began, in *The Perfectionists* (1970) and *Glass People* (1972), with heroines who, though constrained by the patriarchal text of marriage, search for an independent identity. Turning to unmarried heroines striving to define themselves outside the cultural script of womanhood, she explores in *The Odd Woman* (1974), *Violet Clay* (1978), and *The Finishing School* (1984) the crucial role of memory and narrative restructuring in the heroines' solitary struggle for selfhood. In *A Mother and Two Daughters* (1982) and *A Southern Family* (1987), she breaks away from the limitations of a single point of view, creating multiple characters whose individual struggles for identity become embedded in the dialogic interplay of diverse voices. In her most recent work, *Father Melancholy's Daughter* (1991), Godwin further extends the concept of an evolving self by exploring the spiritual aspects of becoming, integrating an individual's quest for identity and the larger drama of humanity's struggle for coherence and meaning.

Contesting the modernist abandonment and the postmodern deconstruction of the self, Godwin creates in her fiction an evolving self that mediates between traditional humanists' rigid presumptions of a centered self and modernists' and postmodernists' radical denial of selfhood. Fluid and in-process, Godwin's evolving self *moves* toward a relatively centered position through decentering dialogic activities, *becomes* more coherent through constant self-examination, *assumes* autonomy from deliberate exercise of memory and interpretive power, *achieves* greater degrees of authenticity by means of continuous self-redefinition. Transforming the concept of self from one of *essence* into one of *process*, Godwin enables her heroines to affirm the humanist ideal in the context of a fragmented modern world that has made the conditions of selfhood problematic. Stressing the search for the self and probing various dimensions of female development—family, place, memory, mother-daughter relationships, female networks—Godwin makes significant contributions toward the making of a contemporary Bildungsroman—the

revitalization and profound transformation of a traditional male genre gradually slipping into self-parody.

This volume examines Godwin's exploration and construction of a self-in-the-becoming. Feminist criticism of fiction in general and of contemporary Bildungsromane in particular illuminates Godwin's representations of female development; its insistence on process, conflict, and plurality underscores Godwin's portrayal of women's complex psychological struggle to seek strong, personal identities. Mikhail Bakhtin's theory of the dialogic imagination, on the other hand, informs my analyses of Godwin's later work—her more expansive and socially informed "major-key" novels, with increasing emphasis on the diversity of individual voices and the way intense dialogue shapes social relations and individual development.

I first became interested in Gail Godwin's work through Lynne Waldeland, who introduced me to *The Finishing School*. I was captivated by Godwin's engrossing narrative, her fascinating characters, and, more than anything else, the thematic thrust of the novel—the idea of persistent struggle for and continuous growth toward female self-definition. Little had been published on Godwin's work while I was completing the study. Consequently, I had both the delight of freely exploring her fictional territory and the frustration of groping for direction. As my mentor and dissertation adviser, Mary Suzanne Schriber provided invaluable assistance, discussing specific thematic and narrative concerns with me and urging me to consider larger theoretical issues. She commented extensively and intensively on successive drafts, suggesting ways to reinforce my arguments and pushing me to sharpen what I was struggling to say. I am grateful to her for her encouragement, support, and critical expertise.

Robert T. Self also provided perceptive critique of my analysis. In particular, he pointed out the changing concepts of the self over time, thus clarifying some theoretical issues I had to grapple with in formulating an analytical framework for my study. Rosalie Hewitt read the drafts with enthusiasm and insight, discussing with me not only specific details in Godwin's novels but also the author's narrative strategies. Sean Shesgreen and David Bywaters read a version of the study, suggesting ways to tighten the theoretical chapter and making fine stylistic suggestions throughout. James Mellard read a revised version and made insightful comments about possibilities for further revision.

Elizabeth Fox-Genovese of Emory University offered detailed, insightful criticism of my writing, sharing with me her incomparable knowledge of southern literature in general and of Gail Godwin in particular. James Woodress of the University of California at Davis, who first wrote me more than a decade ago on the subject of Willa Cather and has since become my friend and mentor, provided continuous support in many respects, including reading and commenting on a draft of the study. Other friends of mine, particularly Rebecca Rice and Lisa Chase Bywaters, also shared my interest in Godwin; they read her novels and shared with me their impressions of her writing. And I thank Lois Geehr for expertly copy-editing the manuscript.

I extend special thanks to Gail Godwin, with whom I have continued a fruitful dialogue for the past few years. My correspondence with her has been uniformly positive and helpful: she has responded to my questions with enthusiasm and warmth and has shared with me valuable information about her writing. In 1990, I had the opportunity to meet her in person, enjoying her hospitality and interviewing her about her work. Her friendship and support have helped bring this project to closure.

My gratitude goes a long way back across the Pacific Ocean to those who taught me English—my former teachers in Beijing University, Beijing, China. Together, they guided me step-by-step into the world of literary imagination and trained my aesthetic sensitivity for artistic appreciation. Furthermore, they set a fine example of intellectual integrity and sound scholarship. I thank them all, especially Professors Zhao Luorui, Li Funing, Lin Yunyin, Zhao Shaoxiong, Zhou Shanfeng, and the late Professor Yang Zhouhan, for their share in my intellectual and personal growth.

Words do not suffice to express my deep love for and gratitude to my family. My parents wrote me often, sending their abiding love and support from thousands of miles afar. Whatever I have accomplished I owe first of all to them, for they have taught me how to love deeply, live honestly, and work diligently. This book, therefore, is dedicated to my father, Xie Yun, and my mother, Guo Lining, with love, affection, and respect. My three sisters, Xie Jinhong, Xie Zhihong, and Xie Youhong, have been an indispensable source of comfort and support. They have shared their lives with me, constantly reinforcing my sense of the joyous, loving, and mysterious bond of sisterhood.

I thank my husband, Allan Kulikoff, who has lived this work with me,

Introduction

In a compelling autobiographical essay, Gail Godwin vividly evokes a heroine who, as "a modern woman living in a high-pressured world abuzz with too many contradictory messages," strives to be the author of her own story, "cutting her unique swath through the landscape of her times, adding her particular style and contribution to the great myth of humanity." The landscape of her times, Godwin points out, is believed by many to be one of utter fragmentation—without meaning, without pattern, without "a consistent, continuous self." "Fashionable cynics" will tell Godwin's heroine that "there is no *self:* just impulses, reflexes, unpredictable causes and effects; just statistics or demographics or determinism or behaviorism." They will tell her that her so-called existence "rains down on [her] as piecemeal and as randomly as hailstones, leaving the memory and the hurt of the blow but melting back into nothingness before [she] can assemble the evidence into any meaningful pattern." They will tell her with great relish that the concept of a "unique, individual character building an examined life out of past accomplishments and mistakes, is as dated, as dead, as the heroes in Victorian novels."

But her heroine, Godwin declares, refuses to "let the fashionable cynics talk her out of taking herself seriously." Carrying around a self-image "as the protagonist in the context of [her] own unfolding story," Godwin's heroine accepts the task of "keeping track of where she's been and where she wants to go"; conscious of the fragmented world in which she lives, she deliberately *"makes connections* between past and present, between the lives of others and the life she wants to make for herself." She discovers "who she is and what she is good for through a process of building on her successful chapters and learning from . . . her discreditable ones." In the process of creating the plots of her life, she gives it "the shape of a good, rich novel"[1]—broad, profound,

---

1. Gail Godwin, "How to Be the Heroine of Your Own Life," *Cosmopolitan*, March, 1988, pp. 194, 196–97, 227.

and complex, "one that would tempt the novelist to explore it at the risk of getting lost, rather than editing any of it or shutting part of it behind doors."[2]

The "heroine-in-progress" that Godwin evokes in her essay describes the many fictional heroines she has created in her novels. Living in an age when "fragmentation" is a fashionable word; when "meaning," "pattern," "certainty," "consistency," and "continuity" have either lost their resonance or, if they have any at all, suggest naïveté, innocence, or blind faith, Godwin's questing heroines engage themselves in a continuing struggle to come to grips with the question of who they are. Take Jane Clifford, for instance, the protagonist in *The Odd Woman*. In face of the modern disintegration of the self and the accelerating "derangements" of contemporary life, Jane expresses her frustration and skepticism: "Sometimes, lately, she wondered if the concept of the 'self' was a myth which had died with the nineteenth century. . . . Was there, then—had there ever been—such a thing as a basic personality, or was that only a bygone literary convention? Could there exist a true, pure 'character' who was nobody but himself—subject, of course, to the usual accidents of existence—but capable of subordinating his (her) terrain as he progressed through time and space, cutting a swath of chapters that would be meaningful in retrospect?"[3]

Violet Clay, the title character of Godwin's fourth novel, successfully achieves artistic self-definition. In her triumphant painting "Suspended Woman," she creates a nude female body, strong and supple, suspended in radiant October morning light, in "her own possibilities" and "vibrant dimensions."[4] Fearing more than death and old age in the atrophy of the self, Cate Strickland, in *A Mother and Two Daughters*, struggles to hold onto her own history, past and future, and to stay in touch with what she thinks of as her best, imaginative self—one that yearns for the intensity of experience, for the forward motion of questing and becoming. Justin Stokes, in *The Finishing School*, makes memory a creative means of self-renewal, revitalizing herself against congealing into a "final" self. Clare Campion, the novelist in *A Southern Family*, passionately defends her belief in the validity of the self: "Yes, damn my nervous

2. Gail Godwin, "Towards a Fully Human Heroine: Some Worknotes," *Harvard Advocate*, CVI (Winter, 1973), 28.

3. Gail Godwin, *The Odd Woman* (New York, 1974), 21.

4. Gail Godwin, *Violet Clay* (New York, 1978), 324.

curtsy to fashionable theories, I still believe there exists a bedrock reality of the self." Julia Lowndes Richardson, Clare's close friend, also seeks a positive connection between self and history: "Her forte, she liked to think, was the human essence: the way, through the study of other lives, however remote in time and place and circumstance, you could locate (and then better understand) aspects of the self. Not just the personal self, but the vast, extended Self that used history to become conscious of what it was . . . and could be."[5]

Despite the loss of the self in modern literature and art, Godwin persistently constructs positive, compelling images of an evolving self striving for fulfillment in a world that has made the conditions of selfhood problematic.[6] Conscious of the instabilities of modern history—mass culture, world wars, totalitarian governments, economic insecurity, and scientific knowledge—that have called meaning, pattern, values, and efficacy into question, Godwin makes the search for selfhood a central theme of her fiction, tenaciously holding onto the possibilities of coherent, mature, and meaningful self-definition, perhaps with greater intensity precisely because of the modernist and postmodernist challenge to the traditional notion of a centered self. In order to better understand and assess Godwin's work, it is necessary to place it in the context of the tensions between a humanist conception of an efficacious, unified self and the modernist perception of a fragmentary, disintegrated self—tensions further compounded by the postmodern deconstruction of the self. Feminist perspectives on the subject on the one hand and Mikhail Bakhtin's dialogic concept of language on the other mediate between the opposition of coherent egos and problematic social identities, and are therefore of crucial theoretical importance to my analyses of Godwin's work. Finally, the development and transformation of the Bildungsroman as a genre, with the maturing of the self at its thematic center, bears significantly on our understanding of Godwin's contribution toward the making of a contemporary Bildungsroman.

5. Gail Godwin, *A Southern Family* (New York, 1987), 385, 40.
6. Wylie Sypher's book *Loss of the Self in Modern Literature and Art* (New York, 1962) traces the changing concepts of the self from the postromantic period to the modern era.

Gail Godwin and the Search for Self

Writing about the quest for selfhood at a time when, according to Jane
Flax, "Western culture is in the middle of a fundamental transformation,"
Godwin invites us to situate her fiction within the larger intellectual context
of modernism.[7] Throughout the twentieth century, many of the assumptions upon which the Western intellectual tradition is based have come under
attack by various schools of modernist and postmodern thought and literature (existentialism, structuralism, poststructuralism, and feminism, for instance). One of the most problematized concepts in current intellectual discourses is the humanist concept of a unified, centered self. From their radically
different perspectives, modernist and postmodernist thinkers, writers, artists,
and critics have posited a disintegrated, fragmented, or "decentered" self in
place of the centered, unified self of traditional humanism.[8]

Bourgeois humanist ideology presumed a rational, unified, autonomous,
and centered self capable of making choices and largely in control of its
own actions and destiny. Beginning with Descartes, Hobbes, and Locke and
sustained by later Enlightenment rationalists, these ideas prevailed in Western
thought until the late nineteenth century. The world begins with individuals, humanists argued, not with some larger social unit; each individual self,
as the "bearer of a consciousness" in dialectical opposition to the external
world,[9] has its own unique subjectivity. Defining everything outside of itself
as the "object of its thinking power,"[10] consciousness assumes the privileged
status as the source of knowledge, the coherent center of meaning and action.
At the intersection of each individual's unique subjectivity and the common
epistemological privilege shared by all individuals, bourgeois humanist ideology builds its "idea of the sovereign self," which exists outside of any spe-

7. Jane Flax, "Postmodernism and Gender Relations in Feminist Theory," in *Feminist Theory
in Practice and Process,* ed. Micheline R. Malson *et al.* (Chicago, 1989), 51.

8. In the past few decades, structuralists and poststructuralists (*e.g.,* Emile Benveniste, Jacques
Lacan, Jacques Derrida, Michel Foucault, and Roland Barthes) have challenged the humanist
notion of a centered, unified self from even more radical perspectives, replacing the concept of
the self with that of the subject.

9. Paul Smith, *Discerning the Subject* (Minneapolis, 1988), xxvii.

10. J. Hillis Miller, *Poets of Reality: Six Twentieth-Century Writers* (Cambridge, Mass.,
1965), 3.

cific time or place.[11] The search for this stable, unique, and authentic core of being—the cohesive and unified self—stands, as we will see, at the center of the traditional Bildungsroman.

As the world entered the twentieth century, this sovereign self became increasingly tenuous. Modern science and technology, the chaos and irrationality of world wars, and the overwhelming sense of disjunction led to a crisis of belief, a crisis of identity. The death of God, the loss of meaning and reason, the failure of civilization, and the disintegration of the self became some of the most frequently recurring literary themes of the modernist period, indicating a radical break from the traditional humanist conceptions of a knowable, verifiable reality, of a self in control of its own action and destiny. Since T. S. Eliot's J. Alfred Prufrock, an insignificant, metaphorically shrunken man without a capacity to choose, images of antiheroes—modern men plagued by a profound crisis of identity and groping aimlessly in the thick of existential despair—have prevailed in twentieth-century literature.

The loss of the self in modernist thought and literature continued into the second half of the twentieth century, taking on an entirely different philosophical universe and conceptual frameworks in the works of postmodern theorists. Today, the critique of the concept of an autonomous, centered self is a focal point in many areas of contemporary intellectual discourse. From radically different perspectives, structuralists, poststructuralists, and some schools of feminists alike contest the humanists' man-centered view of the world. Beginning with Saussure and post-Saussurean linguists; developed by Jacques Lacan's psychoanalytical theories; and used in literary deconstruction, Marxist critiques of capitalism, and radical feminist thinking; contemporary discourses have sought to subvert the primacy of individual consciousness and expose the transparency of self-identity. Replacing the term *self* with *subject*, theorists argue that subjectivity does not occupy the presumed, privileged position that humanism advanced. Rather, subjectivity is constructed in language and discourse. Through linguistic differentiation, these theorists claim, an individual speaker acquires a sense of himself as a subject: only "by referring to himself as *I* in his discourse" does the speaker posit himself as a subject. The "basis of

11. Philip Rice and Patricia Waugh, eds., *Modern Literary Theory: A Reader* (London, 1989), 119.

subjectivity," therefore, "is in the exercise of language."[12] "I" construct my "self" in language acts and language constitutes "me."

Emphasis on language and representation characterizes much of contemporary writing on the construction of subjectivity. Jacques Lacan, for instance, has been much cited as a theoretical basis for decentering the privileged, unified self of bourgeois humanism. His theory of the "mirror stage," contemporary theorists contend, particularly subverts the primacy of a preexisting, harmonious, unified consciousness.[13] Louis Althusser's theory of the ideological interpellation, on the other hand, has also been used to emphasize the construction of subjectivity in language and discourse. According to Althusser, contemporary theorists point out, ideology, not consciousness, functions to constitute "*concrete individuals as subjects.*" Far from being the center of meaning and source of subjectivity, consciousness is, in Elizabeth Grosz's words, "a distorted reflection of real relations."[14] Where traditional humanists presume a centered, coherent self, contemporary theorists see a range of subject-positions from which the individual derives a sense of self, one that is invariably contradictory, conflicted, and continuously shifting, rather than unitary and harmonious.

The influence of Lacan's psychoanalytical paradigm and Althusser's Marxist sociological perspective indicates the degree to which the concept of self has come under radical attack from poststructuralists. Bourgeois humanists championed a classical conception of the self that works efficaciously with rea-

12. Emile Benveniste, *Problems in General Linguistics* (Miami, 1971), 225–26.

13. Jacques Lacan (*Écrits, A Selection,* trans. Alan Sheridan [New York, 1977], 1–7) argues that the infant has no conception of itself as a subject in dialectic relationship to the object, the other. When the infant reaches the mirror stage, it becomes capable of recognizing itself as separate from the outside world. This distinct sense of self, however, is illusory because it is, in Catherine Belsey's words, "an identification with an 'imaginary' unitary and autonomous self." Full subjectivity does not develop until the child begins to speak, learning to differentiate between and identify with various subject-positions, such as "I," "you," "she," and "he." Also see Catherine Belsey, "Constructing the Subject: Deconstructing the Text," in *Feminist Criticism and Social Change: Sex, Class, and Race in Literature and Culture,* ed. Judith Newton and Deborah Rosenfelt (New York, 1985), 48; Rice and Waugh, eds., *Modern Literary Theory,* 120.

14. Louis Althusser, *Lenin and Philosophy and Other Essays,* trans. Ben N. Brewster (New York, 1971), 171; Elizabeth Grosz, *Sexual Subversions: Three French Feminists* (Sydney, 1989), 12.

son in a knowable universe, as well as a romantic conception of the self that works in the realm of the imagination, to achieve some moral, ethical, or aesthetic meaning and order. The increasing fragmentation of the twentieth-century world has bred an existential despair over the loss of that rational or romantic self, evoking in its place a modernist self for whom meaning, order, and efficacy are called into question. In the more radical postmodern deconstruction of the self, one sees an almost unbridgeable space between the self as a rational being capable of knowing and the subject as an "empty 'place' where many selves come to mingle and depart," split, fragmentary, unstable, alienated.[15] This postmodern vision of utter disjunction and fragmentation leaves little room for any coherence and unity, for a self that grows as a discrete thinking individual, however constrained and fragmented.

Feminist scholars, for whom "the cultural construction of subjectivity" has become a central issue,[16] view the poststructuralist position on the self with much ambiguity, caution, and division. French feminists are among those who have most relentlessly challenged the man-centered humanist ideology; in contrast, some British and American theorists have worked toward a feminist reformulation of the concept of the self.[17] Drawing on Althusser's theory of ideology and post-Saussurean linguistic theories, Catherine Belsey defines subjectivity (what humanists would call the "self") as a "matrix" of often inconsistent, incompatible, or contradictory "subject-positions," not the coherent center in the humanist paradigm. Identity, in Belsey's view, is "perpetually in the process of construction," a result of intense negotiation among conflicting subject-positions through both internal and psychological as well as external and social processes.[18]

Belsey's work on subjectivity points to the eclectic, pluralistic nature of feminist thinking. Feminism, Jane Flax argues, is part of that postmodern "deconstructive" discourse that seeks "to distance us from and make us skeptical about beliefs concerning truth, knowledge, power, the self, and language

15. Ihab Hassan, "Prometheus as Performer: Toward a Posthumanist Culture?" *Georgia Review*, XXXI (1977), 845.

16. Belsey, "Constructing the Subject," 45.

17. Some of the most important French feminists are Julia Kristeva, Hélène Cixous, and Luce Irigaray.

18. Belsey, "Constructing the Subject," 45–50.

that are often taken for granted within and serve as legitimation for contemporary Western culture." Feminist scholars such as Jane Flax, Catherine Belsey, and Jean Grimshaw caution us that by placing a coherent, autonomous, unified female subject at the center of meaning and action, as much recent fiction of female development and criticism of these works do, women authors and critics embed their critique of a male-dominated ideology and literary tradition in the very intellectual frameworks and language they attempt to subvert. Jean Grimshaw, for instance, contests the way some feminists reconceptualize "autonomy" by seeing an authentic, inner female self behind the conditioned and nonautonomous female self victimized by patriarchy. To define autonomy and authenticity "as originating in some way from *within* the self" and perceive female development in terms of a "recovery" or "discovery" of that "untainted" core of being, Grimshaw argues, leads to "an overmonolithic account of male power" and a failure to consider the ways sisterhood and female friendship have sustained women's individual development.[19]

Notwithstanding challenges to the humanist notion of a centered, unified self, many feminist critics insist on the search for and the assertion of a female self, finding it necessary, in Judith Kegan Gardiner's words, "to defend the very idea of a female subject."[20] In the internal logic of humanist ideology, they see a possibility to "conceptualise the need women have experienced for [a] greater degree of autonomy and control, for overcoming the fragmentation and contradictions in their lives, and for a capacity for self-definition."[21] In bourgeois society women have never enjoyed full rights as individuals, either in theory or in practice; they have lacked a complete indi-

19. Flax, "Postmodernism and Gender Relations," 54; Jean Grimshaw, "Autonomy and Identity in Feminist Thinking," in *Feminist Perspectives in Philosophy,* ed. Morwenna Griffiths and Margaret Whitford (Bloomington, Ind., 1988), 92–97.

20. Judith Kegan Gardiner, "Mind Mother: Psychoanalysis and Feminism," in *Making a Difference: Feminist Literary Criticism,* ed. Gayle Greene and Coppelia Kahn (London, 1985), 115. Gardiner argues that feminist writers have challenged the concept of a unified, male-centered self by insisting on a female self. Just as Dorothy Richardson, Virginia Woolf, and Gertrude Stein attempted to "melt the [self] into a female choral and collective voice," she observes, contemporary women may feel that "the old unified subject was never a female subject" and see "little advantage in the current project of dismantling it."

21. Grimshaw, "Autonomy and Identity," 105.

vidual identity outside the social scripts of patriarchy, reduced to the Other and deprived of a sense of unique, authentic selfhood. Feminist rethinking and rereading have led literary critics and theorists to explore intensively and extensively the construction of a female self. A "new female literary culture," Elizabeth Fox-Genovese contends, has thereby exploded upon the contemporary literary scene, expressing itself in increasingly powerful "waves of female self-exploration" both in fiction and in feminist criticism, vigorous and diverse, with a "determination to understand female literary culture as an articulation of female being."[22]

Judith Kegan Gardiner, for instance, points out that, "although antihumanist critics consider identity a bourgeois illusion," prominent feminist scholars such as Elaine Showalter and Barbara Christian have identified a search for and the development of a female self as the main theme of novels by women authors since the 1920s.[23] Particularly, feminist critics have investigated the fictional landscapes of recent novels by women, asking whether "there is a new woman emerging in literature."[24] In contrast to the truncated lives that characterize the fate of fictional heroines in the nineteenth century, feminist scholars of twentieth-century fiction are finding heroines portrayed as "whole people or as people in the process of creating or discovering their wholeness."[25] In accord with the humanist paradigm of the self, a heroine's journey of self-discovery, her quest for authentic, autonomous selfhood, and her potential for integrating all aspects of the self into a coherent whole have become central thematic concerns in recent fiction by women authors; hence the revitalization and transformation of the traditional genre of the Bildungsroman.[26]

In critical response to the traditional concept of a rational, unified self on

22. Elizabeth Fox-Genovese, "The New Female Literary Culture," *Antioch Review,* XXXVIII (1980), 202, 196.

23. Judith Kegan Gardiner, *Rhys, Stead, Lessing and the Politics of Empathy* (Bloomington, Ind., 1989), 3.

24. Anne Z. Mickelson, "Gail Godwin: Order and Accommodation," in *Reaching Out: Sensitivity and Order in Recent American Fiction by Women* (Metuchen, 1979), 1.

25. Susan Koppelman Cornillon, ed., *Images of Women in Fiction: Feminist Perspectives* (Bowling Green, 1973), xi.

26. Ellen Morgan, "Humanbecoming: Forms & Focus in the Neo-Feminist Novel," in *Images of Women in Fiction: Feminist Perspectives,* ed. Susan Koppelman Cornillon (Bowling Green, 1973), 183.

the one hand and to modernist debilitations as well as the postmodern deconstruction of that self on the other, many feminist scholars have come to view the construction of a female identity as an ongoing process of conflict, struggle, and transformation. Feminist discourse, according to Jane Gallop, constitutes an effort "to call into question a rigid identity that cramps and binds." Identity, Gallop asserts, "must be continually assumed and immediately called into question." Jean Grimshaw also suggests that feminist critics must see the search for identity and autonomy as "a problem of negotiating contradictory or conflicting conceptions" of oneself.[27] For many feminists seeking a place for themselves in a modern world that has found the conditions for selfhood difficult, self-identity is not an impossible illusion but a process of struggle characterized by conflict and a sense of multiplicity. Identity, they argue, exists "in a constant state of becoming, amid agreement, disagreement, conflict, encounters, understanding, and misunderstandings."[28] This emphasis on process, conflict, and plurality, as we will see, underscores Godwin's fictional representations of evolving selfhood.

Mikhail Bakhtin's work of the 1920s and 1930s intersects with the feminist insistence upon process and multiplicity and is of major theoretical importance in my analysis of Godwin's conceptions of the self. Bakhtin's writing covers a wide range of theoretical issues about the novel, but central to his poetics of the novel is dialogue—in its *"multi-voicedness and vari-voicedness."*[29] Rejecting monologic thinking (the cult of the unity of a single

27. Jane Gallop, *The Daughter's Seduction* (Ithaca, 1982), xii; Grimshaw, "Autonomy and Identity," 102.

28. Marcelle Marini, "Feminism and Literary Criticism: Reflections on the Disciplinary Approach," in *Women in Culture and Politics: A Century of Change,* ed. Judith Friedlander *et al.* (Bloomington, Ind., 1986), 153–54. Also see Joanne S. Frye, *Living Stories, Telling Lives: Women and the Novel in Contemporary Experience* (Ann Arbor, 1986), 26; Dale M. Bauer, *Feminist Dialogics: A Theory of Failed Community* (New York, 1988), 5; Marianne Hirsch, *The Mother/Daughter Plot: Narrative, Psychoanalysis, Feminism* (Bloomington, Ind., 1989), 12; Gardiner, "Mind Mother," 115; Ann Ferguson, "A Feminist Aspect Theory of the Self," in *Women, Knowledge, and Reality: Explorations in Feminist Philosophy,* ed. Ann Garry and Marilyn Pearsall (Boston, 1989), 93–105; Elizabeth A. Meese, *Crossing the Double-Cross: The Practice of Feminist Criticism* (Chapel Hill, 1986), 146–50.

29. Mikhail M. Bakhtin, *Problems of Dostoevsky's Poetics,* trans. and ed. Caryl Emerson (Minneapolis, 1984), 265.

consciousness), Bakhtin defines the novel as "a diversity of social speech types (sometimes even diversity of languages) and a diversity of individual voices, artistically organized." The novel, Bakhtin contends, "begins by presuming a verbal and semantic decentering of the ideological world." In representing "a multiplicity of voices and a wide variety of their links and interrelationships," the novel creates a lively, intensely dialogic context, through which social "heteroglossia"—Bakhtin's term for his unique concept of language—enters and the highest artistic unity is achieved.[30] The interaction of diverse consciousnesses and voices—within the individual self as well as among discrete individuals—constitutes, therefore, the most important act of self-understanding. "Life by its very nature is dialogic," he writes. To live means to communicate, to "participate in dialogue: to ask questions, to heed, to respond, to agree, and so forth."[31]

Language, Bakhtin maintains, "lives only in the dialogic interaction of those who make use of it." Self-consciousness and self-perceptions, he further argues, never exist in isolation but always come into being through the echoing and refraction of different voices, constantly refashioned and reordered out of their intense, mutual interaction.[32] Although gender issues are not Bakhtin's concern, his dialogic principle is congenial to feminist analysis of novelistic representations of female experiences.[33] Specifically, his discussion of the novel's dialogic capacity illuminates Godwin's developing vision of the self and her artistic representation of that vision.

30. Mikhail M. Bakhtin, *The Dialogic Imagination: Four Essays*, trans. Caryl Emerson and Michael Holquist, ed. Michael Holquist (Austin, 1981), 262, 367, 263. Bakhtin's concept of language stresses the multiplicity of voices and the intricate connection between language and context. For him, the "internal stratification" of a language into diverse speech types and various individual voices is "the indispensable prerequisite of the novel as a genre," through which the novel "orchestrates all its themes, the totality of the world of objects and ideas depicted and expressed in it." See p. 263.

31. Bakhtin, *Problems of Dostoevsky's Poetics*, 287, 293.

32. *Ibid.*, 183, 207.

33. Employing Bakhtin's theory in her reading of contemporary women's fiction, Frye proposes a "feminist poetics of the novel," claiming the novel's capacity "both to *represent* women's experience and to *redefine* the premises of representation." See Frye, *Living Stories, Telling Lives*, 16. Bauer's study of Hawthorne, James, Wharton, and Chopin is also vitally influenced by Bakhtin's theory; in it she examines "the play of female voices, misreading, carnivalized textual events, and a sequence of silencing." Bauer, *Feminist Dialogics*, xiv.

The humanist ideal of a coherent, centered self, the feminist principle of process and plurality, and Bakhtin's dialogic vision of an individual in interaction with multiple voices lie at the heart of Godwin's contemporary Bildungsromane. Aware of the increasing tenuousness and the radical problematization of the humanist self yet believing in the possibilities of mature self-definition, Godwin embarks on a fictional quest for a vision of the self by constructing a world in which bewildered individuals continue their search for self-fulfillment, in face of the world's accelerating fragmentation, despite general disbelief and their own uncertainty. Her eight published novels reveal the direction and depth of her struggle for that vision; they constitute a vigorous response to the contested notion of a coherent, centered self, suggesting the distance she goes toward seizing some possibilities of the old "self," lost in modernist existential despair and decentered through postmodernist deconstruction.

Godwin begins, in *The Perfectionists* (1970) and *Glass People* (1972), with heroines constrained by the patriarchal text of marriage searching ineffectually for an independent identity. In *The Odd Woman* (1974), *Violet Clay* (1978), and *The Finishing School* (1984), she constructs stronger heroines striving to define themselves outside the cultural script of womanhood. In these "minor-key" novels—private, psychologically intense, and characterized by the single point of view[34]—Godwin explores the "psychological time of memory."[35] Dramatizing the interplay of past and present, she unfolds the heroine's growth as a dialogic process in which memory, interpretation, and narrative reconstruction become crucial means for self-understanding. By delineating the heroine's inward encounters with sundry versions of herself, Godwin makes the single point of view dynamically multiple, asserting female autonomy and identity as an internal process of self-exploration. Building upon this dialogic imagination, Godwin takes her exploration of

34. In her interview with *Contemporary Authors*, Godwin spoke of three of her novels (*A Mother and Two Daughters*, *The Finishing School*, and *A Southern Family*) in stylistic terms: "I seem to do a major-key thing and then a minor-key thing. I mean, *A Mother and Two Daughters* was major key (I'm speaking musically, not grandiosely). The one I've just finished was most definitely minor key, very sinister and much smaller and very, very private. The one I'm planning now will be major-key: a novel about Southern society. It will have all kinds of people in it." See *Contemporary Authors*, n.s., XV (1985), 159.

35. David H. Miles, "The Picaro's Journey to the Confessional: The Changing Image of the Hero in the German Bildungsroman," *PMLA*, LXXXIX (1974), 989.

selfhood into a new, spiritual direction in her most recent minor-key novel, *Father Melancholy's Daughter* (1991). In this novel the heroine's search for self-identity emanates out of a complex dialogue—past and present—between the heroine and her dead mother, her rector father, and, finally, the God that unites all.

In *A Mother and Two Daughters* (1982) and *A Southern Family* (1987), her two "major-key" novels characterized by a formal expansiveness and a broad social spectrum,[36] Godwin explores more comprehensively the role of dialogic interaction in an individual's growth and self-definition, unfolding the lively interplay among diverse voices, a process that Bakhtin considers the premise of novelistic representation. Through the narrative device of multiple points of view, Godwin shows how individuals shape and mold each other and how their self-perceptions are intertwined with other people's perceptions of them. By probing the nature and implications of the process of perceiving oneself for and through another, Godwin brings increasing breadth and depth to her concept of evolving selfhood, constructing larger social reality through the many mutually reflecting mirrors of individual consciousness.

Throughout her fiction, Godwin is preoccupied with the construction of a self that would adequately express the complexity of contemporary reality on the one hand and embrace the possibilities of continuous growth and fulfillment on the other. She situates her questing heroines in a world quivering with change, fraught with confusion and fracture, and increasingly rich in multiple voices—individual aspiration, feminist consciousness, cultural script, family, region, class, and religion. She portrays their complex responses to social, psychological, and spiritual challenges, and dramatizes their struggle to achieve coherent identities in a fractured society. With each succeeding

36. In a recent interview, Godwin remarked again about her alternate use of "major-key" and "minor-key" techniques: "I can only do [multiple points of view] every other book and then I like a single viewpoint again. The multiple viewpoints make for a long book; you lose a kind of intensity that you get when you just focus on one character and, like Henry James said, have the whole world come filtering through that character. You get a certain pressure and intensity from the world having to narrow itself to get into that one opening. Each kind of book gives a different reward; I like to balance them." See "Gail Godwin," in *A Voice of One's Own: Conversations with America's Writing Women*, ed. Mickey Pearlman and Katherine Usher Henderson (Boston, 1990), 37.

novel, Godwin's concept of the self becomes increasingly multiple; her thematic emphasis shifts from the cultural text of patriarchal oppression and female victimization, through the interior, psychological space of reconstructing past selves, to a thoroughly dialogic context in which diverse voices interact with each other. Constantly contesting and reshaping her concept of the self, Godwin sees growth as continuous and dynamic, encompassing the interpersonal and social process of dialogic interaction as well as the internal process of memory.

What emerges from Godwin's fiction, then, is a concept of an evolving self that mediates between traditional humanists' rigid presumptions of a centered self and postmodernists' radical denial of selfhood. Fluid, in-process, and continually becoming, this evolving self approximates feminist "multiplied versions of the 'subject'"[37] and is informed with an implicit Bakhtinian vision. In developing a concept of evolving identity and constructing the self's struggle toward meaning, order, and cohesion, Godwin affirms the humanist ideal of a centered, coherent self. By delineating the increasing difficulty of self-identity in a fragmentary reality, she brings a modernist dimension to the traditional concept of the self, transforming the concept of self from one of *essence* into one of *process*. Rather than presuming a centered, coherent self, Godwin contests the traditional humanist self, casting it as a sense-making, evolving process—a process, as Jean Grimshaw puts it, of relating "confused fragments of ourselves into something that seems more coherent and of which we feel more in control."[38]

In emphasizing the complex interplay of voices—an individual's internal dialogue and the multivoiced, multicentered dialogue among diverse individuals—Godwin comes to envision the self as becoming increasingly multiple and "decentered."[39] But the decentering process strives toward affirmation, not negation, of the possibilities of constructing a self capable of "building an examined life out of past accomplishments and mistakes," out

37. Smith, *Discerning the Subject*, 149.

38. Grimshaw, "Autonomy and Identity," 106.

39. The term *decentered*, I understand, evokes connotations associated with poststructuralist discourse. Unless in the context of poststructuralist theories about the subject, my occasional use of the term means either the fragmented self that modernism posits or the dialogic process of interaction that Godwin constructs among diverse voices, internal as well as external.

of dialogic engagement with itself and the world around it.[40] Cohesion, unity, autonomy, and authentic self-identity—terms that humanists consider to be self-evident and transparent but modernist despair throws into disbelief—become relative terms in Godwin's fictional world. Out of the diversity of human experience, out of the fragmentation of contemporary reality and individual lives, Godwin constructs complex, compelling images of a heroine-in-progress, one who achieves mature, evolving selfhood through a continuous, dynamic sense-making process. That unceasing process of striving opens up for Godwin's heroine the possibility of greater degrees of unity, cohesion, and control. As long as she persists in keeping track of herself, Godwin tells us, her heroine will find herself suspended in vibrant possibilities of continuous growth, with "more compound interest" accruing to her "in the form of insights and expanding confidence in [her] powers."[41]

Gail Godwin's Novels as Contemporary Bildungsromane

Gail Godwin's fictional portrayal of an individual's struggle for identity and self-fulfillment links her work to a specific genre—the Bildungsroman. A long-established literary tradition, the Bildungsroman originated in eighteenth-century Germany, spread to England and France in the nineteenth century, declined in the twentieth century, only to be revived and transformed by contemporary women writers in their exploration of what it is like to be a modern woman "in a world increasingly responsive to their needs."[42] To understand Godwin's work as an affirmation and transformation of the humanist self (in the face of modernist abandonment and postmodern deconstruction of that self), we need to place it in the context of the Bildungsroman as a genre —its origin, development, and transformation over a history of two centuries.

The Bildungsroman, variously defined as the novel of development, the novel of education, the apprenticeship novel, the initiation or adolescence

40. Godwin, "How to Be the Heroine of Your Own Life," 197.

41. *Ibid.,* 196.

42. Elizabeth Abel, Marianne Hirsch, and Elizabeth Langland, Introduction to *The Voyage In: Fictions of Female Development,* ed. Abel, Hirsch, and Langland (Hanover, N.H., 1983), 13.

novel, and the novel of formation, has been a genre of long-standing interest to literary critics.[43] Theorists from Wilhelm Dilthey in the nineteenth century to contemporary critics such as Jerome H. Buckley, Martin Swales, and
Marianne Hirsch have discussed the origin, development, and characteristic
features of the genre. Although critics debate the definition and value of the
Bildungsroman as a historical genre and a literary concept,[44] and apply the
term to a wide range of novels in accordance with their theories,[45] there is
scholarly consensus on the thematic and formal categories that broadly define the features of the genre.

As a literary concept, the Bildungsroman emerged from eighteenth-
century Germany, deriving its ideological and intellectual impetus from
"the individualism and interest in self-cultivation valued by German culture."[46]
This Idealist understanding of human growth assumes the possibility of full
realization of an individual's inner capacities in an organic, cumulative, and
total unfolding of personality. In the Goethean ideal of human totality—perhaps rarely achieved—successful Bildung (education) is achieved within an
existing social context: the Bildungsheld (hero of education), progressing stage
by stage in the careful tending of his personality, is expected eventually to become integrated into the existing society, whose values have facilitated his
growth and helped to mold his personality.

The Bildungsroman has its characteristic protagonist, plot, conflict, and
narrative structure. It recounts the experiences of a sensitive young man, who
attempts to "learn the nature of the world, discover its meaning and pattern,
and acquire a philosophy of life and 'the art of living.'"[47] The classic plot of

43. Jerome Hamilton Buckley, *Season of Youth: The Bildungsroman from Dickens to Golding*
(Cambridge, Mass., 1974), viii; Esther Kleinbord Labovitz, *The Myth of the Heroine: The Female
Bildungsroman in the Twentieth Century* (New York, 1986), 2; Marianne Hirsch, "The Novel
of Formation as Genre: Between Great Expectations and Lost Illusions," *Genre*, XII (1979), 295.

44. Hirsch, "The Novel of Formation as Genre"; Jeffrey L. Sammons, "The Mystery of the
Missing *Bildungsroman*; or, What Happened to Wilhelm Meister's Legacy?" *Genre*, XIV (1981),
229–46; Abel, Hirsch, and Langland, Introduction to *The Voyage In*.

45. Charles Dickens' *Great Expectations*, Samuel Butler's *The Way of All Flesh*, Thomas
Hardy's *Jude the Obscure*, D. H. Lawrence's *Sons and Lovers*, James Joyce's *Portrait of the Artist
as a Young Man*, W. Somerset Maugham's *Of Human Bondage* are some of the novels variously
considered to be works of the Bildungsroman.

46. Hirsch, "The Novel of Formation as Genre," 293.

47. William Flint Thrall and Addison Hibbard, *A Handbook to Literature*, rev. C. Hugh
Holman (New York, 1960), 31.

the Bildungsroman novel explores the progress of the central character from ignorance and innocence toward maturity, harmony, and fulfillment, tracing each stage of his development: initial alienation from an uncongenial rural environment, departure from the constraints of his provincial home and venture into the big city, various adventures and ordeals in the city, and eventual accommodation to the existing social order. The typical Bildung of the protagonist consists of his schooling, his sexual initiation and ordeal by love, his various encounters with friendships, his search for a vocation and a philosophy of life, and his "ultimate assessment of life's possibilities."[48] The plot thus illuminates the *rite de passage* of a single male protagonist from childhood through adolescence, "leaving him at the threshold of maturity,"[49] with his choice of mate, vocation, and philosophy of life made, and all aspects of the self fulfilled according to a preconceived goal.

The philosophical implications of the Bildungsroman—revealed through its protagonist, plot, conflict, and narrative structure—attest to the humanist notion of a centered, unified self. Defined as a novel form that "is animated by a concern for the whole man unfolding organically in all his complexity and richness,"[50] the traditional Bildungsroman operates within the humanist paradigm, with its assumption that there exists an autonomous, complete, and unified self—an essential core of being—to be discovered and achieved through the process of Bildung. The Bildungsroman charts that process, taking the youthful hero through each necessary stage of development until he reaches the point of maturity, marked by his achievement of full self-identity and self-fulfillment. At that point, the novel closes; the crucial struggle for selfhood is complete, and the hero coheres into a centered, unified being, becoming by and large what he essentially is—mature, wise, competent, in control of his destiny.

In the course of its development, the Bildungsroman has undergone changes and expansions in its definition, its conception of Bildung, its image of the hero, and its narrative form. Two of the most significant changes—con-

48. Charlotte Goodman, "The Lost Brother, the Twin: Women Novelists and the Male-Female Double Bildungsroman," *Novel*, XVII (Fall, 1983), 28.

49. Labovitz, *The Myth of the Heroine*, 3.

50. Martin Swales, *The German Bildungsroman from Wieland to Hesse* (Princeton, 1978), 14.

cerning the definition of the genre and the shifting image of its hero—reveal an increasing skepticism about the humanist ideal of a harmonious, whole self. Realization of the discrepancy between "the ideal Bildung" and "actual human possibility within culture" and of its consequences on the developing hero has led to expanded definitions of the genre, which move it "away from German idealism, from the symbolic and socially conservative aspects of the German novel, toward a vision of individual development as a series of disillusionments or clashes with an inimical milieu."[51] In contrast to the full realization of man's inner capabilities depicted in the classic Bildungsroman, the protagonist in the expanded genre often culminates his journey of self-discovery in withdrawal, rebellion, or even suicide.

The shifting image of the Bildungsroman's hero evokes more explicitly a changing concept of man developed during the nineteenth century. The "post-classical" Bildungsroman of the nineteenth and twentieth centuries, David H. Miles argues, portrays an "intensive-confessional" hero, in contrast to the "extensive-picaresque" hero in Goethe's prototypical Bildungsroman, *Wilhelm Meister.* Whereas the earlier mode emphasizes the picaresque dimension of the hero's experience in "linear, episodic, and chronological" time, the later mode stresses the reconstruction of the self through memory, recollection, and reflection. The isolation of the protagonist, the psychological dimension of his quest, and the sense of "the tenuousness of the self"—in sharp contrast to the harmonized, whole man of the humanist tradition—reveal, Miles suggests, a recognition of the "fragmentation of culture" and the self-alienation of man during the nineteenth century.[52]

Charting the "deep-lying historical changes" in the patterns of the Bildungsroman employed by modern and contemporary writers, Miles also speculates on the future of this long-standing genre. What lies beyond the anguished retrospection and confession that characterize the twentieth-century Bildungsroman protagonist? What could be expected of a literary tradition based on the belief in the evolution of a total, coherent self when contemporary life has become increasingly fragmented and chaotic? Two possibilities, Miles anticipates, exist for the modern writer: "either to take a final step into the world of total breakdown and psychic disorder, into that tan-

51. Abel, Hirsch, and Langland, Introduction to *The Voyage In*, 6.
52. Miles, "The Picaro's Journey to the Confessional," 980–81, 987, 989.

gential sphere—Kafka's Archimedean point—from which all reality becomes problematic; or, in a less drastic move, to raise the entire narrative to the saving plane of self-parody—to write, in other words, an anti-Bildungsroman parodying both picaresque and confessional branches of the genre." In twentieth-century versions of the Bildungsroman, Miles sees not only the domination of the anti-Bildungsroman, but also the threat of the "absolute end of the genre, even within the realm of parody," with a protagonist "mocking his entire literary parentage of the last two hundred years—the picaros, the confessors, and the various tragicomic inversions of both." Parody, Miles concludes, "coming as it does at the end of a historical period, necessarily holds its mirror up to the art and life of yesterday, not to that of today or tomorrow."[53]

Like most literary critics who write on the Bildungsroman before the surge of feminist criticism, Miles perceives the genre from a predominantly male perspective. From its inception and well into its maturity, the Bildungsroman had been a male affair, written by male authors about male protagonists and studied by male literary critics. Although critics frequently include a few selected works by women in their studies of the genre,[54] the majority of these studies, in Charlotte Goodman's words, "not only focus almost entirely on novels written by males about male protagonists, but also define the genre in terms that apply exclusively to male experience."[55] As Elizabeth Abel, Marianne Hirsch, and Elizabeth Langland point out, "even the broadest definitions of the Bildungsroman presuppose a range of social options available only to men." Formal schooling, travel, sexual adventures, political and social involvement, an independent life in the city—none of these aspects of Bildung, vital to the development of a total personality in the traditional Bildungsroman, were available to heroines of nineteenth-century fiction. "While the young hero roams through the city, the young heroine strolls down the country lane," seeking protection rather than adventure. Sexual encounters for the male protagonist are seen as important steps toward adulthood; for the heroine they bring only social ostracization.[56] Whereas the

53. *Ibid.*, 989–90.
54. Buckley, for instance, devotes one chapter of *Season of Youth*, a study of the English Bildungsroman, to George Eliot's *The Mill on the Floss*.
55. Goodman, "The Lost Brother," 28.
56. Abel, Hirsch, and Langland, Introduction to *The Voyage In*, 7–8.

traditional Bildungsroman hero reaches, at the conclusion of his journey, a stage of completeness, marked by his acceptance of his proper place in society and his assumption of his social responsibilities, the heroine of nineteenth- and early-twentieth-century fiction has few options except the entrapment of marriage, psychic fragmentation, or death.

Although critics of the Bildungsroman have expanded the concept of the genre to accommodate historical and cultural variables, moving it far beyond the German prototypes, gender "has not been assimilated as a pertinent category, despite the fact that the sex of the protagonist modifies every aspect of a particular Bildungsroman: its narrative structure, its implied psychology, and its representation of social pressures."[57] The exclusively male-centered concept of the genre, therefore, leaves unexplored, until recently, the muted half of human development.

Despite the androcentrism of the Bildungsroman tradition, women writers, feminist critics contend, have always written their own stories of female development. A considerable portion of fiction by women, Annis Pratt writes, "is devoted to the quest of the youthful self for identity, an adventure often formalized in a ritual initiation into the mysteries of adulthood." Pratt emphasizes, however, the disjunction between the male and female Bildungsroman. Although many novels of female development attempt to conform to the general patterns of the Bildungsroman, gender-role norms "make the women's initiation less a self-determined progression *towards* maturity than a regression *from* full participation in adult life." The most conservative branch of the women's Bildungsroman, Pratt argues, renders women's Bildung as a process of "growing down," rather than "growing up."[58]

Examining novels of female development, feminist critics have focused on women writers' subversion of the male form and have identified features— both thematic and formal—that make the female Bildungsroman a distinct genre. Abel, Hirsch, and Langland, for example, see a history of revision and transformation of the traditional male form by nineteenth- and twentieth-century women writers. In their collectively edited work, *The Voyage In,* one of the most comprehensive and perceptive studies of the female Bildungsroman,

57. *Ibid.,* 5, 13.
58. Annis Pratt, with Barbara White *et al., Archetypal Patterns in Women's Fiction* (Bloomington, Ind., 1981), 13–15, 36.

feminist critics examine both nineteenth-century narratives that depict heroines' truncated development in a society hostile to their imaginative vision,
and twentieth-century fictions that portray heroines confronting difficult options in their modern environment. Together, these critics chart the development of a female version of the Bildungsroman that constitutes three historical phases: nineteenth-century formulations (redefining a male tradition),
twentieth-century reformulations (claiming a female tradition), and contemporary transformations (creating new traditions by expanding the genre's formal and thematic limits).[59] In examining gender-based social expectations and
social pressures in fictions of female development and their influence on the
developing heroine, these critics provide revisionist readings of narratives by
nineteenth-century women that differ from the typical male Bildungsroman
in the developmental plot, in the concept of Bildung, in thematic emphasis,
and in narrative structure.

In the traditional male Bildungsroman, the developmental plot typically
begins with childhood and follows a linear, chronological structure in depicting the hero's progressive journey from innocence to maturity. In contrast,
nineteenth-century fictions of female experience frequently focus on the
later stages of heroines' development; that is, they begin where traditional
Bildungsroman ends, with marriage and family. Whereas the male Bildungsheld
eventually overcomes the obstacles and limitations to self-discovery through
the outward, progressive mode of education in experience, female development is often presented as an act of awakening—inward and epiphanic—to
limitations that social realities impose on women's personal aspirations.[60]
Reversing the conventional male plot marked by progress and linear direction, the female novel of awakening proceeds in circularity, following a pattern of "inward growth, return, and eventual death." The inner self is the only
recourse for the heroine; childhood "not so much the beginning of a continuous progression, the source of a future, but a presence to return to"; and
death "an escape from female plot," the "only means to reverse the growth
into limitation and subordination that is reserved for women 'in song and
story' and in nineteenth-century society."[61]

59. Abel, Hirsch, and Langland, Introduction to *The Voyage In*, 17.

60. Susan J. Rosowski, "The Novel of Awakening," in *The Voyage In*, ed. Abel, Hirsch, and
Langland, 49–68.

61. Marianne Hirsch, "Spiritual *Bildung*: The Beautiful Soul as Paradigm," in *The
Voyage In*, ed. Abel, Hirsch, and Langland, 42, 37, 44.

Formal revisions of the male Bildungsroman occur not only in prevailing narrative patterns but also in the structure of the plot. Because of women's marginal status in a male-centered society, their development is often marked by a vacillation between rebellion and conformity, between self-assertion and submission. "Repeatedly, the female protagonist or Bildungsheld must chart a treacherous course between the penalties of expressing sexuality and suppressing it, between the costs of inner concentration and of direct confrontation with society, between the price of succumbing to madness and of grasping a repressive 'normality.'" Fictions depicting female development and the forces that shape it consequently tend to generate thematic and narrative tensions leading "to a disjunction between a surface plot, which affirms social conventions, and a submerged plot, which encodes rebellion; between a plot governed by age-old female story patterns, such as myths and fairy tales, and a plot that reconceives these limiting possibilities; between a plot that charts development and a plot that unravels it."[62]

If nineteenth-century women novelists wrote fictions of female development by subverting the conventions of the traditional Bildungsroman, twentieth-century women writers, particularly contemporary women writers, are less handicapped in their fictional expressions of women's need for self-definition in a world of social and ideological change. For the first time in history, "women's experience has begun to approach that of the traditional male *Bildungsheld*,"[63] and women's developing self-consciousness has found various fictional expressions in twentieth-century work. Whereas their male counterparts, in response to the existential despair of the age, are parodying the long-established tradition, women novelists are revitalizing and transforming it by peopling their narratives with modern women seeking and, to various degrees achieving, self-identity and fulfillment. The female Bildungsroman, in Ellen Morgan's words, is becoming "the most salient form of literature" for contemporary women writing about women.[64]

Like Ellen Morgan, Elizabeth Abel, Marianne Hirsch, and Elizabeth Langland, most feminist critics speak of women's appropriation of the genre in positive terms. Contemporary female Bildungsroman, Bonnie Hoover

---

62. Abel, Hirsch, and Langland, Introduction to *The Voyage In,* 12–13.
63. *Ibid.,* 13.
64. Morgan, "Humanbecoming," in *Images of Women in Fiction,* ed. Cornillon, 185.

Braendlin believes, allows female authors to "convey the complexity of the female quest for selfhood and confirm its universality" through irony and retrospection; it has therefore become "an attractive genre to modern women intent on expressing female awakening and consciousness-raising and on proclaiming new, self-defined identities." Joanne S. Frye also sees the female Bildungsroman as a "dynamic form" that has "a clear relevance to the urgency of female self-definition." In particular, she emphasizes the "feminist potential" of the first-person narrative process used by women novelists to illuminate "a still more positive enactment of agency."[65]

Representing a dissenting voice, Carol Lazzaro-Weis challenges the claim that the female Bildungsroman has become a literary form most conducive to representations of women's experience. Deconstructive criticism, particularly arguments surrounding "concepts of the self, of experience, and the possibility of representation," Lazzaro-Weis contends, has called into question the very theoretical premises of the female Bildungsroman—the "possibility and necessity of the representation in writing of women's experience and with the goal of finding a new definition of female identity." Using undifferentiated gender as a critical category to interpret works about female development, she argues, separates women from men so radically that men do not have to pay attention to feminist demands, thereby reducing the political to the personal. Her skepticism about the genre notwithstanding, Lazzaro-Weis recognizes the "recent use of the *Bildungsroman* to reconceptualize the mother-daughter relationship, to deny the existence of stable identities, and to unmask the social structures that determine experience." The female Bildungsroman, whatever its limitations, fills a critical and literary need, she concludes, by addressing "the questions surrounding the relationship between experience, subjectivity, and social structures" that are "far from being resolved."[66]

Contemporary female Bildungsroman, the recast form of the traditional Bildungsroman, has stimulated critical interest because it expresses the complex, interrelated forces of gender, family, region, culture, and class that shape individual development. Various terms have been used to describe this

65. Bonnie Hoover Braendlin, "Bildung in Ethnic Women Writers," *Denver Quarterly,* XVII (Winter, 1983), 77; Frye, *Living Stories, Telling Lives,* 79, 83.

66. Carol Lazzaro-Weis, "The Female *Bildungsroman:* Calling It into Question," *NWSA Journal,* II (Winter, 1990), 16–34. See quotation on pp. 17–19, 34.

new form, with close critical attention to its two distinct branches: the "spiritual quest" novel—fiction that emphasizes a process of female self-discovery through mystical identification with nature—and the "social quest" novel—fiction that stresses the social dimensions of female development.[67] For example, Carol Christ defines social quest as a "search for self in which the protagonist begins in alienation and seeks integration into a human community where he or she can develop more fully," and spiritual quest as an interior journey "in relation to cosmic power or powers." Annis Pratt juxtaposes the younger heroes in "the novel of development" and the older women heroes in novels of "rebirth and transformation," seeing Margaret Atwood's *Surfacing* as describing "an immanent naturism achieved by a hero who turns away from society and towards the universe as a whole, reconciling the spiritual to the physical through the vehicle of a green-world Eros." Bonnie Hoover Braendlin, on the other hand, examines contemporary works by women that focus on "secular quests, the struggle for self-actualization restricted to social and psychological planes that admit no transcendent deity or naturistic powers."[68] Such broad division, Rita Felski observes, "derives from the degree of emphasis given to either the inward transformation of consciousness or to active self-realization within the individual text." It does not,

67. Critics have used the following terms to describe contemporary works by women about female development: the novel of self-discovery, the female Bildungsroman, contemporary women's Bildungsroman, the feminine Bildungsroman, contemporary feminist Bildungsroman, modern feminist Bildungsroman, and contemporary Bildungsroman. See Morgan, "Humanbecoming," in *Images of Women in Fiction*, ed. Cornillon, 72; Bonnie Hoover Braendlin, "Alther, Atwood, Ballantyne, and Gray: Secular Salvation in the Contemporary Feminist Bildungsroman," *Frontiers*, IV (Spring, 1979); Braendlin, "New Directions in the Contemporary Bildungsroman: Lisa Alther's *Kinflicks*," in *Gender and Literary Voice*, ed. Janet Todd (New York, 1980); Labovitz, *The Myth of the Heroine*, 1; Elaine Hoffman Baruch, "The Feminine *Bildungsroman*: Education Through Marriage," *Massachusetts Review*, XXII (1981); Rita Felski, *Beyond Feminist Aesthetics: Feminist Literature and Social Change* (Cambridge, Mass., 1989), 126.

68. See Carol Christ, "Margaret Atwood: The Surfacing of Women's Spiritual Quest and Vision," *Signs*, II (1976), 317; Pratt, with White *et al.*, *Archetypal Patterns in Women's Fiction*, 135, 157–58; Pratt, "Women and Nature in Modern Fiction," *Contemporary Literature*, XIII (1972), 476–90; Francine du Plessix Gray, "The Literary View: Nature as the Nunnery," *New York Times Book Review*, July 17, 1977, pp. 3, 29; Braendlin, "New Directions in the Contemporary Bildungsroman," 161; Braendlin, "Alther, Atwood, Ballantyne, and Gray," 18–22; Felski, *Beyond Feminist Aesthetics*, 126–27.

however, "constitute an opposition or signify that these two models of female self-discovery are to be viewed as mutually exclusive."[69]

Although some theoretical questions about the Bildungsroman as "a specific type of novel" still generate debates,[70] feminist scholars, in examining women's appropriation, transformation, and revitalization of this traditionally male form, have identified issues central to an understanding of the question of female identity. These issues encompass a wide range of female experience: mother-daughter relationships,[71] female networks and friendships,[72] female acculturation through fairy tales, psychology of female development, and women's relationship to their body and to language. Emphasizing gender differences, feminist reformulations of the Bildungsroman have profoundly transformed the way the genre has traditionally been conceived and evaluated while acknowledging its vital link to the classic genre. In the words of Abel, Hirsch, and Langland, feminist reformulation of the Bildungsroman "shares common ground with the presuppositions and generic features of the traditional *Bildungsroman:* belief in a coherent self (although not necessarily an autonomous one); faith in the possibilities of development (although change may be frustrated, may occur at different stages and rates, and may be concealed in the narrative); insistence on a time span in which development occurs (although the time span may exist only in memory); and emphasis on social context (even as an adversary)."[73]

The thematic thrust of Godwin's novels coheres precisely at the intersec-

69. Felski, *Beyond Feminist Aesthetics,* 128. Christ also points out that "social quest" and "spiritual quest" may be "united in a single novel or life." See "Margaret Atwood," 317.

70. Susan L. Cocalis, "The Transformation of *Bildung* from an Image to an Ideal," *Monatshefte,* LXX (1978), 399–414; Lazzaro-Weis, "The Female *Bildungsroman,*" 16–34.

71. Lazzaro-Weis points out that "the generational gap, spoken predominantly in terms of the mother-daughter relationship," is a characteristic theme of more recent versions of the female Bildungsroman. Lazzaro-Weis, "The Female *Bildungsroman,*" 24.

72. Speaking of women writers' key transformations of the Bildungsroman, Felski points out that female community and friendship offer "an alternative form of intimacy grounded in gender identification," as opposed to the traditional plot of love and marriage, in which a heroine's identity is grounded in the cultural script of female dependence and subordination, characterized by a sense of alienation. Whether actual or symbolic, female community functions to "complement and extend the protagonist's sense of self rather than to threaten it by absolute otherness, and thus to provide a framework within which a gendered identity can be meaningfully located." See *Beyond Feminist Aesthetics,* 132, 139.

73. Abel, Hirsch, and Langland, Introduction to *The Voyage In,* 14.

tion of the recast contemporary Bildungsroman and the modernist/post-modernist contestation of the traditional concept of the self. One of the most articulate and persistent writers on the contemporary literary scene to pursue the idea of the self, Godwin has developed a mature, dynamic vision of the self and rendered that vision with increasing artistic power. Situating her characters' struggle within the fragmentary landscape of modern reality, she has created an evolving self that embraces the possibility of achieving the humanist ideal through an increasingly decentering process of self-search. In her eight novels, she concentrates on female experiences over the life cycle, from childhood to old age; embeds her characters in family, region, culture, and class; and explores in depth the relationship between social constraints on the development of an individual and her or his struggle to resist cultural scripts. With her focus upon various dimensions of female development—memory, place, family, and friendship—Godwin makes significant contributions to the revitalization and profound transformation of a traditional male genre slipping into self-parody and death.

This volume focuses on Godwin's pursuit of a concept of self that at once encompasses the complexity of contemporary reality—its confusion, discontinuity, and fragmentariness—and affirms an individual's desire and capacity for growth and self-identity. I choose to call Godwin's novels "contemporary Bildungsromane" because the term most comprehensively and accurately describes the breadth of Godwin's work. Contemporary Bildungsromane encompass various dimensions—social, psychological, artistic, and spiritual—of individual development depicted in Godwin's work. Illuminating many of the defining features of contemporary novels of development, with its focus on female self-discovery and growth, the term at once embraces gender implications and leaves room for expansion of narrative boundaries, including crossing gender lines.[74]

In six chapters, I examine Godwin's exploration of how a modern heroine

74. Though most of her protagonists are female, Godwin gives a more balanced treatment of male and female characters in her most recent work. *A Southern Family*, for example, portrays sympathetic male characters struggling to understand the meaning of their lives, as well as a positive male figure who participates in the drama of the story in a significant way, and whose perspective contributes to the realization of the novel's themes. *Father Melancholy's Daughter*, Godwin's most recent work, also constructs a sympathetic male character preoccupied with self-understanding in a religious context.

constructs a coherent, autonomous, authentic and, above all, *evolving* self out of the fragments of her personal experiences, out of her psychological, existential, social, or spiritual struggle. In particular, I emphasize Godwin's use of *process* as an essential mode of Bildung and the primary means of self-definition for her protagonists. Centering my study of Godwin's contemporary Bildungsromane on an understanding of self as process, with its connotations of change, motion, and progress, I use such terms as "centered," "autonomous," "coherent," and "authentic" to define Godwin's fictional representations of the self. While these terms link Godwin to the humanist ideal of a unified self to which she partially adheres, I emphasize their qualified meanings in the particular context of Godwin's fiction. The self *moves* toward a relatively centered position through a decentering process of negotiating conflictual self-conceptions. It *becomes* more coherent through constant acts of sense making, sorting out the fragments of one's experience and "fitting [them] into the ongoing weaves of [one's] life."[75] It *assumes* autonomy from deliberate, conscious exercise of memory and interpretive power toward the possibility of successful self-definition. It *achieves* greater degrees of authenticity—temporary because it is immediately subjected to change but nonetheless real in its moment—by rejecting both the cultural scripts into which one has been inscribed and the various false identities constructed by oneself.

To illuminate Godwin's developing vision of the self and her maturing novelistic technique, I treat Godwin's eight novels in a chronological order, reversing only *A Mother and Two Daughters* and *The Finishing School.* Chapter One discusses Godwin's first two novels, *The Perfectionists* and *Glass People,* both portraying a heroine's frustrated search for an independent identity within a constraining marriage. I consider these two novels tentative explorations of the concept of an evolving self, with a thematic and narrative tension Godwin was unable to resolve at the time. In these two novels, the patriarchal text of oppression overwhelms the feminist text of resistance, leaving in its wake old images of a victimized female self rather than new images of an evolving self.[76]

Chapter Two deals with *The Odd Woman,* which marks Godwin's first

75. Godwin, "How to Be the Heroine of Your Own Life," 227.
76. Kerstin Westerlund emphasizes the psychodynamics of the failed struggle of heroines in

major shift as a novelist. In Jane Clifford, Godwin creates her first heroine-in-progress, a southern daughter alienated from family and region yet psychologically imprisoned in both. Situating her heroine in "the maximum context of culture"[77]—family, female networks, region, and culture—Godwin delineates her struggle to overcome the culturally prescribed endings of female plot in order to become an evolving heroine. However difficult female growth and self-definition, Godwin's characterization of Jane suggests, it is possible, through self-exploration and self-confrontation, to "escape entrapment in plot expectations"[78] and learn to create new, positive, and dynamic identities for oneself.

Violet Clay and *The Finishing School* form the subject of Chapter Three. In both novels, Godwin creates an artist as the narrating heroine, whose recollection and reconstruction of her past selves unfold an internal process of growth and self-definition. Emphasizing memory and internal dialogue, through which the present, narrating self interacts with her previous, experiencing selves, Godwin renders the concept of an evolving self with compelling artistic success. Mature self-definition, Godwin illuminates in these two novels, can be achieved through memory and the dialogic interplay of present and past. In Violet Clay and Justin Stokes's self-assertive voice, Godwin claims both female autonomy and gender identity, affirming powerfully the possibility of constructing a coherent self—again subject to constant reformation and reevaluation—out of a continuous process of grasping and contesting multiple versions of one's self.

Chapter Four examines *A Mother and Two Daughters,* the first of Godwin's "major-key" novels. Breaking through the limitations of a single point of view, Godwin, for the first time, constructs multiple characters and points of view, opening up new thematic and narrative possibilities to explore the concept of

both these novels to break the bonds of patriarchy. She comments on the heroines' subordinate role in a marriage of "hierarchic polarization" and claims that Godwin "points to women's own part in the perpetuation of traditional gender roles." See *Escaping the Castle of Patriarchy: Patterns of Development in the Novels of Gail Godwin* (Uppsala, 1990), Chap. 3, esp. pp. 60–62, 69–70.

77. Elaine Showalter, "Feminist Criticism in the Wilderness," in *The New Feminist Criticism: Essays on Women, Literature, and Theory,* ed. Elaine Showalter (New York, 1985), 259.

78. Frye, *Living Stories, Telling Lives,* 1.

the self. Portraying three very different heroines growing together and creating a dialogic context for their interlocking struggles to achieve an evolving identity, Godwin further decenters the process of self-definition. She perceives diverse modes of self-search, continuing to explore the dimensions of her characteristic, existential heroine while fully developing two previously existing figures—the married young woman and the mother. However crucial the internal process of memory, Godwin suggests, growth encompasses yet another dialogic process, that of "coming to know another's word."[79] By depicting the intense interaction of diverse individual voices, Godwin further accentuates the concept of the self as complex and multiple.

Chapter Five examines *A Southern Family*, Godwin's most expansive novel and her fullest novelistic realization of the dialogic imagination. In this "hybrid" novel, Godwin dispenses with main characters and constructs, instead, a multitude of voices, consciousnesses, and languages. Thoroughly decentering her fictive world, she develops a highly differentiated speaking community in which no discourse is privileged, all truths are relative, and diverse voices are set in intense interaction with one another. Furthermore, she transcends the female-centered plot, embeds family relations in social structure, and grants characters of different gender and class an equal capacity to conceptualize, articulate, interpret, and express. In so doing, she considerably expands her novelistic horizon and affirms with greater power the concept of self as an evolving process of both internal questing and dialogic communication.

The final chapter discusses *Father Melancholy's Daughter*, a novel that continues Godwin's quest for a vision of self but extends that quest into new territory. Alongside the familiar theme of the mother-daughter dialectic, Godwin portrays, for the first time, the significant relationship between father and daughter. In this novel, familial conflict and individual striving take the heroine beyond the social grounding of self-identity. After confronting her past, after understanding who she is in terms of parental heritage and cultural upbringing, Godwin's heroine embarks on a new voyage to understand *what* she is in humanity's spiritual drama of faith and salvation. It is precisely this kind of religious journey toward self-identity and spiritual growth that the young heroine begins as the novel ends.

79. Bakhtin, *The Dialogic Imagination*, 353.

My analysis of Godwin's fiction builds upon what Elaine Showalter terms a cultural model of feminist inquiry—a "contextual analysis" that interprets "ideas about women's body, language, and psyche . . . in relation to the social contexts in which they occur."[80] Feminist studies of fiction in general and of contemporary Bildungsromane in particular frame my assessment of Godwin as a novelist and her contributions to the development of the genre. Bakhtin's theory of dialogic imagination, on the other hand, informs my reading of Godwin's later novels: her artistic development, both in vision and in craft, becomes more visible when situated in his theory. Throughout the study, I examine Godwin's rendering of the dynamic process of growth, noting aspects of gender differences that her characters experience as products and expressions of cultural forces and ideals. In locating the familial, regional, social, and cultural constraints on female self-definition, I emphasize such potent issues as the mother-daughter relationship, female networks, the psychology of place, the cultural script of traditional southern womanhood, and the role of memory and dialogue. All of these play into what becomes Godwin's conception of an evolving self that affirms as well as transforms the humanist belief in a coherent, centered self in the context of an increasingly fragmented modern wasteland.

80. Showalter ("Feminist Criticism in the Wilderness," 259, 266) explains and evaluates four models of differences used by theorists of women's writing to "define and differentiate the qualities of the woman writer and the woman's text": biological, linguistic, psychoanalytical, and cultural. The cultural model incorporates the other three in placing ideas about women's body, language, and psyche in the "maximum context of culture."

I

Female Victimization and Feminist Self-Search
The Perfectionists and *Glass People*

Godwin's first two novels, *The Perfectionists* and *Glass People,* explore in a
tentative yet illuminating way the idea of an evolving self, thereby marking
the beginning of the author's passionate, persistent pursuit of the subject.
Both feature a married young woman struggling for self-identity: *The
Perfectionists* depicts the heroine's gradual disillusionment at what she initially envisioned as a "marriage of the future"; *Glass People* focuses on a
beautiful, pampered young wife's search for self after she leaves her stultifying marriage, only to return to the protection and security provided by her
adoring husband. Despite differences between these two novels in plot and
characterization, they share a thematic and narrative tension that reveals
Godwin's struggle to formulate and render an idea of the self.

   This tension manifests itself in two aspects. First, tension emerges in Godwin's ambivalent, uncertain development of two texts: one of female victimization by patriarchy and the other of feminist self-search.[1] Lacking
narrative strategies to dramatize female empowerment against adversity and

   1. Gail Godwin has vehemently decried the use of "feminist" as a label or category in literary criticism, rejecting its usage on the grounds that it not only lacks precision but also de-
limits. See Godwin, Interview with *Contemporary Authors,* 157–59. I use the term "feminist"
in its broadest sense to describe a range of positions and perspectives, from women's (heroines')
emerging consciousness of and quest for an identity outside the cultural text of marriage and
motherhood to radical demands for restructuring society to ensure female equality.

to create strong, self-defining heroines, Godwin chooses to emphasize the text of patriarchal oppression. By highlighting the war between the sexes—in its binary opposition of oppressor versus oppressed, victimizer versus victimized—she compromises the theme of feminist self-search with that of female victimization. She is unable, finally, to sustain the two heroines' struggle to break out of the bonds of patriarchy, letting one retreat into psychic isolation and sending the other back to marriage and motherhood.

Second, tension exists in Godwin's fictional representation of an evolving self. While she endows the heroines with an emerging feminist consciousness of self-identity, she gives vision and voice to the male protagonists. By having them articulate an idea of self-as-process, constantly striving and continually evolving, she makes the two male characters spokesmen for what is to develop into a vital philosophical concept underlying her fiction.[2] Yet, at the same time, she portrays the male protagonist in each novel as the embodiment of patriarchal power that reduces women to the status of the "other."

Despite thematic and narrative tension, *The Perfectionists* and *Glass People* establish important comparisons in relation to the novels to follow; hence, they constitute points of departure in assessing Godwin's work as a whole. The thematic abstraction that characterizes Godwin's representation of an evolving self in her first two novels is to be replaced by compelling dramatic presentation in later novels. The limited, binary representation that typifies

2. In a different context and with a different focus, Jane Hill also examines this narrative split. *The Perfectionists*, she observes, juxtaposes John's preoccupation with the concept of "enantiodromia"—a spiral pattern of growth aimed at greater self-awareness—and Dane's lack of understanding of it, which prevents Dane from "experiencing the growth typical of Godwin's other protagonists." In *Glass People*, Hill sees Cameron and Francesca as Godwin's "extreme rendering" of the "two dominant strains" in her characteristic heroine—"the impulse to order and control," which is central to the heroine's imaginative self-definition, and the "contrary impulse to torpor and drift, to a completely passive life," an impulse she must resist on her journey of self-discovery. Hill finds this split detrimental to the novel's narrative development but acknowledges its redeeming value: "By separating these impulses, Godwin sacrifices the richer internal conflicts that emerge in the later work when a single character is struggling with the implications of both impulses at every turn in her life. But the aesthetic act of the separation may well have allowed Godwin to clarify and resolve her own struggle with these impulses as an author-narrator and to discover that this essential conflict can provide the source for any number of characters and plots." See *Gail Godwin* (New York, 1992), 28, 38.

her portrayal of the heroines' struggle for selfhood is to evolve into more complex, revealing explorations of female experience in the contexts of family, region, culture, and society. The images of psychic isolation and maternal imprisonment, with which Godwin ends her first two novels respectively, are to give way to dynamic images of female growth and the self-assertive female speaking voice. Of most importance, the split between themes and character development that marks these two novels is to cohere into a continual movement toward a complex, profound dialogic interplay of diverse voices, perspectives, and consciousnesses.

A "Marriage of the Future": *The Perfectionists*

Gail Godwin's first novel participates in the contemporary feminist search for affirmative, evolving heroines as well as narrative strategies to represent themes of female development. Despite its thematic and narrative tension—between a theoretical ideal of self articulated by the hero and the lived struggle of conflicting self-perceptions experienced by the heroine, between themes of feminist self-search and female victimization—the novel does two important jobs. It outlines the underlying concept of Godwin's contemporary Bildungsromane and, with its portrayal of a modern heroine caught between uncertain yet aspiring new roles and secure old ones, sets the stage for a complex, moving drama of self-exploration.

An Evolving Self as a Theory

In *The Perfectionists*, the heroine's husband, John Empson, is an important character through whose theory of self Godwin lays out the conceptual framework for her contemporary Bildungsromane. However, in this early work, Godwin treats the crucial concepts that she later dramatizes compellingly through thematic development and character revelation as explicit, deliberate, and scientific abstractions, articulated by a male voice and severed from the heroine's experience that she unfolds. Notwithstanding its limited rep-

resentation, John's theory of self illuminates our understanding of the philosophical implications of Godwin's work as a whole.

John's intellectual abstraction of the self is a rudimentary version of what is to emerge in Godwin's later work into a dynamic, evolving self that aspires to the humanist ideal of reason, cohesion, and efficacious identity despite the modernist despair at the loss of the self. In Godwin's delineation, John is a character deeply concerned with his development as a unique, evolving individual unbound by any rigid, fixed identity yet capable of coherent self-definition. He perceives himself as someone constantly changing and evolving, assuming different roles and identities at varying stages of his life: "I've been a math scholar, philosopher, computer programmer, doctor who delivers babies . . . and, of course, I was almost a Jesuit. I've been all those things and I'm none of them now. Next year I may be something else again. I'm evolving all the time. I'm not your 'finished' man, I'm afraid. To be finished is to be circumscribed, to have stopped growing. Then one might as well be dead."[3]

In his vehement dismissal of what he sees as futile and stultifying categorization, in rejecting rigid, constraining identities and attempting to continually produce new ones, John advocates a theory of self that brings into harmony seemingly contradictory attributes: fragmentariness and coherence, fluidity and efficacious self-identity. He proposes, furthermore, a mode of self-definition that insists upon process—one of continually contesting previously imposed or achieved identities and moving toward unity and cohesion through constant self-redefinition.

Just as he sees fluidity and coherent self-definition as mutually harmonious, John also embraces the seemingly contradictory concepts of multiplicity and totality, thus affirming the humanist notion of the wholeness of man in the context of the fragmentation of modern reality. He sees himself, for instance, as a "collection of selves" (4), in which some parts have arrived at a higher level of growth than others. His "tender growing parts" (4)— "unintegrated," "blundering," and "nebulous"—need and are capable of cultivation for the formation of a whole, complete self. All parts of the self, all aspects of its life, and all important moments of its history are to be reck-

3. Godwin, *The Perfectionists* (New York, 1970), 41. Subsequent references will be indicated in parentheses within the text.

oned with in its development into a coherent and total self, no matter how unintegrated, blundering, inferior, and embarrassing they may be. The defects, inadequacies, blunders, and chaos are parts of a "natural disorder that precedes growth" (71). And growth is largely a matter of increased awareness and self-knowledge, a path without end yet leading spirally toward a higher plane of consciousness: "No man knows his own dimensions. He's like the iceberg, he *is* much further than he realizes" (72).

Insisting upon a fluid yet coherent mode of self-definition and embracing both multiplicity and unity, John's philosophical self continually creates new possibilities for its development in a spiral pattern of evolution. "Overcoming your contradictions on a given level," he says, "you can swing wider, into the next level of growth" (39). The self, in John's vision of human growth, is "a soul on the prowl" (57) that thrives on making persistent attempts to extend itself into new universes, staying open to alternatives and refusing to be "closed down" (57). Insofar as the world is limitless, so the self, swinging itself wider and higher in each attempt to go beyond the previous one, enjoys infinite possibilities of growth. *"Each step becomes available only after one has taken the step before. . . .* One needs to take [the first] step, . . . before anything further becomes possible" (157). The evolutionary scale for human development is a "constructive sequence" (157), with each step not a mere substitute for the last but an addition to it, so that the completion of each step brings a new dimension to the self, making it larger, richer, and fuller than its previous versions.

John's theory of self entails a philosophical belief in growth, change, and process, and it addresses questions crucial to Godwin's questing female characters—identity, autonomy, and self-actualization. Through such a theory Godwin envisions an ideal self as an evolving process of attending to its multiple versions and creating wholeness out of fragments and inconsistencies. Emphasizing on the one hand fluidity and multiplicity and on the other hand coherence and unity, Godwin incorporates the humanist conceptions of the self into the context of fragmenting modernity. Far from presuming the preexistence of an "authentic or unified 'original' self which can simply be recovered or discovered as the source of 'autonomous' actions,"[4] she leans toward a characteristically feminist perspective which insists that

4. Grimshaw, "Autonomy and Identity," 106.

"identity must be continually assumed and immediately called into question."[5]

The theory of self as process is crucial to our understanding of Godwin's representations of her struggling heroines. Self-definition, for Godwin and her characters, is a continuous process of striving for coherence and control, of contesting versions of the self, with each effort bringing more self-understanding, self-knowledge, and self-awareness. The courage and perseverance with which one contests the confused, contradictory, and fragmented selves and pursues more integrated, defined, and coherent selves constitute the ultimate measure of growth in Godwin's contemporary Bildungsromane.

John's thematic and philosophical significance to her work as a whole notwithstanding, Godwin's presentation of the concepts he embodies leaves much to be desired. *The Perfectionists* lacks the engaging power of dramatization; it spells out the pursuit of a coherent self in a realm of intellectual abstraction that Godwin never manages to integrate into and make inform the actions of the characters and the drama of character revelation. The concept of a multifarious self moving toward its totality emerges as the subject of John's thinking, writing, observation, and conversation. Whatever desirable intellectual dimension this manner of presentation may add, one regrets that the most interesting, compelling, and important ideas of Godwin's fiction are presented here outside of social relations and psychological conflicts, as a cold, scientific project of a domineering and egotistic husband.

In Search of Female Self-Identity

In contrast to the hero's theoretical explorations of an evolving self, the heroine's struggle for self-identity takes place in the context of patriarchal marriage and culture. Attracted to John's vision of an expanding and evolving self yet disturbed by a loss of self-identity through a ten-month-old marriage, Dane Empson feels acutely the chasm between an ideal self she aspires to and a stifled, compromised self she has become.

Godwin launches her troubled heroine on an intense search for self-knowledge and understanding. In portraying Dane's self-images and her con-

5. Gallop, *The Daughter's Seduction,* xii.

ceptions of womanhood, she demonstrates the heroine's inner conflict between responding to individual aspiration and capitulating to cultural scripts
of womanhood.

This internal conflict between striving for authentic, mature self-definition
and surrendering to cultural definitions of womanhood is a crucial aspect of
female self-definition for all of Godwin's heroines, imbued as they are with
a feminist consciousness, yet at the same time deeply immersed in cultural
scripts with which they grew up and which they have to various degrees internalized. In patriarchal culture, Catherine Belsey argues, women as a group
"are both produced and inhibited by contradictory discourses": they "participate both in the liberal-humanist discourse of freedom, self-determination
and rationality and at the same time in the specifically feminine discourse
offered by society of submission, relative inadequacy and irrational intuition."[6]

Belsey's observation about women's contradictory impulses toward self-
definition on the one hand and cultural capitulation on the other illuminates
Godwin's fictional portrayals of struggling heroines. In Godwin's fictional
world, the experience of an aspiring heroine exemplifies what Grimshaw calls
the "problem of negotiating contradictory or conflicting conceptions" of herself, of searching for new, self-creating roles to replace the old, culturally
available, and self-debilitating ones.[7]

Godwin's characterization of her first heroine marks the beginning of a
continuous exploration of the conflict-ridden process toward self-definition.
On the one hand, Dane adheres to a belief in self-actualization and seeks a
state of "her becoming supremely herself, with as few concessions as possible" (115). She commits herself to the pursuit of education in its broadest
sense: knowledge and experience through reading, travel, friendship, love,
and a career, venturing into the world independently for self-fulfillment. She
rejects the traditional ideal of womanhood because it prescribes a female plot
centered on marriage, motherhood, and the virtues of self-sacrifice. In her
perception, Mrs. Hart, the proud "born mother," embodies the fulfillment
of that ideal in sacrificing personal aspirations for security. Mrs. Hart revels
in her nurturing role; Dane sees Mrs. Hart's life as a total deprivation of female autonomy. She "imagined the Mrs. Hart who might have been, had she

6. Belsey, "Constructing the Subject," 50.
7. Grimshaw, "Autonomy and Identity," 102.

stuck up for her ideals, braved London at twenty-nine: Mrs. Something Better—or perhaps supremely herself" (123). In response to Mrs. Hart's self-congratulatory account of her nursing another baby as well as her own, Dane conjures up a repellent image of "a woman turned complacent dairy machine" (117).

Her desire for and claims to self-fulfillment notwithstanding, Dane is a conflicted heroine aware of different roles that culture prescribes for women. Watching Spanish women coming out of church, she expresses feelings contrary to her determined avowals to seek self-actualization. "Dane counted three kinds of women: the young and virginal, with their white missals and fresh skins; the married and pregnant; and the old and widowed, draped in funeral black. She envied them their definitive stages of womanhood. It was all done for them. They had only to flow along with nature's seasons, being courted, bedded, bechilded and bereaved. There were not all those interstices of ambition and neurosis for them to fall into"(17).

In depicting Dane's perceptions of and reaction to the lives of native Spanish women, Godwin emphasizes the heroine's conflicted sense of female self-identity and destiny. Despite her acknowledgment of envy for what she calls stages of definitive womanhood, Dane articulates this envy in a subversive language that belies her overt envy and expresses her profound ambiguity about modern womanhood. In native Spanish women, Dane perceives a series of roles available for women—maiden, wife, mother, widow—all of them defined in relation to a man and each reducing the woman to an object of male desire or the consequence of male action. Describing these roles by using a predominantly passive linguistic structure, Dane covertly reveals her awareness of these roles as expressions of cultural scripts that define and constrain women. Passivity, nonidentity, and stasis characterize the lives of those native Spanish women: their individuality reduced to generalized categories, their personal histories denied in their assigned social roles, their development limited to physical ripening, and their autonomy resigned in their subordination to the status of the "other." Being "courted, bedded, bechilded and bereaved," these women move successively into one after another identity defined in relation to man. Progressing passively through life's journey, along with "nature's seasons," their existence evokes nothing of the "naturistic epiphanies" through which some contemporary fictive women find

spiritual anchorage.[8] Contrary to organic growth and constant renewal in nature's cyclical pattern, these "definitive stages of womanhood" suggest fixity and stagnation, a closing down that Dane finds threatening to her very existence.

Although she is alienated from the self-negating ideal of traditional womanhood, Dane is also troubled by her own "ambition" and "neurosis" and feels the appeal of the cultural script of femaleness. If it leaves little room for female autonomy, self-identity, and development, it provides not only security but a form of clarity and definition that appeals to the heroine's needs for order and control. Dane's envy of the relational and reductive definitiveness of female lives clearly contradicts her gospel of infinite individual growth, showing that she participates both in the bourgeois humanist discourse of individual freedom and self-determination and in the "specific feminine discourse" of dependence, submission, and inadequacy. In delineating the heroine's inconsistent, conflicted conceptions of herself in relation to others, Godwin gives fictional expression to the notion of self as, in the words of philosopher Jean Grimshaw, "*always* a more or less precarious and conflictual construction out of, and compromise between, conflicting and not always conscious desires and experiences, which are born out of the ambivalences and contradictions in human experience and relationships with others."[9]

Dane's conflicted sense of herself is more emphatically revealed through Godwin's delineation of her attitude toward marriage. On the one hand, Dane seeks to subvert the patriarchal text of marriage through a feminist revision, upholding an ideal of egalitarian marriage that promises continuous mutual growth. As an ideal, marriage will no longer be the prison house of the female body and spirit; it will become a metaphorical space, an expanded, boundless universe for two stars to shine equally brightly. Although she admits the difficulty and challenge of such a marriage, Dane affirms her belief in the possibilities such a union opens up: "With us, everything is perpetually in growth." Such a marriage is "a marriage of the future," taking them "further in awareness than either of [them] could go alone" (105).

On the other hand, Dane is deeply embedded in cultural myths and scripts

8. Pratt, "Women and Nature in Modern Fiction," 488.
9. Grimshaw, "Autonomy and Identity," 103–104.

that shape her attitudes and expectations. In patriarchal society, conceptions of female destiny are rooted in notions of romantic love and marriage. In fiction as well as in life, romantic love and marriage have been "the woman's adventure, the object of her quest, her journey's end,"[10] and the mode of her education and development. Centering on romantic love and marriage, cultural ideals and myths of female development have found their definitive expressions in fairy tales, a form of Bildungsroman[11] that states "culture's sentences with greater accuracy than more sophisticated literary texts"[12] because it "reduce[s] a complicated process of socialization to its essential paradigm."[13]

As imaginative and symbolic representations of cultural myths, fairy tales inscribe the ideal of human growth in contrasting patterns of male and female development. The developmental paradigm for heroes is characterized by journeys, trials, and quests for "a rugged independence,"[14] whereas female development in heroine tales based on *Cinderella, Sleeping Beauty,* and *Beauty and the Beast* evolves around patterns of "romantic fantasies of love and marriage" and "patient servitude and waiting."[15] Fairy tales, in Marcia R. Lieberman's view, have given gender a "cultural character" and provided a primary channel of female acculturation: "Millions of women must surely have formed their psycho-sexual self-concepts, and their ideas of what they could or could not accomplish, what sort of behavior would be rewarded, and of the nature of reward itself, in part from their favorite fairy tales."[16] The fundamental, gender-based difference in male and female development,

10. Carolyn G. Heilbrun, "Marriage and Contemporary Fiction," *Critical Inquiry,* V (1978), 309.

11. Bruno Bettelheim's argument, in *The Uses of Enchantment,* that "fairy tales depict in imaginary and symbolic form the essential steps in growing up and achieving an independent existence" has permitted feminist scholars to view fairy tales as "tales of Bildung." Quoted by Ellen Cronan Rose, "Through the Looking Glass: When Women Tell Fairy Tales," in *The Voyage In,* ed. Abel, Hirsch, and Langland, 209.

12. Sandra M. Gilbert and Susan Gubar, *The Madwoman in the Attic: The Woman Writer and the Nineteenth-Century Literary Imagination* (New Haven, 1979), 36.

13. Rose, "Through the Looking Glass," in *The Voyage In,* ed. Abel, Hirsch, and Langland, 209.

14. Karen E. Rowe, " 'Fairy-born and Human-bred': Jane Eyre's Education in Romance," in *The Voyage In,* ed. Abel, Hirsch, and Langland, 75.

15. *Ibid.,* 70–71, 77.

16. Marcia R. Lieberman, " 'Some Day My Prince Will Come': Female Acculturation Through the Fairy Tale," *College English,* XXXIX (1972), 385.

from a feminist perspective, provides a crucial index to our understanding both of gender-role experience for women in a society dominated by male norms and of cultural interpretations of gender-role difference.

Despite her claim to equality and individuality, Dane does not hesitate to make her own fairy tales, surrendering her feminist ideals to "romantic fantasies of love and marriage." While she was living her venturesome life as a single woman, she was also "on the lookout for . . . an event charged with meaning which would signal the turning point of her life" (29). Dane's expectations and sense of destiny are fully revealed through a striking image of an active, galloping hero and a passive, prostrate heroine: "The heroines in her favorite novels all met their destinies face to face: Rochester galloping out of the fog knocked Jane Eyre down" (29). In its striking polarity of male and female, subject and object, agent and recipient, the image expresses powerfully the cultural division between the typically masculine mode of questing and the traditionally feminine mode of waiting.[17]

Juxtaposing male activity and female passivity, Godwin points to Dane's psychological enslavement to cultural scripts of female destiny, to that "gentle but forcible process of acculturation"[18] that prepares women for traditional social roles. The failure of Dane's marriage, therefore, cannot be entirely attributed to John's male egotism and his scientific coldness; Dane, on her part, condones male supremacy and dominance. Not only does she share the culture's idealization of male autonomy, agency, and heroism; she also has internalized cultural assumptions of female inferiority. Her fairy-tale frame of mind makes it hard for her to accept John's weaknesses and vulnerabilities, yet her habit of self-denigration negates her ideal of an egalitarian union. She blames herself for being a terrible wife and repeatedly requests John's reassurance that he has not given up on her. She resents John for "encroaching on her space, trying to collide and merge with her like those horrible zygotes" (97), but she willingly concedes, accepting the position of the "other," content to be the lesser star. As she reflects upon her disintegrating marriage, she sees no way out of the entrapment of female lives: "She couldn't go back to the meaningless editorial waiting game so many girls

17. Kathryn Allen Rabuzzi, *The Sacred and the Feminine: Toward a Theology of Housework* (New York, 1982), 143–45.

18. Lieberman, "'Some Day My Prince Will Come,'" 384.

played at, in publishers' offices all over the world. Waiting for the Big Event. This *was* her Big Event, supposedly. Only, what did you do when it turned out to be not *grand* Big, so you felt yourself expanding, being more than you were before, but *stifling* Big, overwhelming—each thing you conceded becoming another deprivation to yourself?" (97).

Dane's psychological embeddedness in cultural ideals and conceptions of women also finds expression in her self-image and her conflicted attitudes toward the female body, sexuality, and motherhood. Frequently, she engages in the act of degrading herself through fantasy and grotesque self-imaging. She often sees her body in negative terms, measuring herself against cultural standards of beauty. Staring into a glass door, she is shocked to discover that the "pale," "wraithlike" woman she sees is "unfortunately" herself in reflection. Her "short helmetlike haircut . . . made her look sharp as a shrew" (5) in the primeval light of the resort island. Once she imagines herself as a disgustingly fat woman, perversely enjoying the thrill of debasing her body and depriving herself of dignity. Often, her sexual experiences, real or imagined, are delineated as painful and unfulfilling, even repulsive, associated with dirt, stench, low-class status, and obscenities. Dane's grotesque self-images reveal her troubled feelings about the female body and sexuality, a reaction to the cultural overvaluation of male-defined female beauty, which, in turn, is identified with female sexuality.

Motherhood is another cultural text that Dane both rejects and assimilates. Despite her overwhelming resistance to motherhood as a deprivation of selfhood, Dane nevertheless confronts the issue with mixed feelings, often experiencing an uneasiness, even guilt, at her own lack of maternal inclinations, sometimes expressing a vague yearning for the nurturing role. On the one hand, she flatly, with a passionate lack of passion, admits that she is "about as motherly as stone and about as concerned about it as one" (162). On the other hand, she expresses in various ways her profound concerns about motherhood. She questions whether "something has been left out of [her]" (119) and is curious about whether John perceives her as a mother type or a comrade type. She pretends pregnancy to participate vicariously in the "fuss" about biological motherhood. In her acknowledgment that Mrs. Christopher, her stepson Robin's foster mother (surely the "Christopher Robin" conjunction is meaningful), is "a wonderful mother, probably

better than I will ever be" (3); and in her desire to "cope brilliantly with the child" (5) and her persistent attempts to reach out toward him, she expresses a suppressed longing to be motherly and to become a good mother.

Dane's conception of self-identity, then, is riddled with contradictions. Even as she tries to reject the cultural text of patriarchal marriage, she remains immersed in it. Seeking some sort of identity separate from that of her husband, she nonetheless lives in his shadow. Alienated from the idea of motherhood, she cannot entirely reject it as an alternative for female self-fulfillment. Fearing the constraints of female sexuality, she succumbs to perverse sexual fantasy and grotesque self-imaging. Conscious of the seductive power of cultural scripts and of her internalization of these scripts, she must resolve her inner conflict in order to grow.

Female Victimization

If John's neatly theorized self as an evolutionary process and Dane's experienced self as the "site of contradiction"[19] form one aspect of the novel's thematic and narrative tension, themes of patriarchal oppression and feminist self-search form another. In granting the male character a vision of self, Godwin reveals the cultural conceptions of male autonomy and agency. In light of her thematic emphasis on female growth, however, John's characterization as both an embodiment of patriarchal oppression and an advocate of a vision vital to Godwin's novelistic exploration of female growth produces an uneasy tension. Furthermore, the assignment of this vision to the male victimizer serves to highlight and, indeed, to make dominant and even overwhelming, the themes of female victimization, implicitly denigrating the potential of feminist resistance.

Victimization runs through the novel as a prominent, even dominant, theme in Godwin's presentation of the heroine's frustrations and agonies. Apart from being a passionless union rooted in ideas, Dane's marriage to John is exploitative, serving for him as a generative, nurturing force in facilitating his own philosophical quest. In contradiction to his role as passionate acclaimer of a vital idea of self, John emerges as a cold, self-centered,

19. Belsey, "Constructing the Subject," 50.

and intellectually domineering person who married Dane because she could complete him by nurturing his "tender growing" parts. Evoking compelling theories about human evolution and the creative capacities of love, he sees Dane as instrumental in expanding his own horizon so that he can "exist through his partner in new ways of relationship to the world" (72).

Godwin's representation of Dane's marriage resembles the familiar pattern Sandra Gilbert and Susan Gubar describe as "dramatizations of imprisonment,"[20] featuring the use of spatial constructs as "analogues for the female protagonists' existential condition."[21] The image of the "panicked roaches" (1) exterminated by the Orkin man in her father's home at the beginning of the novel establishes the victimization theme through a spatial metaphor of enclosure that suggests the nature of her marriage and her emotional vulnerability. Spatiality, as the novel unfolds, becomes a recurring metaphor for expressing the heroine's boundary anxiety and her sense of constraint and enclosure: John's intrusion into her private space, the dwindling of the virgin territory of her precious self, a flower "planted in a pot too small" (22), a black flower on the verge of bursting through her skull and "blossom at the expense of [her] very sanity" (160). The most emphatic expression of victimization through enclosure is seen in the set of images Dane constructs by which to guide her day: "windows sealed against a molecule of intrusion; . . . monks writing with frozen fingers in chilly monasteries, Jane Austen's world of manners. She would be Victorian. Silent. Circumscribed. Closed" (78).

The theme of victimization is present not only in Godwin's use of spatial constructs as metaphors of patriarchal oppression; it also is evoked through descriptions of Dane's complex feelings about female sexuality. The heroine's first sexual encounter with John, for instance, is delineated as an act of self-obliterating violence. With the heroine feeling a series of unpleasant physical premonitions—vertigo, fainting, vomiting, and numbness—sexual acts become linked to martyrdom: "She had often wondered how martyrs felt, the moment before they were devoured by fire, or nuns, when their hair is being cut off, just before taking the veil. It must be something like this. He

20. Gilbert and Gubar, The Madwoman in the Attic, 85.

21. Roberta Rubenstein, Boundaries of the Self: Gender, Culture, Fiction (Urbana, 1987), 4.

took her rather quickly, but it didn't matter. She lay there afterward feeling totally obliterated by his will" (68).

This sense of victimization that Dane seems to link to female sexuality is evoked even more powerfully in Godwin's description of the heroine's fantasized lovemaking. In the most extreme of these fantasies, Dane imagines herself beaten, insulted, and degraded, totally without control of her own body and utterly at the mercy of male whims. At one point, she imagines herself being turned into a milk machine, her breasts swelling "with milk enough to suckle the hungry mouths of the entire world" and herself transformed into "a universal teat" (125). She also imagines traveling with a nameless, coarse driver across "anonymous, dusty countries." In a third-rate hotel, the driver "tears off her clothes, slaps her twice across the face and knocks her down on the bed. Makes her lie there with her legs open and beg for him. Teases her. Laughs at her. Makes her take it in her mouth" (125). Her reaction to a Walt Disney movie on reproduction, too, reinforces this sense of victimization. She was "appalled" when "the cartoon sperm had whipped himself with a wet resounding *plok!* right smack into the poor defenseless egg." Then, to her utter disgust, "the awful joined thing began going wild, multiplying like a cancer, until there was no trace left of the two separate things" (97–98). Again sexuality is seen as a process of deprivation, a form of male power and an instance of female victimization.

Furthermore, Godwin's depiction of the bizarre relationship between Dane and her stepson Robin also encompasses this pervasive theme of female victimization. Robin, who is "almost a physical copy" (11) of his father, is delineated as a symbolic extension of John, epitomizing male egotism and patriarchal authority in his arrogant denial of Dane. John, for instance, stresses that Robin is himself as a child, and Robin is described as a "regal child" (11), a "shrunken man" (15), and an "ancient, silent king" (11). His look of "pure negation" and expressions of "superior scorn" (210) make Dane feel that he is her "victimizer, critic, silent little judge" (76). In his silence and shrill cries, Dane feels her absolute powerlessness. Her sense of inadequacy becomes magnified in the child's critical surveillance: "The blue eyes, cool and critical, followed her everywhere, but always just skirted acknowledging her. She read in a psychology book that a person could be driven mad by lack of acknowledgment, somebody consistently denying your reality" (15).

Whether she smothers Robin with passionate kisses or perversely exerts physical violence against him, Dane's difficult relationship with Robin can be at least partially seen as an expression of the opposition between male dominance on the one hand and feminist resistance, however ineffectual, on the other.

Retreat into Interiority

Dane's resistance to patriarchy ultimately takes the form of a retreat into psychic isolation, and Godwin's characterization of her demonstrates the difficulty of female self-definition and fictional representation of that process in a society that inscribes female lives in male-centered cultural scripts. Lacking effective narrative strategies to create a "heroine-in-progress," one that she clearly longed to create,[22] Godwin leaves her first heroine locked in increasing alienation and isolation. Incapable of becoming the heroine of her own unfolding story, Dane remains a figure in the background of John's private voyage of discovery. She has, as it were, become a character in John's stories about her, avidly devouring everything John says about her in his scientific "field-notes" and keeping track of herself through his perception and analysis.

Dane's retreat into interiority is marked by grotesque self-imaging and the psychic terror of self-degradation. "With a perverse energy," she indulges in a "self-diminishing" fantasy: "she saw a woman who sat in a chair all day stuffing herself with sweets and pastries until she achieved a disgusting layer of fat which would keep the world away. Dane with fat pendulous breasts drooping toward a mound of swollen belly and thick haunches: the image produced a strange thrill" (76–77). Often, this type of perverse self-debasement occurs in the context of sexuality. For instance, Dane imagines her grotesque, fat self in sexual acts: "she would sneak downstairs, slowly, ponderously, carrying all flesh, to admit her lover: a laborer—no, a really grotesque menial, some teeth missing and dirt under the nails. She laid her hand tentatively between her legs, imagining the lewdly sensual ascent of the menial with his fat lady to her, John's bedroom. He would take off his clothes, smelling of slums, and—

22. See Godwin's comments in "Towards a Fully Human Heroine," 26–28.

prefacing his act with insults and obscenities—plow his way through the folds and folds of unnatural fat" (77).

Disillusioned at the failure of a "marriage of the future" and incapable of developing new, satisfying means of self-definition, Dane sees little possibility for herself but to "retreat wholly into herself, abdicate from her disappointments through various aberrations" (76). Her complete retreat into psychic isolation culminates at the end of the novel in a fantasy of death, not her own but her husband John's imaginary death and her stepson Robin's symbolic one. In her imaginary dialogue with John, Dane tells him that she almost killed Robin, claiming a powerful and private experience that cannot be shared by anyone. Locked in total interiority, Dane shuts herself away from the world, from the possibilities of creating an evolving identity for herself out of active engagement with the world around her.

In *The Perfectionists,* Godwin creates a heroine beset with many of the conflicts and difficulties that her later heroines are to confront: conflicted ideas about female body and sexuality, ambiguous feelings about marriage and motherhood, internalized notions of female behavior and identity, and a sense of confusion and fracture. Godwin's portrayal of the heroine's painful self-questioning anticipates her later heroines' intense soul searching, and her focus on a complex internal movement—marked by interspersed flashbacks and reminiscences—within a relatively short narrative time frame establishes a narrative pattern that is to recur and develop in her later novels. Notwithstanding its thematic and narrative tension, its abstract manner of representation, and its somewhat unsympathetic characterization, we recognize in Godwin's first novel a heroine becoming aware of her conflicted selves and striving for coherent self-identity. Although the dynamic process of growth—integral to the Bildungsroman—has yet to be envisioned, Godwin, in delineating a heroine's frustration and exasperation, has made us feel the pains preceding the birth of a "heroine-in-progress."

A Woman on the Pedestal: *Glass People*

Portraying a pampered wife's quest for self-identity, Godwin's second novel both differs from and bears affinity to her first. *The Perfectionists* empha-

sizes the interior movement of the heroine; *Glass People* focuses on the hero-ine's picaresque adventure. While both novels lack the deep sense of place that marks Godwin's later work, *Glass People* situates its heroine in the so-cial worlds of California and New York, in contrast to the secluded island of *The Perfectionists,* devoid of social context. Although both focus on mar-ried women, *The Perfectionists* portrays its heroine outside the framework of her family of origin, whereas *Glass People* touches upon the important theme of the mother-daughter relationship, though it does not explore it.

Despite differences, *Glass People* and *The Perfectionists* both lack the qualities that distinguish Godwin's mature work—focused thematic con-ception, dramatic rendering, convincing characterization, and mature nar-rative execution. Like its predecessor, *Glass People* reveals a thematic and narrative division between the hero and the heroine and between themes of female victimization and feminist self-search. The characterization of the male protagonist, Cameron Bolt, exhibits the same tension we recognize in the characterization of John Empson: he embodies on the one hand the ex-ploitative and repressive patriarchal culture and on the other an articulate, captivating vision of an evolving self postulated upon existential quest and inner growth. In contrast to her characterization of Dane Empson, whose self-search is largely reflective and interior, Godwin portrays Francesca Bolt, the heroine of *Glass People,* as actively pursuing an identity outside a stifling marriage. "Francesca," Godwin wrote, "interested me: what happens when the man's ideal woman decides to descend from her pedestal and go off in search of a self."[23] Her delineation of Francesca's self-search, however, is de-terminedly external, lacking the dimension of inward search and inner growth she otherwise insists upon—first through the philosophical abstraction of her male characters and later through dramatic representation of her questing heroines. Furthermore, Francesca's characterization at times ex-hibits an uneasy discrepancy: the Francesca to whom Godwin attributes the consciousness of an expanding self at times contradicts the Francesca who emerges from the unfolding events of the narrative as a heroine failing to grow in self-perception. On the whole, Godwin's second novel, like her first, is more interesting in revealing the author's search for a vision of an evolving self and for satisfying narrative strategies commensurate with that

23. Gail Godwin to Lihong Xie, June 22, 1989.

vision than it is as a viable portrayal of what she calls a "heroine-in-progress"—someone who continually builds the plot of her own story by consciously and persistently making sense and meaning out of the fragments of herself.[24]

The Battle of the Sexes

More emphatically than *The Perfectionists, Glass People* delineates an exploitative and debilitating marriage, juxtaposing patriarchal oppression with feminist self-search. The marriage of Cameron and Francesca, the powerful district attorney and the beautiful young wife he puts on a pedestal, embodies a dominant pattern governing the male-female relationship in patriarchal culture—the disciplinary, manipulative male gaze that reduces women to the status of signs.[25] Despite his lip service to the emancipation and individual autonomy of women, Cameron turns his wife into an object. Perceiving his wife through the cultural lens of male egotism and authority, he sees her youth and beauty a prize object useful in embellishing his career and enhancing his sense of ownership. Subject to his relentless male gaze that scrutinizes and defines, Francesca exists only as "signifier for the male other."[26] Her identity is purely and exploitatively relational: Cameron is the subject who possesses, evaluates, admires, and criticizes; Francesca is the object of his possession, evaluation, admiration, and criticism.

Through what Cameron proudly calls a theory of containers, Godwin exposes his patriarchal conceptions of women—their identities and roles as defined by culture and tradition. Relationships, Cameron declares, are containers that "provide a finite form in which we can store our identities."[27] Marriage, according to him, is a particular form of container: "In a marriage, a traditional marriage let us say, the husband is the public container. He gives his wife his name, his social and financial backing, he insulates her from certain outside infringements in order that she may have the leisure and secu-

24. Godwin, "How to Be the Heroine of Your Own Life," 227.

25. Bauer, *Feminist Dialogics,* 3.

26. Laura Mulvey, "Visual Pleasure and Narrative Cinema," *Screen,* XVI (Autumn, 1975), 7.

27. Gail Godwin, *Glass People* (New York, 1972), 99. Subsequent references will be indicated in parentheses within the text.

rity to develop her inner life, to blossom forth as a container for their private life" (99). Although such an idea of separate (even hermetically sealed) spheres, common in bourgeois discourse on women since the early nineteenth century, slowly dissipated as women received the right to vote, gained full property rights, and demanded full equality, it by no means disappeared, as the feminine mystique, a vision of domestic motherhood common in the 1950s and early 1960s, attests. In characterizing Cameron as the advocate of a politically reactionary ideology, blind to the historical process of change and growth, Godwin may be suggesting both the persistence of such strong patriarchal ideologies and the difficulties women couched in them may have in breaking free.

Cameron's theory of containers, with its relegation of women to objects, is reiterated throughout the novel in imagery and diction. Consider, for instance, the image of gazing with which the narrative begins. Cameron, "a tall skinny figure in dark, well-fitting clothes," stands "gazing down" at Francesca. "You are not your old dazzling self," he tells her. "I want you to go somewhere and revive. I want you splendid again." Coveting that "dazzling," "splendid" woman who used to dress up and accompany him to the court—"to watch him wither his opponents" (4) and enhance his public success with feminine touches of beauty and elegance, he urges his wife to take a vacation, to be "hurled back into life" (39) and made to "open out like a flower" (4).

By making Cameron the agency of action ("gazing down") and the subject of discourse ("I want you to"), and Francesca the recipient and grammatical object—whether the withered flower in need of recovery or the dazzling, showy one that gives visual pleasure—Godwin establishes the dichotomy of male dominance and female passivity. Exclusively physical and sensual, the male gaze reduces the female to a passive object, existing merely to make an impression, to receive, and to be acted upon, entirely deprived of agency.[28] Repeatedly, Godwin shows Cameron in the act of gazing down at his wife and making a visual statement about his privileged position as the subject

28. Karen C. Gaston offers a reading of *Glass People* based on the fairy tale of "Beauty and the Beast" and contends that Godwin uses the fairy tale's structure and theme "as a means for ironic commentary." Gaston, " 'Beauty and the Beast' in Gail Godwin's *Glass People*," *Critique: Studies in Modern Fiction*, XXI (1980), 94–102. Westerlund also discusses *Glass People* in terms of its use of myths and fairy tales—"Beauty and the Beast," "Snow White," and the Demeter/Kore myth. Westerlund, *Escaping the Castle of Patriarchy*, 64–69.

and Francesca's subordinate status as the other. The dynamic of the male gaze is most strongly evoked through Godwin's description of the couple's love-making, cast as a visual process of Cameron's "cold, passionate scrutiny" (12).

> He undressed her slowly, folding each garment and laying it on a chair. He touched each piece of her clothing as though it were very delicate, very valuable. At last she stood naked before him. This was the part that terrified her, when he knelt in front of her, still fully clothed himself, and kissed each of her bare feet, then let his eyes travel slowly, very slowly upward, inspecting inch by inch of her. As a collector might go over a piece of precious sculpture, examining it for chips or flaws. At such times, she thanked the fates for her beauty, she needed every bit of it. A woman a gradation less beautiful would have died under that cold, passionate scrutiny. (12)

The characterization of Cameron here is reminiscent of the antagonist in Hawthorne's "The Birth Mark," whose murderous gaze kills, spiritually and symbolically, by reducing his lover to lifeless, decorative art.

Godwin's emphasis on Cameron's lovingly meticulous care in undressing his wife on the one hand and his "cold, passionate scrutiny" on the other underscores the paradox of the situation. Cameron's superficial, deceptive lovingness conceals a destructive strategy for reading women's lives. By equating Cameron's adoring gaze with the professional scrutiny of an art collector, Godwin protests against male insistence upon reducing woman to her "traditional function as sign"[29]—as "bearer of meaning, not maker of meaning."[30] At the same time, her description of Francesca's reaction to that dangerously reductive male gaze points both to the powerful authority of the patriarchal text and to the distance women have yet to travel toward self-liberation. Francesca's terror, coming from her fear of not passing the beauty test, reveals her entrapment in male values about women. Deeply immersed in ideals of femininity, Francesca can find no alternative way of

29. Bauer, *Feminist Dialogics*, 3.
30. Mulvey, "Visual Pleasure and Narrative Cinema," 7.

self-perception and self-definition except capitulating to male standards of feminine beauty and grace.

Patterns of male dominance and female passivity are further reinforced through Godwin's emphasis on female silence or absence. Portraying Cameron in the habit of visiting Francesca's closet in her absence and transferring the male gaze from the female body to her clothes, Godwin exposes the pervasiveness of Cameron's sense of ownership of his wife. For Cameron, self-indulgent worship of Francesca's closet is a most gratifying assurance of his ownership of a beautiful woman. When Francesca fails to come back to him after her visit with her mother, for instance, Cameron assuages his feelings of rejection by a trip to her closet, where his sense of marriage as container is restored. Breathing her perfume, Cameron "wished he could break every other bottle of this perfume in the world, so that this scent would be identified as his wife's alone!" He loses himself in touching Francesca's dresses and shoes in the same possessive way he touches her naked body in lovemaking. Fixing his gaze on a white Roman toga Francesca once tried on but has never worn, he becomes wildly thrilled at the thought that he "alone had seen Francesca in this garment" (79). Carrying the garment to the bed, Cameron abandons himself to enormous sensual pleasure, identifying his absent wife with a piece of clothing and assuring his proud sense of ownership.

Later in the novel, when Cameron goes to New York to a bedridden Francesca, Godwin depicts another scene in which the male gaze violates the integrity of a silent female. Francesca is asleep. Cameron sits in the chair, watching, his gaze traversing her body in slow motion, zooming in at some prominent parts: legs, the curve of her body, "a smooth forehead," "a flushed half-moon of cheek," the "firm and shapely" upper part of an arm "made for sleeveless dresses," and its "rich, ripe golden-pink" color (185). Godwin's attention to detail here—her use of a cameralike point of view—turns Cameron's gazing into a figurative act of dissecting the female body into individual parts, deprived even of physical wholeness. Under the reductive male gaze, Godwin suggests, Francesca exists only as physical fragments—arm, leg, forehead, body, skin, shape, looks, hair, clothes—as "instances of a femaleness considered essential rather than existential."[31] In possession of these individual items that make a beautiful woman "her own excuse for being"

31. Morgan, "Humanbecoming," in *Images of Women in Fiction*, ed. Cornillon, 184.

(15–16), Cameron does not need a thinking, speaking female subject. He wants Francesca to remain as sign, the muted "other": "To tell the truth, he preferred his wife's silences. He wished there were more of them. Then her ineffable beauty shone out and she was his mysterious, beautiful woman again" (45).

Whereas Godwin portrays Cameron as the culturally sanctioned male gaze demanding female silence, she draws Francesca, the female antagonist, as a victim of that repressive cultural gaze. Put on the pedestal, infantilized, and reduced to object, Francesca loses her vitality and devolves into a "tiresome invalid" (16). She is protected from any work in the house because Cameron, wanting to preserve her beauty, does not mind doing such traditionally female work as cooking, cleaning, and washing. Her single task is to sit there looking perfectly beautiful. Totally dependent on her husband for even the smallest activity, Francesca lapses into a parasitic and stagnant existence, the highlight of which is getting dressed for dinner and tweezing her legs.

Beginning the narrative at the moment when the heroine is in the thick of inertia, Godwin portrays her emerging sense of self as she leaves Cameron to embark on a journey of self-discovery. As in *The Perfectionists,* however, Godwin emphasizes the binary opposition between male and female and the power of the patriarchal text of marriage. By establishing a stark juxtaposition between victimizer and victim, imprisonment and escape, Godwin develops a critique of patriarchal marriage as the cause for the heroine's inauthentic mode of living and the impediment to her growth, but she fails to develop an effective text of feminist resistance. In marked contrast to succeeding novels, in which complex personal struggle and ultimately growth dominate the narrative, *Glass People* leaves little room for the heroine to change and grow.

By delineating the heroine's resentment against and fear of her husband's power, Godwin exposes the way patriarchal marriage sustains female victimization. Francesca complains to her mother, for instance, that marriage is suffocating her, that she feels as if she is being "frozen," "hypnotized," and "slowly becoming paralyzed" (63). She describes her feelings of suffocation and fear to her one-night lover: "I can't breathe sometimes, after I've talked to him. He makes me feel full of . . . fear, something" (51). In a night-

mare that Francesca narrates in her letter to Cameron, she dreams of running away from black-masked doctors and nurses who have an operating table set for her. But her escape is stopped by the appearance of Cameron wearing the same black mask as the doctors and nurses, reinforcing the heroine's perception of herself as a terrified victim running away from adversity.

As in *The Perfectionists,* Godwin uses spatial constructs as images of imprisonment and entrapment to emphasize female victimization. Three times in the novel, Cameron visits Francesca's closet to reinforce his sense of ownership. The closet thereby becomes a metaphor for expressing Cameron's capacity for *containing* Francesca and maintaining a marriage commensurate with the cultural script of womanhood that has persisted for centuries. Gazing, the visual expression of reductive male perception, also evokes a sense of imprisonment and enclosure. Consider Francesca's premarriage nightmare of walking down the city streets and failing to see reflections of herself in the windows. Terrified at the nightmarish reality of nonidentity, Francesca wakes up screaming and finds Cameron "gazing down on her" (35). Raising her arms to him "like a child," she "searched his eyes and saw herself again" (35). The image of the infantilized female seeing herself safely contained in male gaze illuminates the hegemonic power of husbands over wives—their ability to enforce, and gain acquiescence in, their demands for control.

Godwin's use of Cameron's last name, Bolt, provides another example of using spatial constructs as "analogues" for the female protagonist's "existential condition."[32] She describes, for instance, Francesca's reaction to the media's play on her husband's name: "Recently cartoonists had begun drawing bolts all over the place: arrows, lightning flashes, locks on doors and gates, the crucial part of a firearm. She had never known there were so many kinds of bolts" (4–5). Through the sinister punning of "Bolt," which takes on a special meaning in light of Cameron's theory of containers and the tyranny of the male gaze, Godwin evokes a powerful sense of patriarchal imprisonment. Locked into an oppressive marriage in a multitude of ways and pierced by arrows and lightning flashes (potent Freudian phallic symbols),

32. Rubenstein, *Boundaries of the Self,* 4.

Francesca, Godwin suggests, could claim an autonomous identity only by "unbolting" Cameron and leaving the place owned by his name.

Finally, Godwin employs the motif of sickness—a dominant motif in fictions about and by women—as an important means of thematic development. She describes the heroine's preoccupation with "the girl in 313" (132), next to her own room in a cheap New York hotel. During her week-long stay there, Francesca constantly hears her next-door neighbor, a crying woman frantically shouting into the telephone and frequently running into the bathroom, suffering from diarrhea. She meditates on the girl's suicidal loneliness, writes Cameron about her situation, and tells her employer about her anxieties and concerns over the "mad" woman. By having Cameron claim that, upon inquiry, there is nobody in Room 313, Godwin leaves the existence of the crying woman ambiguous. But this nameless woman—only one of those "women in rooms alone, weeping, waiting" (169)—could well be interpreted as a phantom character—the madwoman in the attic of Francesca's mind—constructed to serve as a mental projection of Francesca's own psychic isolation and disintegration. Significantly, Cameron comes to Francesca, toward the end of the novel, when she is bedridden, "too weak to move, to think" (178), overwhelmed with a feeling of "her body beginning to dissolve, slowly, naturally, as if she were a candle thrust into a fire and held there" (176).

Godwin's emphasis on female victimization in *Glass People* leaves few avenues for her heroine to achieve even minimal autonomy. Patriarchal oppression, as Godwin presents it in this novel, is simply too strong. If Francesca remains tied to Cameron, she suffers invidious infantilization; if she rejects patriarchal authority, she becomes sick, physically bedridden and mentally lapsing into psychic disintegration. Without developing a positive, satisfying metaphor for her heroine's journey of self-discovery, Godwin is forced to bring her heroine back to the prison house of marriage, thereby failing to sustain a vision of successful female Bildung.

Failure of Self-Exploration

In its exploration of a concept of self, *Glass People* exhibits the same narrative tension we recognize in *The Perfectionists*. While making Cameron a

patriarchal victimizer, Godwin also grants him an achieved vision of an existential self that, though lacking full development in the novel, reflects the author's central concern about the status of "self" in a world of increasing uncertainty and contingency. This vision of self, expressed in the language of golf playing, emphasizes what the heroine of *Violet Clay* is to call one's "inner necessities"[33]—one's responsibility for creating challenges from within and continually moving toward higher, fuller forms of self-actualization.

For Cameron, playing golf is not just a sport but a form of self-definition: "It is a game in which I compete with myself and judge myself. On the golf course, I am my own constituency of one" (123). Even when playing with other people, he sees challenge coming from within: "it is always my own score I am striving to beat" (123). The challenge, in his view, comes not from competing and measuring himself against others but from "finding the most challenging and most complete use for [his] capacities" (123).

Underlying Cameron's ideas about golf is a vision of self that posits "the existentialist shaping of identity through projected goals,"[34] through constant self-creation to realize its fullest potentials. This vision entails a belief both in the *possibilities* of achieving positive and coherent self-definition and in the vital *process* of struggle for the fulfillment of a goal—two crucial components of Godwin's contemporary Bildungsromane.

Godwin's characterization of Cameron, like that of John Empson, reveals cultural conceptions of male self-definition. In patriarchal culture, male is perceived to be the carrier of a concept of self, whereas female is deprived of the possibilities of self-definition, except in the relational capacity as wife and/or mother. But, making Cameron both the embodiment of patriarchal force antagonistic to female growth and the articulator of a vision of self potentially expressive of Godwin's poetics of female self-definition creates tension in the novel's thematic and narrative development. Furthermore, Godwin's emphasis on the male protagonist's strong sense of destiny and agency and the heroine's limited self-awareness also contributes to the novel's tension resulting from its uneasy division between male and female, between the patriarchal text of oppression and the feminist text of self-search.

When we examine Godwin's development of the theme of feminist self-

33. Godwin, *Violet Clay,* 242.
34. Frye, *Living Stories, Telling Lives,* 116.

search in the novel, we recognize its inadequacy. At the same time as she makes Francesca aware of her stultifying marriage, sends her out into the world of social reality to find an identity outside marriage, and at times allows her to articulate a clear vision of self-exploration, Godwin nevertheless stresses the heroine's lack of a conscious, strong, and informed sense of gender identity and destiny that distinguishes her later heroines. Godwin shows Francesca at her most self-conscious in protesting against her debilitating marriage: "How she wanted to venture forth, experiment with life, explore her limits and extensions, feel passion . . ." (70). At moments like this (rare in the novel), Francesca expresses a desire for self-exploration and growth close to the "inner necessities" that compel all of Godwin's later heroines to take on their anguished journeys of self-discovery. Throughout the novel, however, Francesca's characterization reveals a limited capacity for experience, a nearly total lack of survival skills (she can find work only as a part-time domestic after she decides to leave her husband and stay in New York), and an impoverished self-consciousness. Her dependence on an exclusively physical sense of self severely qualifies her claim to self-expansion, and the external form of her quest reveals a lack of the "unceasing inner activity of perception" that marks the Bildung of Godwin's later heroines.[35] Just as her "extensions" beyond the patriarchal prison of her husband's home are determinedly superficial, her "limits" as a heroine of self-discovery are unmistakable.

In Godwin's portrayal, Francesca's limitations are primarily limitations of perception and consciousness. Having internalized a reductive self-image through the male gaze, Francesca perceives herself entirely through the limiting vehicle of the physical eye. She has no other conception of self than the cultural scripts of a beautiful woman, a woman who can wait contentedly for "destiny" to come and seek her when single and, when married, live her protected and "useful" life as ornament to her husband's public success. The "old, dazzling self" to which Cameron wants to restore her has been the only self whereby she derives purpose and identity. Though repelled by Cameron's gaze, she nevertheless subsists on a fragile, reductive, purely physical sense of self, needing constant reassurance of her beauty and youth.

Throughout the novel, Godwin employs mirror images as external rein-

35. Miles, "The Picaro's Journey to the Confessional," 988.

forcement of the heroine's feeble sense of selfhood.[36] Making mirror images Francesca's crucial means of self-definition after she leaves her husband, Godwin emphasizes her firm inscription in cultural definitions of femaleness and her lack of creative means to define herself. The male gaze, Godwin shows, not only reduces the female to a mere object but becomes an internalized condition. Francesca, for instance, needs her reflection in Cameron's eyes to grasp an image of herself she frantically searches for in her nightmare street windows. While she contemplates her projected emancipation from Cameron, mirror images become her single means of self-affirmation and are instrumental in reducing her again to an object of gaze: "As she walked back and forth in the terminal, enjoying the sway of her own body, reaffirming herself in a mirror here and there, a man kept watching her" (70). This kind of self-affirmation only lands Francesca in the arms of a stranger, who helps construct more mirrors for the heroine. Once, the bathroom mirror—figuratively "*her* territory" (87)—in the hotel where she and her lover are staying becomes an important vehicle for enhancing her feminine appeal in the eyes of her lover: "Going away from him, even for a little while, would make him cherish her again. She would go down and use her bathroom in peace and splash water on her face and brush her hair till it shone. He would be struck anew by her" (87). At another time, the street windows showing reflections of her walking with her lover reinforce a culturally inscribed fantasy: "Francesca looked at herself walking beside this graceful, serious man, in the plate glass of the windows they passed. She imagined herself married to him" (88).

After her unsuccessful interview at an employment agency, Francesca again resorts to a mirror to salvage her injured sense of self. The interviewer's disapproval of her lack of experience and self-knowledge does not seem to register, but her remarks about her body make a powerful imprint. "She was relieved to find herself alone in the restroom. She went at once to the mirror. Was she fat? . . . The mirror gave back the same reflection she was used to. For the first time, it seemed insufficient. For one thing, the hair . . . what a mess!" (106). After much work in front of the mirror, Francesca leaves the

36. Gaston writes: "That Francesca's entire identity exists in her appearance is reflected in the mirror imagery of the novel." Gaston, " 'Beauty and the Beast' in Gail Godwin's *Glass People*," 98.

employment agency feeling defeated. "She spent the morning wandering up and down the streets, in a kind of stupor, occasionally checking herself in the windows to see if she had gotten ugly, to see if she was still there" (107).

Mirror images, finally, play the central, determining role in Francesca's decision to go back to her husband. Taken by Cameron to Bergdorf's to shop for winter coats—Cameron's gifts to his wife after she informs him of her decision to leave him—Francesca again becomes prey to the seductive power of mirrors. "As they went up, Francesca began to feel more secure in herself. Shopping, trying on clothes, was one thing she could do as well as anyone in the world. It was one thing in which she could not be called inexperienced" (190). Here, Godwin points to the role of mirrors, especially mirrors in clothing stores, in female internalization of cultural conceptions of their self-identity. The triple mirrors in the dressing room where Francesca tries on "the stunning reproduction from a Byzantine mosaic of the Virgin" (187) then perform the miracle of reviving Francesca's self-confidence with a multitude of mirror images of herself: "Francesca observed the little pageant in the triptych. She remembered how she and Kate had trooped dutifully through all those cathedrals in Europe. Scenes from her past life flashed before her, clothes she had tried on over the years, reflections of herself at six, at ten, at eighteen, at twenty, reflections in so many mirrors, all over the world" (196).

Describing Francesca's reaction to various mirror images of herself, Godwin emphasizes on the one hand the pervasiveness of the cultural lens through which women are perceived and on the other women's enslavement to cultural conceptions of femaleness. Staring into the triple mirrors, Francesca becomes "transfixed" by the image of "three Camerons kneeling at her feet" and adoring her with his head "bowed over the luxuriant folds of the costume" (196). Framed in Cameron's and culture's gaze, Francesca regains a sense of her assets as a woman of beauty and grace. The motif of female imprisonment in male frames is further developed when Godwin links the mirror image to the spatial metaphor of the closet. Cameron tells Francesca that he wants to take the costume back with him: "It will hang in your closet. I'll take it out sometimes and remember the morning you tried it on, when it touched your skin" (197). Surrendering to a vision of herself recontained in the private spheres of domesticity, security, and subordination, Francesca

lets Cameron literally purchase her "the identity of his choosing"[37] and thus brings to an end her abortive journey of self-discovery.

Thus the pervasive cultural text of femaleness overpowers the emerging feminist consciousness that Godwin grants her heroine. Francesca returns home with her husband and, pregnant with her one-day lover's child, buries her urge toward self-definition in the expectations of motherhood. Resuming her status as sign, she nevertheless muses over these junctures "where things might have taken different turns"—if she "had not gotten sick"; if "it had not been the weekend"; if she "had not underestimated [Cameron's] terrible love for [her] and gone with him to the airport"; if she "had not agreed to come home and wear that dress 'just for the party'" (204). Pregnancy, the ultimate rescue from a lonely struggle for identity, is the "final If" that has compromised the lives of many women. Contemplating on that "final If," Francesca wonders "how many women there are in the world whose stories would be different had it not been for *that* If!" (204).

Francesca's musing is as far as Godwin could go in envisioning a heroine's struggle for self-definition and her "extensions" beyond the constraints of patriarchal culture.[38] Godwin's first two novels reflect the uneven development and the contradictions found in the women's movement of the 1970s. Seeking to explain female victimization *and* to gain female equality, many women turned to an analysis of male oppression. In so doing, they ironically devalued the abilities that women, living in a society with increasing freedom and opportunities for female growth, already possessed or could have developed to overcome oppression and create positive and evolving identities for themselves. *The Perfectionists* and *Glass People* participated in this early phase of feminist consciousness by portraying women with stunted identities, tied to dominant husbands, unable to achieve autonomous selfhood.

37. Hill, *Gail Godwin,* 30.

38. Gaston contends that at the end of the novel, Francesca contemplates self-exploration and becomes empowered: she "feels free to express herself, laughing for the first time in the novel and saying what she thinks." Her pregnancy, Gaston argues, becomes her source of inspiration and power; she "contemplates the possibility of giving birth to a giant." Gaston, "'Beauty and the Beast' in Gail Godwin's *Glass People,*" 102. Hill speaks of Francesca's "ironic triumph"—presented in "mythic rather than realistic terms" at the end of the novel, claiming the heroine's empowerment, however limited. Hill, *Gail Godwin,* 30.

With her first two heroines' self-search ending respectively in psychic isolation and impending motherhood—two contrasting themes that encapsulate
fictional female experience—Godwin leaves unanswered the question feminist critics as well as women writers ask in great frustration: "What can a
heroine do?"[39] Where, beyond the suicidal withdrawal into psychic isolation
and the institutional definition of woman as wife and mother, could a
heroine go to forge a meaningful existence for herself? What could she do to
become the heroine of her own life?

Read in isolation, *The Perfectionists* and *Glass People* expose patriarchal
culture by delineating on the one hand its victimization of women and on the
other the heroines' inability to break out of the bonds of patriarchy and grow
into mature, autonomous human beings. In the context of Godwin's controlling thematic concern about female growth, these two novels raise
questions about novelistic possibilities of creating complex, evolving heroines and representing their growth through compelling characterization and
dramatic revelation. In "Towards a Fully Human Heroine: Some Worknotes,"
written after the publication of *Glass People,* Godwin seriously probes the
question of fictional representation of female characters.[40] The conventions
of fiction and those of life, she suggests, cooperate in making it difficult to
create a "fully human" heroine. Fictional heroines are scripted into a limited
range of roles, and literary conventions impose far greater limitations on the
fictional development of female characters than that of male characters. "Why
is it so much easier," Godwin asks in frustration, "to create doomed heroines, flawed, chipped and hardened heroines, heroines more than half in love
with easeful death (whether it be cutting her wrists, developing an interesting psychosis, or finding a man who will say lie down and stop trying now,
I'll take over), heroines who maim and destroy the spirits of those around
them, castrate their men or let themselves be welded naked to chairs by men,
heroines who become agile demonstrators of fellatio in novels which
would better be called recipe books for adultery?"[41]

Although Godwin was talking about fictional representations of female

39. Joanna Russ, "What Can a Heroine Do? Or Why Women Can't Write," in *Images of
Women in Fiction*, ed. Cornillon, 7.
40. Godwin, "Towards a Fully Human Heroine," 26–28.
41. *Ibid.*, 26.

experiences in general, her statement conveys a strong sense of dissatisfaction with her own first two heroines. Writing these notes in the spring of 1972, at the time she "was embarking on *The Odd Woman*,"[42] Godwin envisions an image of a "better," "fully human" heroine, one that she "would like to meet" and "can be proud of." A "fully human" heroine, she tells us, "would be the subject of her own destiny, not the object of 'Blind Destiny' nor a character in somebody else's destiny." She would be committed to the work she feels "called to do with the dedication of a priestess." She would live "within her moral center, carefully furnished by herself, consisting of items she needed and liked to see around"; she would "refurbish it and spring-clean it and throw away or replace items when they wore out." She would have problems, but "they would be problems of growth more than problems of fear." She would, in conclusion, "have a name, a face, furniture, an occupation and a future."[43]

Godwin's later novels constitute a continuing exploration of a "fully human" heroine, an evolving self capable of creating mature and positive self-identities. An oppressive patriarchal world remains, but fruitful struggle against cultural scripts is possible. By developing new narrative strategies—the use of memory, mother-daughter bond, first-person narrative, and dialogic interplay of many voices—Godwin continually explores the possibilities of female growth in contemporary life and of fictional representation of women's struggle for autonomous selfhood. Her portraits of determined heroines struggling with both externally and internally imposed false self-definitions express a belief her first two novels do not foreground—that "the responsibility for self-discovery clearly lies with the individual who must cut through many forms of self-indulgence in order to recognize the truth about herself."[44]

42. Gail Godwin to Lihong Xie, June 22, 1989.

43. Godwin, "Towards a Fully Human Heroine," 26, 28.

44. Karen C. Gaston, "The Theme of Female Self-Discovery in the Novels of Judith Rossner, Gail Godwin, Alice Walker, and Toni Morrison" (Ph.D. dissertation, Auburn University, 1980), 153.

2

Becoming a Heroine
The Odd Woman

The Odd Woman is the first of Godwin's novels that portray a heroine's growth toward a positive self-identity outside the constraining cultural definitions of femaleness. Situating her heroine in the rich, complex frameworks of family, region, and culture—in sharp contrast to the secluded resort island in *The Perfectionists* and the vast, unknown city of New York in *Glass People*—Godwin begins to seek new ways of narrating female lives. Moving out of the binary representation of patriarchal oppression and feminist self-search of her first two novels, she now focuses on the text of feminist resistance to cultural scripts, depicting the heroine's embeddedness in them yet emphasizing her awareness of that embeddedness and her struggle to break free. Where she was unable to envision evolving patterns of female development earlier, Godwin now explores such potent themes of female growth as the mother-daughter relationship, female networks, place, and memory. Where she earlier resorted to spatial metaphors of patriarchal imprisonment to emphasize impediments to female growth, she now devises a dynamic literary metaphor to describe her heroine's growth: by struggling to "escape entrapment in plot expectations,"[1] the "odd woman" Jane Clifford develops a potential capacity for "writing beyond the ending"[2] and creating new texts of feminist self-definition.

1. Frye, *Living Stories, Telling Lives,* 1.
2. Rachel Blau DuPlessis uses "writing beyond the ending" to refer to the "invention of

Writing Beyond the Ending

In writing *The Odd Woman,* Godwin confronts the question of how to create what she envisions as a "fully human" heroine, a heroine with "problems of growth," not "problems of fear," one who is the protagonist of her own unfolding story, not a victim or "a character in somebody else's destiny." In her autobiographical essay "Towards a Fully Human Heroine: Some Worknotes," Godwin expresses a deep concern about fictional representations of female lives. She compares the experiences of her mother and herself as writer to show the constraints literary conventions impose on female-centered plots. In the 1940s, Godwin tells us, literary tastes dictated her mother's writing career. A writer of romantic love stories for pulp magazines, Godwin's mother "worked mostly from a single plot"—girls meeting men, courtship, complications, resolution (proposal or marriage). Her mother could paint the heroines' looks and wardrobes with lavish imagination, but she had little latitude in her choice of their occupations. "Her heroines," Godwin writes, "were stuck behind desks and counters in banks and stores, behind typewriters in offices (though they often got to marry the boss). They were models (but with impeccable morals), aspiring actresses who were always rescued just this side of the wings by a man who had a full-time part in mind for them." To meet the deadline and her family's financial needs, Godwin's mother stepped up the pace of her plot: she "resorted to having the girl meet the man as she rode or descended the bus or train . . . which took her to the city where she would look for a job." With a minimum amount of survival money in her heroine's purse and "thrifty paragraph management," she "could usually succeed in getting her heroine a man before she had to get a job, including the complications necessary to the course of love, which, even in pulp magazines, must not run smooth."[3]

Writing at a time of greater freedom and opportunities for women than in her mother's era, Godwin herself nevertheless faces the same restrictions on

strategies that sever the narrative from formerly conventional structures of fiction and consciousness about women." See her *Writing Beyond the Ending: Narrative Strategies of Twentieth-Century Women Writers* (Bloomington, Ind., 1985), x.

3. Godwin, "Towards a Fully Human Heroine," 27–28.

fictional heroines. Once, she tells us, she was forced to turn her writer-teacher-heroine into something else in order not to "complicate things" for a magazine editor. The revised heroine would be someone who "scribble[d] her *angst* on 4 × 6 notecards," instead of on paper, and *put them away*, to fulfill her creative aspiration. She would be someone who gave birth "quickly to a few children of her own," so that she could fulfill *at home* her talent for teaching. Of course she had to find herself a husband first, "even if he were a mere shadow."[4] So runs the same old plot for female lives: romantic love, marriage, and motherhood.

Godwin discarded her revised story because she did not like her heroine anymore. But the questions she raises—of literature's limited capacity for rendering female experience and the constraints novelistic conventions place on female-centered plots—remain a central concern in feminist literary criticism, expressed urgently in Joanna Russ's question "What can a heroine do?"[5] Heroines, Joanne S. Frye writes, "do not kill bears or set out to travel the world; they do not prove themselves in battle or test the boundaries of human survival; they merely fall in love or fail in love." Even in an age increasingly responsive to women's aspirations for freedom and self-realization, fictional heroines are still trapped in that single available plot, the Love Story, "with its tragic and comic variants, concluding in death on the one hand and marriage on the other."[6]

Plot expectations, Frye points out, are closely linked to gender expectations in a society dominated by male norms, and this connection bears importantly on feminist transformations of the Bildungsroman. As a male form, the traditional Bildungsroman facilitates the portrayal of its male protagonist achieving maturity. In its recast form, the contemporary female Bildungsroman faces the challenge of affirming the heroine's femaleness while claiming her mature selfhood—the difficulty of resolving the culture-specific conflict between female sexual self-definition and autonomy. Successful contemporary Bildungsromane, then, call for narrative strategies that enable the novelists to create authentic, fully human heroines who "escape entrapment in plot expectations."[7]

The Odd Woman is Godwin's first attempt to subvert plot entrapment

4. *Ibid.*, 27.
5. Russ, "What Can a Heroine Do?" in *Images of Women in Fiction*, ed. Cornillon, 7.
6. Frye, *Living Stories, Telling Lives*, 1.
7. *Ibid.*, 1, 5.

and create a heroine with "a capacity for complex selfhood in interaction with contemporary realities, resisting the old stories and telling lives in new ways."[8] The old stories, familiar to writers and feminist critics, are various versions of the Love Story, which has dominated the fate of fictional heroines, with death or marriage as alternative endings. New ways of telling female lives, on the other hand, had only begun to be invented in the early 1970s when Godwin wrote *The Odd Woman*. The novel was published in 1974, a midpoint of the decade that saw the publication of such feminist works as Mary Ellman's *Thinking about Women* (1968), Kate Millett's *Sexual Politics* (1969), Elaine Showalter's *A Literature of Their Own* (1973), Patricia Spacks's *The Female Imagination* (1975), Ellen Moers's *Literary Women* (1976), and Sandra M. Gilbert and Susan Gubar's *The Madwoman in the Attic* (1979). *The Odd Woman*, Rachel M. Brownstein observes, is a novel of a particular historical moment, exploring "literary-feminist themes" and illustrating the era's fascination with literary women. In the 1970s, Brownstein writes, reading and writing became an important channel for female self-understanding; and literary women—readers, writers, and English professors—seemed themselves "attractive role models, professional women who thought professionally about love and its images and stories, achieving, as they did so, an enviable integration of love and work."[9]

As an expression of what Brownstein terms "literary feminism," Godwin's conception of Jane as a heroine who seeks to become the author of her own book constitutes an act of feminist reconceptualization of female lives. A dedicated student of literature and a passionate believer in the power of words, Jane is preoccupied with a literary conception of life, seeing her life as a book and herself as its author. "If my life were a book," she contemplates, "I would like it to make sense to the careful reader."[10] Amid the existential despair of the modern era, with its pronouncement of the death of the author as well as the book,[11] Jane takes upon herself the task of writ-

8. *Ibid.*, 8.

9. Rachel M. Brownstein, "*The Odd Woman* and Literary Feminism," in *American Women Writing Fiction: Memory, Identity, Family, Space*, ed. Mickey Pearlman (Lexington, 1989), 176–77.

10. Godwin, *The Odd Woman*, 45. Subsequent references will be indicated in parentheses within the text.

ing the book of her own life, of creating herself as a heroine, "the kind," in Godwin's words, "who sits by herself in a room and sends alternative versions out into the world to inform—and extend—her experience."[12]

When "people don't plot anymore" (45) and linearity no longer exists, Jane insists on the Aristotelian definition of plot as progression from possibility to probability to necessity, safeguarding her moral well-being with George Eliot's motto "Seek a sure end." When things are no longer thought of as being nameable and explicable, Jane clings tenaciously to the defining power of words, firmly believing that the ability to truly name things corresponds to the degree of control one has over one's life. When "patterns of alienation, despair, disgust, denial, disintegration, and derangement" (118) permeate contemporary literature, Jane yearns to risk being a "visionary," for the ability to "utter phrases of unfashionable hope," to create "a few more lonely patterns of desire" (118).

To become the author of her own life story, Jane must sustain an "unfashionable hope" of discovering patterns and meanings from personal struggles for self-identity. For Jane, the concept of self is inextricably linked to literary representations of it. With her penchant for order and clarity, she laments the modern disintegration of the concept of a coherent self: "Was there, then —had there ever been—such a thing as a basic personality, or was that only a bygone literary convention? Could there exist a true, pure 'character' who was nobody but himself—subject, of course, to the usual accidents of existence—but capable of subordinating his (her) terrain as he progressed through time and space, cutting a swath of chapters that would be meaningful in retrospect?" (21). In face of the maddeningly accelerating derangements of modern society and its ruthless assaults on the humanist ideal of a centered self, Jane is well aware of the fragile and precarious position "self" has taken in today's world. She poses for herself squarely the inevitable, "everpresent problem of her unclear, undefined, unresolved self" (21), setting out on her frustrating, painful struggle for meaning, coherence, and self-definition.

11. John Barth, "The Literature of Exhaustion," *Atlantic Monthly,* CCXX (August, 1967), 29–34; Roland Barthes, "The Death of the Author," in *Image, Music, Text,* trans. and ed. Stephen Heath (New York, 1977), 142–48.

12. Godwin, "How to Be the Heroine of Your Own Life," 196.

The difficult task that Jane must confront in becoming the heroine of her own life is to resist and break free of the gender-specific plot expectations culture and literary conventions have imposed on fictional heroines. Contemporary literature fails to provide Jane with "pure" characters, whole personalities, and coherent meaning. But when she looks into the past she finds personal, familial, cultural, and literary values resounding with many distinctive voices, each articulating an aspect of the "culture text" of femininity.[13] Her great-aunt Cleva's tragic death, her grandmother Edith's gracious fulfillment of traditional womanhood, and her mother Kitty's ambiguous compromise between cultural expectations and self-fulfillment represent for Jane various versions of the same prevailing plot in female lives, the Love Story, revealing their entrapment in gender-specific plot expectations.

Life in the present, on the other hand, provides opportunities for change but also evokes confusion and conflicts. Although modern versions of female subordination persist in the behavior of many women like Jane's colleague Marsha, feminist consciousness has enabled others to choose a path different from that of traditional womanhood. Jane's colleague and friend Sonia's successful integration of love and work, her younger half sister Emily's presumption that she can attain professional and personal success, and her former college friend Gerda's radical rejection of patriarchal culture are examples of feminist resistance to the entrapment of cultural scripts. A heroine "in transit," caught between the old and new ways of living and perceiving, Jane must chart her own development and fashion a meaningful identity for herself out of conflicting conceptions of female destiny.

Nineteenth-century literary representations of female experience provide Jane with another frame of reference against which she tests her conceptions of her own identity. On days when the shape of her life threatens to disintegrate, Jane plays the game of "literary self-imaging,"[14] re-creating herself as a character in a Victorian novel: "'If Jane Austen were putting me in a novel, how would she define me? In that first succinct sentence where I "come on," how would she present me?' Or: 'If George Eliot were making

---

13. Adopting the term *culture text* from J. M. Lotman, Frye addresses the cultural perception of women as "sexually relational female beings." Frye, *Living Stories, Telling Lives,* 3.

14. Brownstein, *"The Odd Woman* and Literary Feminism," 184.

me a heroine in one of her books—though I doubt my character would meet her standards for a heroine—what would she say in that long, involved, philosophic passage where she justifies who and what I am and how I got that way?'" While she allows herself the satisfaction of the game as a means of self-conception, Jane is keenly aware of the limited boundaries for female development that literary conventions demarcate for fictional heroines. Being an Austen or an Eliot heroine, Jane understands, means being a protagonist in the Love Story and fulfilling the plot expectations for female lives, her identity merely relational and her destiny contingent on man. She self-deprecatingly disqualifies herself, living in an age of social mobility and sexual freedom, as a heroine in the fiction of Jane Austen, whose characters "lived in the same village all their lives" and concerned themselves with "marriages and the making of marriages." Even in an Eliot novel, where she would have a "better chance," she would still be a figure in the background of someone else's story: "she might even marry a nice man at the end and lead a useful life helping him" (21–22).

Jane's preoccupation with literary conceptions and representations of female lives and the way images of women in literature bear on and shape the lives of real women has been noted by several critics. Susan E. Lorsch, for example, sees this preoccupation as a "retreat from sexuality and the world around her."[15] By attributing Jane's unhappiness to her immersion in literature, Lorsch ignores Jane's critical interrogation of literature's capacity for representing female self-identity as well as the potential value of a literary conception of life in assisting the heroine's self-definition. Rachel M. Brownstein, in contrast, perceptively sees Jane's literary self-imaging as an imaginative and constructive strategy for revising the traditional plot of women's lives.[16] In Godwin's conception of her heroine as a potential author of her own book, Jane's "literary emplotment"[17] can be seen as a complex process of negotiation, marked by the conflict between a deeply psychological embeddedness in femininity and a conscious resistance to it, between the dangerous need to repeat the traditional female plot and a desire to write her

15. Susan E. Lorsch, "Gail Godwin's *The Odd Woman*: Literature and the Retreat from Life," *Critique*, XX (Winter, 1978), 24.

16. Brownstein, "*The Odd Woman* and Literary Feminism," 174.

17. I borrow the word *emplotment* from Frye, *Living Stories, Telling Lives*, 39.

new story. A literary conception of female destiny, then, poses the threat of entrapment, but it also opens up for the heroine potentials of mature self-definition in face of all contradictory possibilities that she perceives around her, in literature as well as in life.

Godwin makes clear the ambiguities of Jane's literary conception of female destiny and its implications. On the one hand, she depicts Jane's passionate immersion in literature to seek patterns that could impose meaning on her fragmented existence. Jane "ransacked novels for answers to life" (24) and continued to believe that "if only she kept on reading the right books, doing research on the things she did not understand, the mystery of her life would come clear" (19). Such a regressive form of self-search runs the risk of foreclosing her own destiny in preconceived gender roles prescribed by cultural scripts and inscribed through literary conventions. On the other hand, however, Godwin emphasizes Jane's awareness of the danger of self-imprisonment such an approach entails. Stories, Jane realizes, are other people's versions and interpretations of things. They can serve as warnings or lessons, but even the longest stories have to "end somewhere." Trying to squeeze oneself into a particular story entails a denial of self-identity, with "vital parts of [oneself] lopped off" or, even worse, without the ability ever to "get out again" (43).

Godwin's most revealing use of Jane's literary conception of life as a potential means of self-definition is the mistress plot she devises for the novel. As a single woman in a sterile love relationship with a married man, Jane is trapped in the plot of the Love Story, playing the role of "mistress," one of the few available roles assigned to heroines in literature. As a literary woman of the 1970s, on the other hand, Jane is well aware of literature's many mistress stories and the limitations of the role. Furthermore, Jane is preoccupied with the mistress story in her family—her great-aunt Cleva's tragic death at the hands of a "villain," a story with rich literary associations, narrated both within and outside the family so recurrently that it has become a kind of fiction. Jane's growth as a heroine, Godwin shows in the course of the novel, lies in her ability to see parallels between Cleva's story and her own, to grasp the ambiguous relationship between life and literature, and to truly "name" herself.

Throughout the novel, Jane carries the conflicting images of a heroine

stuck in fixed roles and of one creating her own new roles. Toward the end of the novel, she sums up her struggle to become a heroine in a succinct literary metaphor: "we are always in some play or other. Some of us move about, trying different plays, others of us stick doggedly to one role throughout our lives. What I am interested in is: do we create the roles, or do they create us" (349). The distinction between creating one's own roles and letting the old, fixed roles define and constrain oneself is one between, in Godwin's own words, "a passive victim" and a "heroine-in-progress."[18] To become a heroine-in-progress requires a capacity for "writing beyond the ending," beyond the institutional definitions of womanhood, beyond the cultural scripts of femaleness, beyond all imposed plot expectations—marriage, death, madness, and psychic isolation.

For each single role, Jane observes, there will be many different versions, and one remains "indestructible" by "eluding for dear life the hundreds and thousands of already written, already completed stories," reminding yourself "that you were more than they were, that you had to write yourself as you went along, that your story could not and should not possibly be completed until *you* were . . . dead" (44). Jane's growth as a heroine evolves, as we will see, around the dynamic literary metaphor of writing beyond the ending. To become a "fully human" heroine in control of her own destiny, Jane must "[negotiate] contradictory or conflicting conceptions" of herself.[19] She must overcome the scripts of the Love Story, codified through familial and cultural heritage, literary convention, and psychological internalization. She must write and rewrite her life as she lives it, remembers it, and reflects upon it, composing sentences, paragraphs, and chapters, designing the shape of her book as she discards, revises, and creates portions of the plot. By equipping her heroine with such a creative approach to the construction of the self, by situating her struggle for selfhood in the social constructs of family, place, and culture, and by emphasizing the role of memory as a tool of self-definition, Godwin enables her to break through encrusted traditions and the ambiguities of modern female identity in order to embrace the potentials of a "heroine-in-progress."

18. Godwin, "How to Be the Heroine of Your Own Life," 194, 227.
19. Grimshaw, "Autonomy and Identity," 103.

A Woman in Transit: Family, Place, and Female Networks

"I think I was one of those people who have the misfortune to grow up with one foot in one era and the other foot in the next. I wanted to write books, but my body got in the way; yet I wanted my babies, when they came." To her mother's bitter confession, Jane responds wistfully: "Sometimes I think those persons raised in the interstices of *Zeitgeists* are the ones most punished" (169–70). Depicting this rare, intimate moment of mother-daughter exchange, with Jane perhaps understanding that she, too, has been "raised in the interstices of *Zeitgeists*," Godwin evokes powerfully and movingly generations of women struggling to fulfill themselves, caught between personal aspirations and cultural scripts.

Bringing Jane back home one more time to attend her beloved grandmother's funeral, to the place that she has tried to escape from yet has remained psychologically bound up to, Godwin unfolds her heroine's ongoing struggle for self-identity in the rich context of family and region. Each homecoming for Jane amounts to a psychological test: she must fight to resist her family's image of her as their "same old Jane" (85), raised with the cultural ideals of the South, and affirm the image of herself as an independent woman seeking new ways of self-definition. The test of identity becomes more urgent and intense in the atmosphere of "home," an atmosphere at once alienating and seductive, rich in its revelations of region and culture. Despite her mental preparations for the encounter with the family and the place that have shaped her development, Jane cannot escape feeling "uncomfortably restless" (157), even downright defeated: being home turns her into "an anachronism" (129), into a helplessly "dependent" and "undeveloped" wife with "only her inferior emotions and terrors to keep her company," severed from her "better half"—her mind—that resides in the Midwest, possessing "rationality and discipline" (160).

This image of a conflicted self split between culturally defined "feminine" and "masculine" traits vividly captures Jane's awareness of herself as a woman "in transit between the old values, which threaten to engulf her every time she comes home, and the new values, which she must hack out for herself" (132). One side of her—the "feminine" side that ties her to traditional womanhood, to the lives of her mother and grandmother—is still embed-

ded in the cultural script of a region where, according to Anne Firor Scott, middle-class women were long burdened with fulfilling the role of "lady," a role that reduced them to ornaments for their husbands and deprived them, even more than their northern sisters, of personal and psychological histories.[20] The other side of her—the "liberal humanist" side that strives for independence and personal fulfillment—urges her, at this time in history, to pursue feminist modernity.

Feminist consciousness—the spirit of the 1970s—permeates *The Odd Woman,* in Godwin's portrayal of Jane's struggle to seek new ways of understanding female lives—their body, sexuality, and identity—and in her exploration of the role of female networks in promoting self-understanding. Writing about an age when new possibilities for female self-development abound while old cultural scripts still retain a psychological grip on many modern women, Godwin captures the confusion and agony the heroine experiences in response to the profound changes of a unique historical moment. Surrounded by conflicting voices and choices, Jane explores her own limitations and possibilities through the framework of family, place, and female networks. She looks both ways—horizontally and vertically—for inspiring role models, perspectives, and solutions. She "ransacked novels for answers to life, she wheedled confidences out of friends, investigated and ruminated over the women she had sprung from, searched for models in persons who had made good use of their lives, admirable women who, even if not dramatic, might guide her through their examples" (24).

Unclear about what her "best life" would be, Jane sees around her women who provide role models other than traditional womanhood and who seem, unlike herself, to be confident of the choices they have made and the identities they have built. She observes with wonder, for instance, the "female power"—"something much older and stronger than any cultivated practices of the subtle and delicate art of Being a Woman" (95)—of her young half sister, Emily. Self-assured and unbound by tradition, Emily seems to Jane to be free of the inner conflicts and ambiguities that afflict her own troubled selfhood. Emily had "spotted the man she wanted when she was twelve" (23), "begun her campaign to annex him to her life" (59), and married him at

20. Anne Firor Scott, *The Southern Lady: From Pedestal to Politics 1830–1930* (Chicago, 1970).

fifteen "with the approval of family and Church" (23). Getting things done cleanly and efficiently is the dominant pattern of Emily's life, and, not the submissive and docile wife of her mother's and grandmother's generation, she quickly takes over her lazy, passive husband's life, directing his career, organizing his resources, and supervising the implementation of the plans she makes for him. Jane finds Emily an enigma, whose "basic order, solid inner principles, a precocious maturity arrived at without the intervening stages of confused adolescence" (107) contrast sharply with her own "ever-present problem of her unclear, undefined, unresolved self" (21).

In her colleague and friend Sonia, on the other hand, Jane sees the best of modern feminist endeavor. Sonia excels with ease in everything that Jane wants to achieve for herself. As Rachel M. Brownstein points out: "with her children, the already-married lover she got to marry her, her intellectual intensity, her charismatic classroom style, her long list of publications, and her tendency to blush endearingly to the roots of her beautiful hair," Sonia is "a bright female college student's ego ideal." Jane's friendship with Sonia, intellectual and literary rather than intimate, provides her with important perspectives on literary representations of female lives and on the relationship between literature and lived experience. Their intense discussions about literature and life give Jane a strong sense of sisterhood, a kindred feeling, Brownstein states, through their "ecstatic shared flight into a heady realm where forgetfulness of the small, confining self becomes a sense that that self has been enlarged to include sister selves, of women writers and of women who have been written about."[21] Admiring her friend, Jane nevertheless feels her extraordinary success beyond reach.

If Sonia represents for Jane the inspiration and ideal of feminism, Gerda, Jane's friend from college, epitomizes its many ambiguities and conflicts. After flinging herself into every trendy cause "with a zealous, greedy intensity" (35), Gerda now edits a feminist newspaper, *Feme Sole,* renouncing love and the expectation of being "fulfilled or emotionally completed by a member of the opposite sex" (40). Though Jane finds Gerda's radical perspectives on love and female self-fulfillment unsettling, she continues to feel stimulated by her friend's "continued ability to re-create herself" (36).

Godwin's delineation of the experiences of Emily, Sonia, and Gerda points

21. Brownstein, "*The Odd Woman* and Literary Feminism," 176.

to new possibilities for female fulfillment in an age quivering with fervent feminist ideas. Yet the clarity, perfection, and absolutism that she ascribes to the lives of these three women—a modern matriarchal queen, a superwoman, and a radical feminist—express her skepticism about any easy solution to the difficult problem of mature female self-definition, a complex process riddled with contradictions, ambiguities, and conflicts. Though she grants all three successful self-definition and fulfillment in the lives they have chosen, Godwin does not make them adequate role models for the heroine. Instead, she emphasizes Jane's unique problem of making sense and meaning of her own life out of the conflicts and ambiguities that inform modern female identity. Alienated from Emily's generation, with its self-assured expectations of success; estranged from Gerda's radical feminism, with its renunciation of many things she continues to desire; and awed by Sonia's easy and complete success, Jane must grope for her own path, seeking new ways to live her life and define who she is.

Her groping takes her back to her past, to the family and place that converged to shape her development as she grew up socialized with traditional southern womanhood, resisting it yet remaining psychologically married to it. That family consists of a grandmother who "stayed home and minded Jane 'like a mother'" and a mother who "went out and worked 'like a father'" (90). Mother and grandmother both remain crucial figures in Jane's life, continuing their share in shaping Jane's development. Jane's psychological journey into this past of family and place is part of her Bildung; coping with her maternal and cultural heritage allows her to assess her own experience in the context of generational, social, and cultural interaction.

Godwin's exploration of the mother-daughter plot in *The Odd Woman* again places her in the forefront of current feminist thought. The centrality of the mother-daughter relationship to the question of female identity has become a key issue in feminist scholarship. Since the midseventies, the "great unwritten story"[22] of this primary relationship in the life of every woman has engaged feminist scholars of various disciplines, ranging from sociological, anthropological, and historical to philosophical, psychological, and literary. Of all feminist scholarship on the mother-daughter relationship, "the most

22. Adrienne Rich, *Of Woman Born: Motherhood as Experience and Institution* (New York, 1976), 225.

complete and complex work . . . to date," Marianne Hirsch points out in a review essay, "has been undertaken in the area of feminist psychoanalysis."[23]

Hirsch points to three major trends in recent feminist psychoanalytic works about mothers and daughters. Drawing respectively on "Freudian oedipal paradigm and neo-Freudian theory, especially object-relations psychology"; Jungian archetypal theories; and Lacanian theories, these three approaches to the mother-daughter relationship, according to Hirsch, show revealing points of intersection. Whether they attribute the gendered identity to the dynamics of the mother-infant bonding, to Jungian symbols and archetypes, or to the Lacanian symbolic order and semiotic logic, they all feature "a similar insistence on the ultimate lack of separation between daughter and mother and an emphasis on multiplicity, plurality, and continuity of being." Women's being, they all claim, is interpenetrating, "continuous, plural, in-process."[24]

The view of female identity as continuous, relational, and plural provides a useful perspective for examining Godwin's fictional portrayals of the mother-daughter relationship in *The Odd Woman* and in subsequent novels.[25] Godwin, however, perceives the mother-daughter dyad in social, cultural, and psychological terms, rather than focusing on its psychosexual dimensions. In *The Odd Woman,* the dynamics of the mother-daughter relationship reveals the social construction of female identity, a process of "generational interconnection of body experience, sexual ideology, and feminine consciousness."[26] Depicting it as the most important relationship in the heroine's development of gendered identity, Godwin explores not only the continuities between mother and daughter but also the conflicts between them as the daughter grows to maturity and questions her inherited values, attempting to separate herself from her mother.

Edith, the beloved grandmother to whom Jane is deeply attached, is portrayed as the embodiment of "the perfect Southern lady"—"elegant, snobbish, beautiful to the very end" (56). Born in the 1890s and living into the

---

23. Marianne Hirsch, "Mothers and Daughters," *Signs,* VII (1981), 202–203.

24. *Ibid.,* 204, 209, 211.

25. I use the term "mother-daughter relationship" to refer to Jane's relationship to both her mother, Kitty, and her grandmother, Edith, who was a mother figure to Jane.

26. Nancy M. Theriot, *The Biosocial Construction of Femininity: Mothers and Daughters in Nineteenth-Century America* (New York, 1988), 2.

1970s, she has, in Carolyn Rhodes's words, "carried intact through the murky twentieth century the clear standards of her nineteenth-century Southern heritage."[27] In her youth, as the family story goes, she managed to faint dramatically into the arms of a man she would marry—a Good Man who would take good care of her and protect her from the life she calls "a disease." In her old age, she remains the "voice of respectability" (101), awing everybody with her green bottle of smelling salts. She endured sex as a duty and necessity while married and devoted herself to child rearing when a widow, feeling fulfilled and taking pride in knowing who she was and having the "propriety of fine manners, carriage, and dress"[28]—a perfect life for a woman of her generation.

What is the legacy Edith leaves to a granddaughter living in the last third of the twentieth century? By portraying her heroine as a rebellious southern daughter who flees her place of birth and upbringing and lives her single, independent life, Godwin shows that Jane has in rationality and actuality rejected the protected, restricted life of Edith's generation. Yet, at the same time, Godwin depicts Jane's psychological rootedness in the cultural ideals out of which women of her grandmother's generation have built their identities and found their proper roles in society. This psychological marriage to conventional expectations, Godwin demonstrates, expresses itself through the mother-daughter bond. Edith, the mothering woman of Jane's childhood and adolescence, the consummate expression of the "culture text" of femininity, has played a significant role in shaping Jane's sense of body and gendered identity. Her emphatic use of her sister Cleva's stories—her tragic experience with the "villain" and her riding a horse on the day her period began—made a lasting imprint on the impressionable young girl, linking biology and destiny, alienating the adolescent Jane from her own body and her rapidly approaching womanhood.

What Godwin emphasizes is not so much Jane's adolescent experience itself as the effects of her adolescent socialization on her gendered development. She portrays Jane in the act of constantly remembering her past with Edith, showing the relationship between Jane's self-perception and maternal-

27. Carolyn Rhodes, "Gail Godwin and the Ideal of Southern Womanhood," *Southern Quarterly*, XXI (Winter, 1983), 58.
     28. *Ibid.*

cultural indoctrination. In particular, she depicts Jane's love relationship with Gabriel as a revelation of the heroine's maternal legacy.

Waiting for another brief encounter with Gabriel in a hotel room, Jane recollects the anxiety, guilt, and terror she experienced at puberty. Disgusted with her own budding womanhood, she "wished more than anything to have it over with, to be respectable and old, with no taint of men and the blood that seemed to go with them, like Edith was" (238). As a mature woman, Jane cannot escape the repressive sexual ideology that Edith has infused into her consciousness. She suffers constipation because she cannot stand her lover hearing the sound of her bowel movement; she draws pornographic pictures that express her conflicted feelings about female sexuality. Her lovemaking is best when she fantasizes it. When she is with Gabriel, she has to "put some imagined frame around the real scene, . . . to make it work" (139). Once, to sustain the sexual act, she has to rustle up Aunt Cleva's villain, herself becoming a little girl again, "trying to understand the menacing relationship between blood and impurity and a dead aunt she had never seen, who was done in by her womanhood" (239).

More than sexual inhibition, more than proprieties and etiquette, Godwin shows how Jane has inherited from Edith the "feminine discourse" of subservience, dependence, and relational orientation. Despite her rejection of the restricted, self-abnegating life Edith has lived, Jane vacillates between the conflicted desires for the freedom of individual pursuit and the security of a traditional marriage. As a modern, independent woman, she prides herself on having escaped early from the fate of many women deprived of autonomous selfhood through marriage and motherhood. She despises the life of her cousin Frances, Cleva's illegitimate daughter, "safe and secure on [her] husband's thousand acres, hostessing meetings and teas for the D.A.R. and the U.D.C., having [her] red hair washed and set each week" (132). As a single woman, however, who must confront alone all "phantoms" of herself, Jane cannot escape a strong yearning for the protection and security of marriage. Even though she infuses equality and mutuality into her ideal of marriage, using the marriage of George Eliot and George Henry Lewes as an abiding example, she betrays her deep immersion in traditional plot expectations through a dream in which she transmutes that ideal into just another story of a woman running away and seeking her destiny through a man.

Because of her entrapment in plot expectations, Jane initiates and persists in a sterile love relationship to fulfill her needs for relational self-definition. She compromises her feminist modernity by consenting to male norms of female identity, accepting Gabriel's chauvinistic definitions of his wife and mistress as "apples" or "oranges" (8) and thinking of herself in terms of "how large a place she filled in his life" (7). In her last year of a temporary academic appointment, she refuses to search for a job, hoping to spend the next year in England with Gabriel if he gets a Guggenheim. She becomes angry when she has to act as the strong "husband" in the presence of her weak, dependent, and submissive colleague Marsha, and she fantasizes about being taken care of by a man she sees on the airplane. Even at the moment she leaves Gabriel—the climax of the novel—she still cannot sever herself from the scripts Edith has helped her to internalize. Painfully torn between the prospect of traveling alone in the dismal rain and of nestling complacently in the embrace of a man, she surrenders to the image of Edith fainting conveniently into the arms of her future husband, hearing—with great self-pity—her grandmother's dramatic line: "I give up, you take over; life is a disease" (360).

Against Edith's beautifully fulfilled life—by the standards of traditional womanhood—Godwin juxtaposes the ambiguous, conflicted existence of Jane's mother Kitty, an early version of rebellious southern daughters, whose search for self ends in compromise. Portrayed as a "flamboyant" belle in her youth, Kitty "enjoyed her heyday as enchantress, beset by suitors, though none of them were quite the flawless gentleman her mother wished."[29] Like Godwin's own mother, Kitty taught literature and wrote romantic love stories for pulp magazines, creating heroines stuck in the only role available to them but aspiring to a different, more satisfying future for herself. "There was a time when I wanted every one of the things you want," she says to Jane. "I wanted love. I wanted a career. I wanted everything eternally beautiful, and with no compromise. I wanted a kind of marriage I knew my parents had not had: a marriage of passion *and* esteem. I wanted so many things it makes me sick to remember" (169).

In sharp contrast to a past of active pursuit, sustained by a yearning for self-fulfillment, Kitty's present life is one of subservience and self-resignation. Marriage to Ray Sparks, a younger, intellectually inferior, and domineering

29. *Ibid.*

man, deprives Kitty of the independence she once desired, but it gives her the protection and security she needs. Suppressing her bitterness about her unfulfilled dreams, she now self-complacently celebrates the end to the anguished struggle to be the heroine of her own life, thankful that all the "yearning," "choosing," and "dreary, endless agonizing over what you cannot have" (169) are finished for her. Accepting this ending to the plot of her life story, she settles quite comfortably into her present existence, playing her dual role of the subservient wife and the elegant, elusive "lady."

In her characterization of Kitty, Godwin emphasizes the chasm culture insists upon and perpetuates between a woman's femaleness and her autonomy. Kitty struggled to claim both, only to write herself into one of the "premature endings" (44) of the female plots that culture and literature prescribe for fictional heroines, entrapped in the prison house of patriarchal marriage and of her own body. Kitty's failure of self-fulfillment, Godwin suggests, is a product of a particular time and culture. Brought up "to believe woman's best virtue was that of renouncing herself" (170), Kitty had no role models that she could draw on to sustain her creative vision of life; she had few alternatives in a society that denied women what it presumed for men— sexual and autonomous self-definition. Like many other fictional heroines of the era, Kitty chose to capitulate to culture's ideals of womanhood, secure in the knowledge that she had the privilege to "close off the uncertain option, . . . and stay home at nights where [she] belonged, building [her] own interior castle" (11).

The threat and appeal of such a premature ending to one's lonely struggle for selfhood, Godwin shows, lie at the center of Jane's ambivalent relationship with her mother, Kitty. Once Kitty's sisterlike confidante, Jane may very well see her mother in her younger years as an earlier version of herself, a woman with a "dimension of longing" (250) for a life beyond what the ideal of southern womanhood prescribes. When she was five years old, Jane remembers, she knew her mother was different from the heroines she created for the love stories she was writing. In her childhood imagination, her mother would make a much more interesting, appealing heroine, someone who taught literature and wrote stories and had a little girl like herself. Growing up watching her daring, independent mother turning into a subservient, dependent wife, Jane forms a complex, divided relationship with

her mother, one that fuses rejection and longing, envy and fear, intimacy and distance.

At times, Jane sees her mother's choice as "sensible," envying her for gaining security "against old age and death" (11). At other times she resents Kitty's display of an assurance—"born perhaps of her own security" (210)—that seems to mock a stubborn idealism she herself has given up but her daughter is still pursuing. Observing Kitty in one of her performances as "the tightrope walker" (119) between her demanding daughter and her domineering husband, Jane reinforces her resolution not to repeat Kitty's life: "*I would rather die an old maid in my own private space, . . . being as undiplomatic as I like to the morning shadows in my house, than live a 'protected' life under such domination, such chaos*" (120). Yet in times of distressing solitude, she indulges in private fantasies of life with Gabriel, with its welcome domestic boredom, even a degree of male domination.

As in *The Perfectionists,* Godwin portrays the heroine's profound ambivalence about motherhood, a revelation, in Jane's case, of her conflicted response to her mother's life. Motherhood, what Nancy M. Theriot calls "the quintessential expression of femaleness" in nineteenth-century America, remains an important symbol of womanhood in the twentieth century.[30] It entices with the illusion of self-fulfillment and threatens with the danger of self-destruction. Jane is afraid of motherhood, imaging it as a metaphorical prison house and a baby factory, yet in her sexual fantasies, "it was just that, being made into a baby factory, that had the power to excite her most" (298). Furthermore, as Judith Kegan Gardiner points out, she "thinks of loneliness ultimately in terms of mothering,"[31] fearful of being "doomed always to be her own child, the 'only lonely'" (297). As she grows older, "moving inexorably toward the last of her childbearing years" (298), motherhood as a choice takes on greater urgency, pressing with all its ambiguous implications. Crossing off all other options of "self-fulfillment" chosen by George Gissing's characters in his novel *The Odd Women,* Jane stops short of the word *child.* Not only does she refuse to "close all doors of her mind to the possibility of such a creature someday knocking," but even when she affirms

30. Theriot, *The Biosocial Construction of Femininity,* 45.

31. Judith Kegan Gardiner, "Gail Godwin and Feminist Fiction," *North American Review,* CCLX (Summer, 1975), 86.

her ability to forgo that possibility, she expresses, implicitly, a yearning for motherhood as a satisfying means for female self-fulfillment. She feels a saddening loss in relinquishing "the satisfaction of razing the mess she had made of herself to the ground and building a nice clean one in its place in order to justify her own disappointed existence (starting all over again in a small, fresh creature)" (298).

What does she really want? Where is she on the Aristotelian scale of plot? Jane asks herself these questions as she views Edith's dead body, saying goodbye to a certain role in her life as well as to her beloved grandmother. She is no one's granddaughter anymore; one day she will cease to be anyone's daughter. Yet she is not—perhaps never will be—anyone's mother. She has pursued the goal of feminist self-definition as determinedly as other women seek marriage or motherhood. Now, with the terror of solitude, the disappointment of an unfruitful love relationship, and the insecurity of her job situation, she feels the same kind of void other women feel after their children grow up and leave home. What is female destiny beyond biological and sociocultural definitions of womanhood? What is the truth of her individual life?

Though she envies, in Carolyn Rhodes's words, "the certainty of Edith's choices" and longs for the security Kitty's life provides, Jane could not forgo her feminist pursuit of selfhood and let herself sink "in a heap at somebody's feet" (360), as Edith did beautifully in her time, or write herself into premature endings, as Kitty was forced to do in an earlier age. What lies ahead of her if she, "spiritually the daughter of both,"[32] sustains her lonely journey of self-search before death puts an end to her story? She does not know and expects no simple answer.

Portraying a heroine so divided in her desires and needs, seeking the new text of feminist self-definition yet psychologically married to the old "culture text" of femininity, Godwin again illustrates, as she does in *The Perfectionists,* how the construction of female identity is a matter of negotiating between conflicting self-conceptions and transcending the culturally available roles for women. In *The Odd Woman,* however, Godwin suggests that such conflicted self-conceptions are part of the heroine's maternal heritage she must cope with in order to make sense and wisdom out of lived experience. For Jane, understanding Edith's and Kitty's lives means understand-

32. Rhodes, "Gail Godwin and the Ideal of Southern Womanhood," 58, 60.

ing the ambiguities of her maternal heritage; it is her way of paying off her debts so that she can start growing on her own account[33]—debts to the family and the place that have shaped her development, from which she can flee geographically but cannot escape psychologically.

It is easy yet unkind and futile, Jane realizes, "for the 'daughters' of the world to announce to the 'mothers' that, yes! everything was still possible, from outrageous happiness to fulfilled and unbroken selves" (397). It is difficult, yet necessary, Godwin insists through her characterization of Jane, for the daughters themselves to break from the culturally available patterns for female lives—patterns that have restricted and enslaved the lives of their mothers—and to forge a new, meaningful existence for themselves. In delineating Jane's complex psychological responses to her maternal legacies, Godwin emphasizes the role of the mother-daughter relationship in reinforcing the heroine's awareness of her conflicted self and of the necessity to escape the entrapment of plot expectations in order to become the heroine of her own story. For her heroine, Godwin illustrates, the process of "writing beyond the ending" is intimately tied to the social construction of memory.

Memory, Consciousness, and the Growth of a Heroine

Using what David H. Miles terms "the psychological time of memory,"[34] superimposed upon the chronological time frame of the story, Godwin fully establishes in *The Odd Woman* a dominant, recursive narrative pattern that defines growth in her contemporary Bildungsromane. The use of memory, a narrative feature in *The Perfectionists*, becomes in *The Odd Woman* a crucial design for the portrayal of the heroine's growth in self-understanding and toward self-definition. Through the prism of memory, Godwin stretches the relatively brief, uncomplicated narrative present—the heroine's weeklong visit home on the occasion of her grandmother's death and her subse-

33. Gail Godwin quotes Doris Lessing's heroine Martha Quest, "Towards a Fully Human Heroine," 28.

34. Miles, "The Picaro's Journey to the Confessional," 989.

quent meeting with her lover—into an expansive, complex psychological space, where the heroine encounters her past, assesses her present, and speculates on her future. Making memory Jane's primary means of perception, Godwin enables her heroine to use her past to understand and define herself in relation not only to family, place, and culture but also to her previous selves.

Godwin's extensive use of memory in *The Odd Woman* as an aid to self-definition links the heroine to a specific type of Bildungsroman hero David H. Miles calls the "confessor." The "confessor," according to Miles, is "the hero of personality growth, the introspective hero, the protagonist of consciousness, memory, and guilt." In opposition to the "picaro" for whom time is "linear, episodic, and chronological," the "confessor" experiences time "as being complex, multilayered, and psychological." Whereas the "picaro" moves from adventure to adventure in "infinite expansions and 'continuations,'. . . the self of the confessor does not exist a priori, but must be recollected, summoned up out of the remembrance of things past—a process usually launched by crisis and ending in a 'conversion' to a new self."[35]

The increasing stress on consciousness and memory as the locus of growth began in nineteenth-century Bildungsromane and continued into the twentieth century, reflecting changing concepts of social reality and human personality. This trend has found emphatic expressions in contemporary female Bildungsromane, and the significance of memory in self-discovery and self-definition, Bonnie Hoover Braendlin argues, explains the prevailing use of first-person narration in the fiction of female growth.[36] Even though Godwin does not use the first-person narrative in *The Odd Woman*, her focus on the interior movement of the reminiscing heroine, largely the center of consciousness, results in a pattern of fictional time Miles describes as "complex," "multilayered," and "psychological." By making memory and consciousness the "moving forces"[37] behind the heroine's growth, Godwin explores the possibility of creating a "heroine-in-progress," with potential capacity to write

35. *Ibid.,* 980–81.

36. Braendlin examines contemporary authors' use of first-person narration in delineating a heroine's self-development in both "Alther, Atwood, Ballantyne, and Gray," 18–22; and "New Directions in the Contemporary Bildungsroman," 161–71.

37. Miles, "The Picaro's Journey to the Confessional," 986.

beyond the prescribed endings of the female plot, to invent new texts of evolving female selfhood.

The structure for the heroine's "odyssey to self-awareness"[38]—composed of memories of her family history, her personal experiences, her female friendships,[39] and her literary readings—reveals a new level of craft and sophistication in *The Odd Woman*. In delineating the heroine's mental and psychological journey into the past, Godwin makes memory a process of selection, interaction, and interpretation, through which the heroine grasps the meaning of her life. Memories of particular events and people from Jane's past recur persistently in her consciousness, recollected again and again by the reminiscing heroine in various contexts. Progressively, these remembrances take on fresh, added significance as the heroine becomes increasingly aware of the familial and cultural contexts of her personal struggles. Through memory and consciousness, Godwin brings Jane into contact with not only those forces of her past life that have helped shape her development as a woman but also her earlier selves molded by such a past. Through memory and consciousness, she enables the heroine to achieve an enhanced awareness of her conflicted selves—the self psychologically bound up to traditional plot expectations and the self in resistance to its entrapment. Memory and consciousness thus assume primacy in Jane's Bildung, instrumental to her self-understanding in the context of cultural scripts of femaleness.

Godwin's careful craft manifests itself at the very beginning of the novel. Portraying an insomniac woman besieged with thoughts of her past, both remote and immediate, Godwin lays out the landscape of her heroine's inner life. The internal act of memory and reflection, she suggests, is for the heroine an important means of naming. Jane's profession is words, and she believes firmly in their defining power. The degree of one's control over something, Jane insists, corresponds to one's ability to truly name it.

The degree of control Jane presently has over her life, as she lies awake reminiscing, is far from what she desires. Her temporary academic ap-

38. *Ibid.*, 981.

39. Hill points to the "diminished importance of the male-female relationship" in novels following *The Perfectionists* and *Glass People*. In *The Odd Woman* and *Violet Clay*, she comments, "the women find themselves involved in much richer, much more complex relationships with other women than is possible in the stories of Dane and Francesca." See *Gail Godwin*, 41.

pointment is about to end, and her love relationship with Gabriel—twelve intense, brief meetings over two years—is stalemated. In face of the over-whelming uncertainties of her life, Jane tries to imagine herself either in Eng-land with Gabriel, if he gets the Guggenheim, or, if he does not get it, in the same bedroom of her apartment waiting for his infrequent visits. Either way, the shape of her present life revolves around a limited number of available patterns of the Love Story. Variations lie in the where and when and how, but the constant theme remains intact—a woman in subordination to a man, waiting for him to give meaning and purpose to her existence.

Establishing the theme of the Love Story in the beginning of the novel, Godwin proceeds to depict the heroine's internal movement and the role memory plays in her growth out of traditional plot expectations. Turning her thoughts from the uncertain present to the past, Jane reconstructs from mem-ory her favorite family stories of female destiny: her great-aunt Cleva's tragic elopement, her grandmother Edith's fortuitous fainting, her mother Kitty's colorful romance and marriages, and her half sister Emily's swift "capture" of her future husband at the age of twelve. She also retrieves from memory fictive and literary female lives, which impinge upon her consciousness as variant versions of the Love Story. The glamour of romantic love her mother wrote about in her stories for pulp magazines juxtaposes sharply to the painful isolation of George Gissing's heroines in his novel *The Odd Women,* and the happy union of George Eliot and George Henry Lewes represents for Jane an ideal of a mutually completing marriage. The lives of her female friends, too, provide alternative patterns for the fulfillment of female destiny: Mar-sha's modern version of female passivity contrasts sharply with Gerda's radi-cal feminism; and even Sonia, the "emancipated" woman whose successful integration of love and work points to a modern ideal, loves to hear one more time the "old, old story" (58) of how a woman goes to work to get herself a man.

These remembered female lives constitute for the heroine a cultural back-ground—a world of love and marriage (or the failure of love and marriage)—against which Jane reviews her own life as it unfolds in memory. Of all these variant patterns of female lives, Cleva's story is of most importance to Jane's struggle toward self-definition. Cleva, Jane's long-dead great-aunt, ran away with an actor playing the villain in the melodrama *Fatal Wedding,* only to be

brought back home in a coffin ten months later. The cause of her death could only be speculated about from the note she sent to Edith before her tragic return: "*Sister I am in grave trouble please can somebody come the villain has left me*" (22–23).

Jane became acquainted with Cleva's story—as a family cautionary tale—when she was still a small girl, with her grandmother brandishing Cleva's last letter as a warning against misbehavior. As an unresolved family mystery, Cleva's story has since preoccupied Jane: she frequently recollects it for private contemplation and narrates it to her female friends for discussion. As Jane embarks on her psychological journey into the past, the tragic story of Cleva's life becomes a key issue in her conception of the heroine. The literary quality of the story—the villain as a concept in life and as a role in the melodrama in which he played; the viewer of the melodrama turned, in the narrative that has passed from Edith to Kitty and Jane, into a heroine in distress herself; and the dramatic denouement of the story—appeals to Jane's literary conception of life and provides an analogue to her own situation as a female reader of literature struggling to become a heroine.

The analogy Godwin establishes between Cleva's life and Jane's reveals the feminist dilemma a heroine in the 1970s faces. Rejecting the text of patriarchal marriage and male domination and seeking new identities, she may feel, without man and marriage, a complete lack of means of self-definition. By portraying a heroine deeply immersed in the plot of the Love Story yet eventually capable of breaking free, Godwin at once illuminates women's psychological entrapment in plot expectations and affirms the possibilities of escaping that entrapment and achieving feminist self-definition. In *The Odd Woman*, the heroine's goal of "researching her salvation" (415) is accomplished through a constructive use of memory: by making connections between Cleva's story and her own and developing a capacity for naming, Jane finally frees herself from entrapment in culturally available female roles and embraces the possibility of new plots.

First remembered by the heroine for its "crashing, dramatic denouement" (22), Cleva's story serves as a most illustrious example of a female life written into premature endings. Together with other stories of female lives in Jane's family, Cleva's story points to the prevailing pattern of female plots—a pattern of female relational orientation, their lives defined and their des-

tiny determined in relation to men. The choice of man predisposes the ending to the story of a woman's life. "You had your choice," Jane remembers her grandmother Edith saying, "a disastrous ending with a Villain; a satisfactory ending with a Good Man" (23). For Edith, it was as simple as this: a woman either lands safely in the sanctuary of marriage and motherhood or gets in trouble and must die.

As she contemplates the question of female destiny revealed through the lives of her family members, Jane also ponders her own "unclear, undefined, unresolved" (21) self in relation to a married man. At thirty-two, she "continue[s] to lie in a double bed alone" (23–24), disturbed by her "odd" status as a single woman. Despite her desire to elude "the hundreds and thousands of already written, already completed stories" (44) and to write herself as she goes along, she betrays, in her love relationship with Gabriel, a deep psychological bond to the gender-role expectations of female relational dependence. She has become accustomed to thinking of herself largely in terms of her relationship to Gabriel. Memories of her conversation with her friend Gerda reveal her desire for marriage and her reluctance and fear to express it. She recollects her thoughts and imaginings of Gabriel's wife, perceiving herself in relational terms with the married couple. She remembers saying to Gabriel in jest: "If I live till 2030, and you become free one day, I suppose you might marry me" (8), betraying the side of her as a patiently waiting woman. Recollecting her mother's life and her "sensible" choice to marry for security and protection, Jane surrenders to a vivid image of herself as one of those women who "spread their wings and use up all their metabolism soaring up and out into cold nights, across state lines, to perch shivering outside storm windows of imagined houses and wait and watch to see what time lovers went to bed with their wives" (11).

Jane's tangled memories of her family history and personal experience all point to the plot of the Love Story, conjuring up an image of a heroine stuck in the role of "mistress," entrapped in the feminine mode of passive and patient waiting. However, she has yet to develop a capacity to name the role she herself is playing in the Love Story and the cultural implications of it. In the beginning of the novel, Jane is able to name only one side of her, the "liberal humanist" side defined in such terms as "career woman," "professor of English," and "intellectual." She is, in contrast, incapable of naming

the other side of herself, the side embedded in the "feminine discourse" of passivity, dependence, and relational self-definition. When Jane does use the naming word "mistress," which precisely describes the role she has assumed, she dismisses it as a literary type, without seeing its relevance to her own situation: "There were many 'mistress' stories, for instance. There were sinister mistresses, villainesses, home-breakers, with whom the reader understood he was not to sympathize on the very first page. . . . There were many kinds of mistresses, but they were all single visions, limited characterizations. The word 'mistress' itself was a story" (43–44).

Through her characterization of Jane, Godwin once again illuminates the struggle that Jean Grimshaw sees as fundamental to female self-definition—the negotiation of conflicting and contradictory self-conceptions, a phenomenon Godwin describes in a recent autobiographical essay as the "two warring sides of the same woman."[40] Her portrayal of Jane, however, emphasizes the heroine's slow yet gradual growth toward an understanding of her own entrapment by art and an ultimate rejection of reductive, delimiting identities. For the heroine of *The Odd Woman,* the capacity to truly name her experience, to put "a nebulous 'something' into precise words" (3), develops gradually as she persistently pursues the mystery of Cleva's story to understand its cultural significance and its usefulness to her own self-definition.

The meaning of Cleva's story for the family members had always been a complicated matter, despite Edith's determined effort to use it as a cautionary tale to deter her daughter and granddaughter from their wild adventures. Although it worked for preadolescent Jane, who "could be manipulated so easily through a few dramatic images" (172), with Kitty, it often had the opposite effect from that intended. Studying an old photograph of Cleva, Kitty comments to Jane on the outlived usefulness of Cleva's story: "Cleva's been worn pretty threadbare, if you ask me. Her symbolism has been worn out—on our family, at least. I hardly see how her plight can be of any use to Emily. . . . No, as a preventive measure, Aunt Cleva has become as outmoded as . . . certain forms of birth control" (173).

40. Gail Godwin, "The Many Masks of Kathleen Godwin and Charlotte Ashe," in *Family Portraits: Remembrances by Twenty Distinguished Writers,* ed. Carolyn Anthony (New York, 1989), 110.

Not so for Jane. Fascinated by the literary quality of the story, she continues to want to "get to the bottom" (175) of the family mystery, narrating it to her friends, discussing it with her mother, and replaying it again and again in her own mind. She wonders how Cleva managed to meet a man and get to know him well enough during intermissions. As she prepares to leave her family for another stolen meeting with Gabriel in New York, she reflects upon "the perennial old urgencies of having to make the train, the plane, to keep a tryst" (191), thus making herself part of the symbolic train story that vividly captures the relational pattern of the lives of women in her family: Cleva's tragic train ride, Edith's dream of her missed train, and Kitty's train ride turned into unexpected comedy. She speculates on Cleva's fate as she purchases a copy of Edith Wharton's *House of Mirth*: "The novel was copyrighted 1905, the same year Cleva came here with her villain, expecting what? Hoping for what?" (233). She digs up Cleva again to place her side by side with those literary heroines who "get in trouble" and must die according to the literary convention of the time. The themes of Cleva's tragic story, repeatedly retrieved from memory, reiterate for Jane a variant pattern of the single plot available to fictional heroines: getting a man, hoping and expecting, yet a disastrous ending.

As Jane stands purposeless in the New York Public Library, waiting for the time to pass before she meets Gabriel, Cleva's story comes to her rescue: she would research the old melodrama that led to Cleva's undoing, *The Fatal Wedding*. Thrilled to see the printed evidence of "Edith's sensational cautionary tale" (324), Jane begins to work herself into the plot of that melodrama. She first imagines herself in conspiracy with a friend to get Gabriel, as Cora Williams the jealous cat does in the melodrama. Then she compares the swiftness of the melodrama's action with the slow moving of her own idyllic love: "How fast things went, how fast the 'jealous cat' Cora had worked, if Scene One, Act One, took place in 'the happy home of the Wilsons,' and Scene Two 'the New York Divorce Court.' No two years' tact for Cora Williams, waiting around for the man she wanted" (327). Weaving together the plot of her own love story and that of the old melodrama and discerning the similarities between the two, the heroine makes a conceptual leap toward the liberating knowledge of her own entrapment in the Love Story, thereby preparing herself for the final act of naming.

Here, Jane's recollection of Sonia's note about soap opera illustrates brilliantly memory's centrality in aiding the heroine's self-understanding. "Too many women's lives," Sonia had written in her note to Jane, conform to the scripts of soap opera. "Do you think," Sonia asked, "the soap opera follows life or do we pattern our lives with their innumerable crises and catastrophes and shifting casts of characters on this model?" (327). Sonia's observation about literary entrapment of female lives takes on greater significance as Jane now remembers it again in the context of family and personal history, merging it with her recollections of Cleva's story, not only to shed light on Cleva's situation but also to bear on her own. Imagining Cleva holding an old program and reading coming attractions such as *Lured from Home,* Jane achieves a deeper insight into a question central to conceptions of female growth and fictional representations of female experience—the question of, in Rachel M. Brownstein's words, "how literature and the values a woman reader derives from it reflect and determine women's lives."[41]

Cleva's case, Jane reflects, "seemed almost a dramatization of" Sonia's statement about soap opera: "Ridiculously clear-cut, in fact. You wondered how she could have missed seeing it. But the Age of Ironic Distance had not arrived in December of 1905 as a Southern girl, raised on a farm, a little in arrears of her *Zeitgeist,* waited in a theatre in Wilkes-Barre for her villain, looking down at 'coming attractions' and failing to connect them with her own future" (327–28). Further identifying her own story with that of Cleva's, Jane projects into a future with Emily's granddaughter commenting on great-aunt Jane's unhappiness, viewing it with her wisdom of the ironic distance. The old melodrama, Cleva, and herself—the line of connection illuminates the question Sonia asks: Do women pattern their lives on existing models of female destiny and enact their own entrapment in plot expectations?

The dramatic moment for Jane comes after her thrilling discovery of the old program in the library. The frustration of her love relationship that has accumulated during the two-year-long "stately waltz" (330) now explodes, escalated, revealingly, by the recurrence of a pattern that reiterates not only the particular theme of her own two-year love life but also the general theme of the culturally scripted Love Story. Jane finds herself kept and *keeps*

41. Brownstein, "*The Odd Woman* and Literary Feminism," 176–77.

waiting for her lover to come to her, when he first cancels his dinner plans with Jane to dine with a colleague—for the sake of respectability and secrecy —and then calls to postpone his return. Filled with shame, hate, anger, and self-pity, Jane comes to the painful naming of herself as "mistress." The Understanding Mistress finally failing to understand, Jane identifies herself with those abused Indian women "raped by enemy soldiers and then abandoned by their own husbands" (332).

Quickly, however, she dismisses such an easy identification. She had no right, she reflects, "to compare her plight to the betrayal of those Indian wives":

> She had not been betrayed. Not at all. She had, all but legally, contracted to this arrangement with full knowledge of the circumstances and conditions. She had accepted the invitation—no, she had done most of the inviting herself—to perform a certain slow and restricted dance with a certain sort of man. She had known in advance the formation of the dance pattern and the type of man. . . . Was this what she had wanted: this stately dance, leaving her mind free to construct its fantasies around this cool man? And, in the interims between dances, did she enjoy another kind of fantasizing, a playacting at "hoping for more," watching herself play the abused mistress hoping gamely for a future that might change everything? (333)

Through this penetrating self-analysis, Jane comes to full recognition of her own responsibilities for her entrapment in plot expectations. Despite her resistance to cultural definitions of womanhood, despite her insistence on being her own person, and despite her achievement of financial independence, she is, Jane realizes, deeply entrenched in the culture text of femininity. She has permitted herself, contrary to her feminist determinations against it, to play one more time a role that has survived time and social change, creating her own version of the Mistress Story and reducing herself to a limited characterization.

In the intensity of self-understanding, Jane remembers once again her conversation with Gabriel about their prospective marriage in 2030, projects once again into the future when Emily's granddaughter wonders about great-

aunt Jane, and reconstructs once again her love relationship in her imagined conversation with Sonia. She recollects Marsha's account of being told by her lover to be the "most maidenly woman" and restructures her day of frustration and revelation when she visits her feminist friend Gerda. With memory's aid, Jane eventually develops a capacity to name that side of herself she was unable to name in the beginning of the novel. She finds words to describe her story: she "dreamed" Gabriel, created him out of her need to have a lover, made his acquaintance "almost totally through her own devisings and dreams" (222), and practiced love on him for two years, playing alternately the Understanding Mistress and the Abused Mistress, patiently waiting to define and fulfill herself through him. However painful the naming process is, it enables Jane to grasp the truth about her own conceptions of female destiny, expressed so forcefully and revealingly in the image of a "patient," "waiting" woman, stuck in her reductive and subordinate role, restricted to a stunted, fixed, culturally scripted identity.

Throughout the novel, Godwin asserts memory's crucial role in the heroine's Bildung, and her depiction of Jane's ultimate escape from plot expectations emphasizes both the possibilities such escape opens up for the heroine and the difficulty that she has yet to overcome in her ongoing struggle for feminist self-definition. Jane begins to "undream" Gabriel, timidly staging her own walk-out scene. Assailed by conflicting impulses, she could not be a "heroine of clear bold lines and colors" (338) and stage it neatly and cleanly. She falters, she hesitates, she vacillates. But she finally leaves Gabriel, deeply torn between the agonizing choices of staying and leaving, between the ease Edith's kind of life represents—"I give up, you take over; life is a disease" (360)—and the hardships in a life of solitary struggle. By emphasizing Jane's rejection of the restricting role of mistress and waiting woman, her severance from the traditional plot of love achieved, and her determination to embrace the lonely struggle, Godwin shows her heroine in the act of preparing herself for new roles, roles that are not yet defined, that are prone to be challenged, but promise potentials of growth and fulfillment.

In this sense Jane's story ends in "a 'conversion' to a new self"[42] and the birth of a heroine. At the end of the novel, Godwin's heroine has not solved "the ever-present problem of her unclear, undefined, unresolved self"

42. Miles, "The Picaro's Journey to the Confessional," 981.

(21); nor has she achieved a distinct sense of identity. But Godwin shows that her heroine has grown in perception, insight, and self-knowledge, that she has given shape to her experience and achieved a sense of coherence and a greater degree of control over her life. Such progress presages future growth, allowing the heroine the potential to write beyond the ending of the single available female plot, to produce new texts of feminist endeavor, with, in Godwin's own words, "the goal of solvency always before her."[43]

43. Godwin, "Towards a Fully Human Heroine," 28.

3

Narrative Restructuring of the Self
Violet Clay and *The Finishing School*

"I am a painter. I like to listen to music while I work. On that hot August morning on which my story begins in earnest, . . ."[1] The title character of *Violet Clay* begins her narrative with this "assertive self-definition."[2] The story she tells is one of her anguished struggle toward an artistic vision that informed her first major painting—a woman suspended in the radiance of October morning light, "her arms reaching up, her eyes raised toward whatever it is she is reaching for or has got" (308).

"Maybe it's because I'm more confident of my own powers now, not so afraid of losing myself, of being molded by other people's needs of me, of being overwhelmed by them, that I can live in those strange, green days again and willingly be that girl,"[3] reflects Justin Stokes, the heroine of *The Finishing School*, at the end of the novel. As she completes her psychological journey into the past, "on the conveyance of memory, propelled by imagination" (6), Justin reaps the reward of a profound revelation: "But I also

---

1. Godwin, *Violet Clay,* 3. Subsequent references will be indicated in parentheses within the text.

2. Frye, *Living Stories, Telling Lives,* 111. Jane Hill also emphasizes the "straightforward assertion" of Violet Clay's identity in the novel's "short, simple, declarative" opening sentence. Hill, *Gail Godwin,* 55.

3. Gail Godwin, *The Finishing School* (New York, 1984), 321. Subsequent references will be indicated in parentheses within the text.

know something else that I didn't know then. As long as you can go on creating new roles for yourself, you are not vanquished" (322).

The image of the heroine as the speaking "I" distinguishes *Violet Clay* and *The Finishing School,* both featuring a female artist narrating her own story of growth as a means of self-definition. The distinctly female speaking voice and the narrative control that Godwin ascribes to her two artist heroines embody the fusion of two traditionally opposing culture texts: one of autonomous selfhood and the other of female self-definition. Speaking of the "cultural contradiction between adulthood and womanhood," Joanne S. Frye argues that whereas manhood is perceived to be in harmony with autonomy, womanhood is seen to be in conflict with it. "Ideologically defined through their sexuality and its attendant roles," Frye writes, women face the "impossible dilemma of being perceived as either competent autonomous adult human beings or sexually relational female beings, but not both." The dominant cultural ideology, Frye asserts, limits narrative possibilities for female protagonists because it sets in inevitable conflict female sexual identity and autonomous self-definition. Whereas the male protagonist can achieve adulthood "as a simultaneous affirmation of his manhood and his autonomy," the female protagonist often encounters a "painful denial of a crucial portion of self."[4]

The question Frye raises—"why is it so difficult for women writers to create female protagonists who are both autonomous and affirmatively female?"[5]—echoes Godwin's own frustrated inquiries about creating a "fully human" heroine. In *The Perfectionists* and *Glass People,* Godwin struggled with the dual theme of female victimization and feminist self-search, groping for ways to develop a feminist text powerful enough to resist the patriarchal text of marriage and motherhood. In *The Odd Woman,* she portrays the heroine's struggle to escape entrapment in plot expectations and develop a capacity to write beyond the ending. While she celebrates the heroine's ultimate rejection of reductive self-definition within the context of the Love Story, hence her potential to become the author of her own book, Godwin also demonstrates how deeply female lives, even those marked by financial independence and feminist inclination, are trapped by cultural ideals

4. Frye, *Living Stories, Telling Lives,* 9, 2, 3, 5.
5. *Ibid.,* 5.

of femininity. Yearning for an integrated life of love and work, the heroine of *The Odd Woman* nonetheless channels her energy toward self-identification through love, not work. Though the novel ends with the heroine leaving her lover and preparing herself for new roles, it also strikes a note of indeterminacy: disillusioned at her ideal of achieving self-completion in love, Godwin's third heroine is left at the end of the novel wondering in frustration why a woman cannot have both—love and work, relational fulfillment and individuation, female sexual identity and autonomy. Such an ending suggests that although it is possible for heroines to write beyond the prescribed endings of female lives, new ways of self-definition have yet to be invented.

The binary opposition between femaleness and autonomy in literary representations of female experience becomes even sharper when the heroine is an artist, because, as Mary Ellmann points out, the "concept of creation is profoundly intellectual and self-directed" and is in direct contradiction to cultural perceptions of womanhood.[6] The "either-or" choice a heroine is forced to make, feminist critics point out, forms especially "a vital part of the novel of the artist as heroine."[7] Bonnie Hoover Braendlin comments on the "halved" lives of heroines in *Norma Jean the Termite Queen* and *Kinflicks,* who are torn between the "demands of marriage and motherhood" on the one hand and their "artistic, expressive inclinations" and their "wish for personal accomplishment" on the other. Grace Stewart argues that, because the "procreative, other-directed, and nourishing role of woman is antithetical to the role of the artist," the artist as heroine may "remain disintegrated, estranged, or unsuccessful—a failure as a woman or as an artist." Rachel Blau DuPlessis claims that "the figure of a female artist encodes the conflict between any empowered woman and the barriers to her achievement." The choice of the female artist as heroine "dramatizes and heightens the already-present contradiction in bourgeois ideology between the ideals of striving, improvement, and visible public works, and the feminine version of that formula: passivity, 'accomplishments,' and invisible private acts."[8]

6. Mary Ellmann, *Thinking About Women* (New York, 1968), 64.

7. Grace Stewart, *A New Mythos: The Novel of the Artist as Heroine 1877–1977* (Montreal, 1981), 15.

8. Braendlin, "Alther, Atwood, Ballantyne, and Gray," 19; Stewart, *A New Mythos,* 14–15; DuPlessis, *Writing Beyond the Ending,* 84.

This binary opposition in literary representations of women between autonomous selfhood and female self-definition has become a crucial issue for writers and feminist scholars seeking ways to empower women. Joanne S. Frye, for example, claims the novel's inherent responsiveness to its social context and emphasizes the possibilities of developing novelistic strategies to reinterpret female lives, to affirm both femaleness and autonomy. One such strategy, she points out, is the use of the first-person voice, a traditional novelistic strategy that has "provided surprisingly fertile resources for a renewed interpretation of women's lives." The first-person female voice—the narrating "I"—Frye contends, has allowed contemporary women novelists to explore new ways, thematically as well as structurally, to "avoid narrative entrapment" and "subvert the power of old stories."[9]

Violet Clay and *The Finishing School* reflect Godwin's success in finding new ways of telling female lives. Using artist as heroine, for whom the cultural contradiction between female identity and autonomy poses extraordinary challenges, she unfolds Violet Clay and Justin Stokes's retrospective journeys into the past, portraying them in the act of remembering, narrating, and interpreting that past. Through the creative process of restructuring the past, assessing previous experiences, claiming and interacting with multiple versions of the self, Violet and Justin enable themselves to integrate the two culturally contradictory texts: by narrating their lives with what Frye describes as a "controlling sense of agency,"[10] they claim autonomous selfhood; by speaking in an assertive, female voice, they claim affirmatively their sexual identity. The evocative image at the end of *Violet Clay* of a woman suspended in the "vibrant dimensions" (324) of her own possibilities and the wistful daughterly tribute at the end of *The Finishing School* to the mother muse articulate eloquently Godwin's success in creating heroines who achieve continuous, evolving selfhood.

The narrative restructuring of the self as a crucial means for the heroine's growth and self-definition gives Godwin's exploration of an evolving self a Bakhtinian dimension. "Dialogue and its various processes," Michael Holquist, a Bakhtin scholar, points out, "are central to Bakhtin's theory."[11] Language,

9. Frye, *Living Stories, Telling Lives,* 5–8.

10. *Ibid.,* 114.

11. Michael Holquist, glossary to Mikhail Bakhtin's *The Dialogic Imagination: Four Essays,* 427.

according to Bakhtin, "lives only in the dialogic interaction of those who make use of it," and dialogic relationships encompass various processes of interaction between one's own and someone else's consciousness, discourse, and language, including the relationship of a speaker to his own discourse and his earlier selves. In such a dialogized world, everything takes place on the boundary, assuming meaning and significance in the tension-filled encounter of diverse consciousnesses, languages, discourses, and various versions of the self.[12]

In *Violet Clay* and *The Finishing School*, the heroines' growth revolves around the activity of encountering their past experiences and making sense of each encounter. Through her characterization of Violet and Justin, Godwin suggests that successful self-definition can be achieved by means of memory and internal dialogue, through the dynamic process of interaction between the present and the past and the continuous, complex interplay of one's multiple versions of one's self. By juxtaposing the heroine's present, narrating self with her previous, experiencing selves, Godwin creates a vibrant, highly interactive novelistic world. In this world, traditional liberal humanist insistence upon the centered self, feminist recognition of women's conflicted self-conceptions and of the multiple scripts and roles that women must negotiate in their struggle toward self-definition, and Bakhtin's vision intersect, forming complex sets of dialogic relationships.

From "Wasteful Sea" to "Suspended Woman": *Violet Clay*

Violet Clay is the first of Godwin's heroines who attempt to define themselves in relationship to their work, outside the traditional confines of romantic love, marriage, and motherhood. Her artistic self-definition evolves through a process of reassessing her past selves embedded in various self-imprisoning discourses—romantic myths, falsified identities, evasions, and illusions, all obstructions to the development of a serious artist. Through the internal process of recollecting and restructuring, through constructive dia-

12. Bakhtin, *Problems of Dostoevsky's Poetics*, Chap. 5, esp. pp. 182–207; also App. 2, pp. 283–310.

logue with her past selves, Violet achieves greater degrees of control over her life, integrating multiple, fragmented versions of herself into a more coherent, evolving whole.

The Young Woman as Artist Versus the Fleeing Heroine

As Violet begins the narrative of her growth as an artist, she juxtaposes two images of herself: one of "The Young Woman as Artist" (16) she initially appropriates for herself; the other of a fleeing heroine she comes to terms with through memory and narration. Born into a rapidly declining Charleston gentry family, orphaned at six months, and sent away by her alcoholic grandmother to a boarding school at age six, Violet has little sense of family history and regional identity that so deeply mold Godwin's other southern heroines' personal identity. Yet the artistic impulses in the family—her grandmother's talent for music and her uncle's for fiction writing—provide her with a personal heritage. Choosing the discourse of "The Young Woman as Artist" for herself, she rejects the cultural text of femininity that had compromised the artistic vision of her grandmother, Georgette Clay. Her grandmother sacrificed a brilliant musical career for the "pageantry of upper-class Southern wife-and-motherhood"; Violet can take full advantage of feminist modernity by flirting with "Roads Not Taken" (22), congratulating herself for "having achieved a modern girl's sexual rights without having to marry and ruin [her] career" (23). Her grandmother deluded herself with the image of "the accomplished wife and mother who turns her gifts to the enhancement of Home" (29); Violet, as early as her adolescence, envisions a totally different future for herself, conjuring up images of herself granting interviews as a successful young artist.

As an artist, she would write her own success story, making art out of life, reaping artistic gains out of personal losses, just as her uncle Ambrose had done in writing his popular, romantic novel about his unrequited love for Violet's widowed mother. Following Ambrose's suit, Violet is to paint her own version of her mother's death—"Wasteful Sea," a "symbolic and sinister" (19) refashioning of her mother's romantic suicide. She has full confidence that this painting, her project for her last summer in Charleston before entering the art world of New York, will establish her as a serious

artist. Everything "pointed toward the success of this venture" (18). Her uncle had written his successful first novel in the very room where she was staying. He had been twenty-one at the time, the same age Violet was that summer. And he had taken the same subject, creating a romantic and positive version of his love for his brother's widow in *Looking for the Lora Lee*. How could her projected painting be "anything less than brilliant, suffused as it was with personal meaning!" (18). With her grandmother's warnings of failure and her uncle's example of success, Violet dreams of her shining achievements; the image of "The Young Woman as Artist" seems within easy reach.

"Wasteful Sea" never materialized from the summer designated to mark the beginning of Violet's career as a serious artist, and its fate is emblematic of the heroine's nine-year sojourn in New York. At thirty-two, Violet is a commercial illustrator, not an artist, "spending [her] skills on other people's visions" (5) rather than creating her own. Employed with Harrow House Gothics, which publishes romantic suspense fiction, she paints gothic heroines who are "programmed" into their script—running away from sinister-looking houses destined to be their happy abodes and rescued by the Villain who "would show himself to be the Good Man All Along by the end of [the] night" (5). Over her nine years of employment, she has painted over two hundred covers with fleeing heroines, tenuously maintaining the illusion of art by seeking variations in the "Book of Old Plots": "I had sponged off everyone from Giotto to Whistler, varying my medium between watercolor, gouache, or oils worked thin to dry by deadline time. It was my way of keeping my hand in, I told myself, my underground system of staying in touch with Art until the day when I had enough energy (and money) to pack in this job-beneath-my-talents and throw myself into full-time creation" (7). On the morning she begins her story, she is painting her latest fleeing heroine from a photograph of herself, heartily ready to make last-minute modifications—rounding the "stubborn square" and blending the "alertness and flaring" into something "approaching acquiescence" (7)—to make her own face qualify for the cover of romantic suspense fiction.

By having Violet use her own face as a model for the gothic heroine's, capturing her in the conscious act of painting a reductive self-portrait, Godwin evokes the escape motif of the heroine's life that she must reject in order to

grow. From her postgraduate summer until the day that her story begins "in earnest," Violet has been running away, "not from the glowering gothic hero lurking in the shadows but from herself,"[13] from "The Young Woman as Artist"—the fulfillment of what she considers to be her authentic identity. She has been escaping into false, inauthentic, and limited self-definitions to avoid the challenge of taking "real voyages" (4).

Beginning with the summer of the dissipated "Wasteful Sea," the discourse of the fleeing heroine gradually takes over the discourse of "The Young Woman as Artist." Fearful of "an edgy, lonely struggle" that the artist must embrace, Violet first escapes into the "sweet juices of traditional womanhood" (32). Couched in the romantic vocabulary of the Book of Old Plots— the myth of a hero rescuing "the orphan of War and a Romantic Suicide" (31)—her marriage to Lewis Lanier is not so much the result of "cunning" manipulations of her grandmother and godmother (a story she chooses to believe) as her own willing surrender to what Joanne S. Frye calls "the story of the wife."[14] This capitulation numbs her creative urges: "I didn't touch a paintbrush those first months of captivity. What for: The colors of satisfaction oozed out of my very pores. I posed for myself in front of the mirror turning this way and that, thinking: I am now a wife. I breathed the odor of flowers, arranged them in vases, but was not tempted to turn them into still lifes. I lapsed, I gave myself up to my senses, to Womanhood" (32). Content with her identity as wife, Violet forsakes the story of "The Young Woman as Artist."

A recurring nightmare about taking a taxi in New York but never reaching her destination—the art galleries on Madison Avenue—finally leads Violet to break off from the culture text of femininity and resume the story of the artist. She leaves her husband for New York with the painful realization that she had "sold out":

> I hadn't played square with my myth of The Young Woman as Artist. This myth had specified a certain order of events, a certain progression in the development of Self, and I had betrayed that order. I had snatched

13. Gaston, "The Theme of Female Self-Discovery in the Novels of Judith Rossner, Gail Godwin, Alice Walker, and Toni Morrison," 139.
14. Frye, *Living Stories, Telling Lives,* 121.

my security before I'd made a real try for my dream. And thus I was being forced by my undeceived and forthright unconscious, night after night, to seek out the confrontation I had avoided. "New York" in the dream represented this confrontation. That I never arrived at the galleries with my work intact, or that I settled in despair for sexual annihilation, was my dream life's metaphor and parody of my real situation. (16)

Marriage, however, is only the first of Violet's "escape clause[s]" (190) that define her unsuccessful pursuit as an artist. Her arrival in the city is followed by a brief "Euphoric Era" (122) when, basking in the golden light of promise, Ambrose and Violet dream of their future success—Ambrose in completing his second novel about an existential hero creating inner challenges for himself in an age of chaos; Violet in establishing herself in the art world of New York. After a few setbacks such as rejections from galleries and loss of a job, Violet quickly settles into an "Era of Compromise," squandering her artistic energies in various forms of distraction—unrestrained sexuality, alcoholic self-pity, commercialized art, and fantasies of her prospective success.

What emerges from her nine years in New York is not a "distinctive personal vision" (242) or an inspiring story of a young artist struggling to fulfill her potential. Rather, her nine "fallow years" yield a record of evasions, failures, and self-deceptions. Fleeing from art, she has invented one escape clause after another to salvage her from the terror of loneliness, to disguise her fear of failure, or to create the illusion of progress. She finds refuge in the concept of Violet Clay as Victim, frequently resuscitating the label of herself as The Orphan to elicit "the currency of sympathy" (4). She uses Georgia O'Keeffe's example—her commercial artwork and her late success—as justifications for her own excuses and evasions. Her story of "The Young Woman as Artist," lacking its essential elements of commitment, discipline, and perseverance, lapses into inflated images of herself as a successful painter, where even her failure takes on significance in its retrospective blaze of glory: "I could even look back on the Gallery Fiasco Day as an important spiritual lesson for me, and—after I had made my name—a story both touching and encouraging to other young artists coming up" (122).

Without true artistic endeavor, Violet deludes herself with "the illusion of [her] 'progress'" (163): "I was always rushing somewhere now—down to the art store to pick up more illustrator's board, uptown to meet Stewart for a tête-à-tête lunch at that dark little pub, or to Michel's for an evening of fun and games, or to deliver another maiden in distress to Williamson, who would give me tea and praise and write out a voucher for two hundred dollars" (163). Living her life of false commitment and pride, Violet loses sight of the text of "The Young Woman as Artist." She once readily decided to take up pornography, creating her "porno portfolio" with an intense absorption she had not felt since leaving art school and "already imagining [herself] bringing a fresh dimension to the old art" (155). For two years, she escaped into a purely physical relationship with an instructor at the Art Students League, deluding herself with the spurious challenge of his artistic manifesto and her flimsy belief that he was leading her "into a conjunction with Art" (276). For nine years, she has painted nothing but gothic heroines fleeing away from their destiny, "the lovely false consolation of the deadline" contributing to her "illusion of momentum" (163). The few promising canvases she had brought to New York have been collecting dust "in their neglected corners" (55), and her "fizzled-out" (163) self-portrait finally merges into the reductive image of Violet as a fleeing heroine for the cover of gothic fiction.

On the morning that she paints her self-portrait, Violet experiences painful flashes of self-realization but still attempts to soothe her "alarms of failure" with more escape clauses—"the comfort of the Task" (5) and the false optimism that has sustained her for the past nine years: "I hadn't yet reached that point of resignation where I surrendered the image of my greatest self. . . . There was still time, I told myself, though not as much as there had been" (4–5).

Toward Authentic Self-Definition

"The freedom of a character," Bakhtin writes, "is an aspect of the author's design."[15] Underlying Violet's seemingly haphazard reminiscences is a complicated process of narrative restructuring that Godwin unfolds through her

15. Bakhtin, *Problems of Dostoevsky's Poetics*, 65.

speaking female subject. Neither mechanical nor linear but purposefully me-andering, this narrative process zigzags between flashes of self-realization and the sluggish habits of self-capitulation. By positing the heroine as the narrating "I" with a capacity to select, conceptualize, interpret, and com-municate, Godwin gives her the power to contest and reject those self-imprisoning discourses she has previously appropriated for herself as escape clauses—conceptions of herself as Orphan, Victim, Gothic Heroine, and artist-near-success. Furthermore, by depicting the painful, internal dialogue the heroine engages with her previous selves for purposes of self-definition, Godwin makes Violet's narrative, in Joanne S. Frye's words, not "a simple linear success story" but a process by which the heroine comes to reclaim and redefine herself "toward the possibility of success." In "exhuming her past selves" and breaking "free of those falsely constrained selves," the hero-ine "moves closer to formulating a self that meshes with her narrating self without denying her past experiences and without foreclosing future evolu-tion."[16]

For Violet, her uncle Ambrose's suicide symbolizes the death of her long-harbored myth of the artist-near-success, holding dark implications for her own life. Assuming narrative control by choosing the August morning on which Ambrose committed suicide to begin her narrative "in earnest," Violet reconstructs her own past nine years of what she believed to be artistic striving, perceiving two parallel threads of experience linking Am-brose and herself in their self-deluding journey toward an illusion of artis-tic self-definition. As she weaves into narrative pattern her fragmented ex-periences over nine years, she comes to recognize patterns of evasions, compromises, and failures on her part, previously disguised under the myth of near-success that she and Ambrose mutually nourished. In the act of remembering and narrative restructuring, she begins to "shift responsi-bility for her life away from external forces and toward her own controlling sense of agency."[17]

Violet selects, for instance, the evening she met Ambrose nine years ago, upon her arrival in New York, as a point of departure and comparison in her

16. Frye, *Living Stories, Telling Lives*, 117, 113, 114.
17. *Ibid.*, 114.

narrated self-definition. She recalls vividly their eagle's-eye view of Manhattan at sunset. Inspired by the dazzling light and motion and the vital throbbings of promise the city represents to them, they "had clinked [their] glasses to mutual success" (60). As she proceeds with her narrative, Violet keeps returning to that evening, informing it with her interpretive consciousness and superimposing her present, narrating self upon the experiencing, narrated self. At one point, she describes her recollection of that evening as "a memory guaranteed to render its saturation point in remorse" (60), highlighting, as Frye puts it, her "implicit presence of narrative selection and judgment."[18] At another point, she contrasts her markedly different self-perceptions in color images: the evening she spent with Ambrose is blue, "the color of dreaming and of infinite time and space," whereas the August evening nine years later is "a garish, sickening pink" (70). The contrasting color image reflects the heroine's altered state of mind. The blue of her evening with Ambrose generated hope; the pink of her August evening, with her "swilling vodka and stewing [herself] in a lethal brew of self-hatred and remorse" (70), breeds only despair. Her studio, "swathed in the pink of the sun gone down," was "the color of dreams that had lain around too long and were starting to smell at the edges" (70).

As we follow Violet's storytelling, which moves back and forth between her earlier and later experience, we become conscious of Godwin's narrative design. By making her character remember, narrate, and restructure her past, Godwin establishes multiple versions of the same character and multiple time schemes: the younger and hopeful Violet in eager anticipation of artistic success; the older, struggling Violet facing her darkest realization of failure in Ambrose's suicide; and the present narrating Violet who "has lived through all these experiences, past and present, and is assessing *both* from yet another temporal distance."[19] Through such juxtaposition, Violet's struggle toward self-definition assumes a dialogic character, marked by an intense interplay of different discourses and multiple versions of the self. Such dialogic activities, Godwin shows, give the backward movement of memory a forward motion of searching, opening up the possibilities of successful self-definition.

Persistently and circuitously, details of the separate lives of Ambrose and

18. *Ibid.,* 116.
19. *Ibid.,* 115.

of herself in the past nine years come back to the reminiscing and narrating heroine, filtered through her present, interpreting consciousness and yielding new self-perceptions. Switching back and forth between Ambrose's story and her own, Violet becomes painfully aware of their shockingly parallel patterns of evasion. Whereas Ambrose substitutes professional dilettantism for artistic endeavor, throwing himself into such escape clauses as barhopping, salesmanship, marriage, extended honeymoon, divorce, working vacation, and constantly created yet never completed new projects, Violet succeeds in "professionally avoiding [her] profession" (58), sacrificing her urge toward artistic self-definition for cheap emotional gratification. Whereas Ambrose's story of the artist-near-success expires along with his "great shape-shifting novel" (299), Violet's story of "The Young Woman as Artist" degenerates into her reductive self-portrait as Gothic Heroine. Aiming for an artistic rendering of "modern man awash in the flux of too many complexities and possibilities" (79), Ambrose's fragmentary novel, as Frye puts it, gradually "loses all possibility of narrative design and eventually disintegrates into the three speculative 'outlines' of his own last memory-fantasy constructions."[20] In face of his darkest self-realization, Ambrose seeks his final escape clause in death, the message of his living and dying compressed into one short sentence: "I'm sorry, there's nothing left" (264).

Emerging from these memory sequences is the narrator-protagonist's realization of her greatest act of inauthenticity—pretending that Ambrose is an attractive role model in order to cover up her own compromises and failures. For years, Violet has tried to keep alive a romantic, mythical vision of mutual success expressed in Ambrose's cryptic statement during their enchanted evening overlooking sunset Manhattan: "You got to go through me" (64). Despite evidence to the contrary, she has chosen to sustain an initially naïve and increasingly defeated faith in Ambrose's promise of success. She turns the potentially useful model of Ambrose's prior success into a self-destructive myth, deliberately ignoring the warning his continued compromises communicate in order to preserve her own illusion of herself as an artist-near-success.

Restructuring their parallel experiences and engaging dialogically with her previous selves, Violet becomes increasingly aware of her self-deceptive use

20. *Ibid.*, 124.

of Ambrose as a symbol. For example, in blaming Ambrose for her own lack of accomplishment, she self-consciously observes the "weird patterns of cause and effect" that her mind is accustomed to: "My uncle's failure to finish his big novel I saw as a breach of promise to *me*. Nine years ago, . . . we had stood beaming at each other in his apartment and sworn to be true to our dreams. It now seemed perfectly logical that if he had kept up his side, I would have kept up mine" (60). Candidly, she admits to a friend her complete dependence on Ambrose as a shield between herself and hopelessness: "Even when I didn't see him for months . . . years . . . I felt he was there for me to refer to, living his life a little ahead of mine, wanting the things I wanted. Even his flaws and mistakes have given me a certain comfort. I could sort of measure myself, judge myself, by him" (97).

"Where all that time went I just don't know" (79)—Violet remembers Ambrose repeating these despairing words concerning his seven-year-long working vacation in Mexico. She remembers acutely, too, her sharp disappointment at Ambrose's inability to "rekindle [her] own low-burning hopes" (77). Furthermore, she remembers her ambivalent reactions to Ambrose's near confession of his failure and her reluctant admission of her psychological dependence on his success: "I wanted both to reassure him and be gone. To set him back on the road ahead of me in order to give myself a little more time" (78). Until that August morning when she begins her story "in earnest," Violet has willfully deluded herself about Ambrose's success story, using him as her greatest escape clause to avoid confronting the challenges of authentic artistic self-definition.

Ambrose's suicide irrevocably shatters all myths and illusions, forcing Violet to recognize the stark reality of her artistic impoverishment. For the first time in nine years, she begins to learn to use him constructively, acting from a "new-found sense of urgency" that she deems "the most important legacy [her] uncle had left [her]" (212). Leaving her apartment in the city, she moves to upstate Plommet Falls, into the cabin where Ambrose shot himself, determined to make something out of her uncle's living and dying.

During her solitary existence in the woods, Violet experiences the most intense of her dialogic encounters with her past. As she relives the dark despair that smashed Ambrose's sense of himself, she is acutely aware of the undeniable parallel patterns of their lives: "Today it really hit me how some-

one could get so sick of his same old act—the false starts, the fresh failures, the noble resolutions leading in turn to new false hopes and starts—that he'd prefer to have done with it altogether" (258). Despite her determination to confront nakedly her self-delusions and false self-definitions, Violet falters and vacillates, slipping into self-indulgent memories of past love affairs, concocting fresh fantasies, or consoling herself with the image of Violet as a dignified loser.

Such intense interaction with another person's discourse and with her own past selves finally enables Violet to confront all her "personal demons" (257) with honesty. She commits herself to "going through" Ambrose by experiencing his utter despair, again filtered through her informing consciousness as she recollects, narrates, interprets, and communicates with her past. Her dialogic encounter culminates in a symbolic death, with her reenacting Ambrose's suicide as a means toward self-understanding, a creative use of Ambrose's legacy to help herself persevere where he gave up, to triumph where he failed.

Only after the anguish of such dialogic activities can Violet make constructive use of a woodswoman she encounters and befriends during her sojourn in Plommet Falls. In Samantha, a self-made woman, a new kind of heroine who thinks of herself as "the person mainly responsible for making things happen,"[21] Violet finds an inspiring role model for herself. A victim of a sexually abusive stepfather, a rejecting mother, and three rapists, Samantha manages to build an "indestructible edifice" from "the shoddy materials" (310) she was given to work with. In living an energetic, productive, and self-sufficient life, constantly projecting herself into the future and creating possibilities for herself, Samantha teaches Violet that "the test of a person is, in the end, how well she's used what she was given to use" (310).

From Samantha—and her "indomitable spirit" (310)—emerges Violet's first major painting that establishes her as an artist. It is a painting of a nude female body suffused in light, affirming female sexual identity while claiming autonomous, evolving selfhood. Translating vision into visual details, Violet's painting suggests an infinite range of possibilities for female self-definition. Reflecting upon her finished work of art, Violet observes the remarkably wide range of human images Samantha's painted body is capable

21. Godwin, "How to Be the Heroine of Your Own Life," 194.

of suggesting: "Turn her three-quarters away and have her bend as though to pick up something and you had the rib cage and torso of a warrior; have her sit facing you, her shoulders in a relaxed position, and you had a fully mature woman who had borne a child. Stretch her out lengthwise and see tender angles counterposed against tough ones. She was like some hybrid woman, a composite of what had always been and what could be" (304–305).

Whereas Ambrose escapes authentic artistic self-definition in suicide, his vision of a modern man creating his own inner challenges collapsing into total disillusion, Violet achieves it through memory, narration, and dialogic interaction. The role of internal dialogue as an essential part of the heroine's Bildung, stressed throughout the novel, is further illuminated toward the ending, when Violet reflects upon her artistic success. The October morning on which she grasps the vision of a female suspended in her own possibilities becomes, like the August morning of her "Day of Lost Options," one of her deepest mental resources. "I like to remember that October morning. I like to go back into it from the 'future,'" she speaks in her self-assertive voice, affirming the role of memory and the dialogic process of self-definition. From where she lives now, she tells us, she makes her positive time travel, sending her "mental spaceship to points past or future," which "frequently comes back with old buds of present blossomings (like that October morning); or sometimes a bold design of fruits to come" (306).

A Double Bildung: *The Finishing School*

"There are two kinds of people," says Ursula DeVane, in that rich, bewitching voice of hers, to her young friend Justin Stokes. "One kind," Ursula tells Justin,

> you can tell just by looking at them at what point they congealed into their final selves. It might be a very *nice* self, but you know you can expect no more surprises from it. Whereas, the other kind keep moving, changing. With these people, you can never say, "X stops here," or, "Now I know all there is to know about Y." That doesn't mean they're

unstable. Ah, no, far from it. They are *fluid*. They keep moving forward and making new trysts with life, and the motion of it keeps them young. In my opinion, they are the only people who are still alive. (4)

Ursula's voice, resounding with challenge and conviction, vividly recollected by Justin Stokes, the mature, successful artist and the narrator-protagonist of the novel looking back into the summer when she turned sixteen, gives us Godwin's most articulate and persuasive expression to date of the evolving self, a concept that Godwin has pursued persistently in her contemporary Bildungsromane. In the character of Justin Stokes and the dramatized process of her continual growth, Godwin triumphantly evokes a self "in the process of becoming."[22] Complex, creative, and future-oriented, it thrives by means of existential, internal self-search, resisting stasis, closure, and rigid categorization; constantly contesting achieved self-definitions; continually striving to create new, evolving identities. Deeply dialogic, the self-in-the-becoming achieves continuity and totality by embracing past and future, claiming multiple versions of itself, and imparting meaning to the fragments of its personal history.

Rich in mood, engrossingly dramatic in its execution, and profoundly moving in characterization, *The Finishing School* narrates simultaneously the story of young Justin's initiation into the world of love, friendship, and betrayal, and the story of her adult self joyfully continuing to strive for the creative mold of being. As in *Violet Clay*, Godwin establishes multiple versions of the heroine as artist, superimposing the successful artist upon the adolescent girl experiencing her haunting friendship with her forty-four-year-old mentor. Centering on the process of "intensely remembering" (49) and dialogically encountering the past, Godwin produces a narrative of double Bildung: that of the younger, experiencing self and that of the older, reminiscing self. Celebrating a fluid and evolving self, affirming the mother-daughter relationship, and making memory the action of the novel, Godwin in *The Finishing School* weaves her three crucial themes into a moving and finely crafted *Künstlerroman*.

22. Josephine Donovan, *Feminist Theory: The Intellectual Traditions of American Feminism* (New York, 1985), 118–19.

The "Taut Drama of Youth": The Bildung of Adolescent Justin

Through the recollected story of Justin's adolescent summer in Clove, a rural community in upstate New York, Godwin explores in full detail the "taut drama of youth" (49), extending the boundaries of her contemporary Bildungsromane to include that painful, turbulent period between the harmony of childhood and the maturity of adulthood, a time of intense conflicts, desires, and fears as well as a time of "great possibilities for growth."[23] Justin's adolescent Bildung, Godwin shows, evolves around the absorbing friendship she forms with Ursula DeVane, her mentor and an alternate mother figure. As Justin recollects and narrates her story, she unfolds an adolescent's painful initiation into the adult world—a world of moral and sexual complexity—and the accompanying psychological struggle between the urge toward individuation and the need for subordination.

The harmony of Justin's childhood had resided in the strong regional and social identity provided by her southern existence. The peculiar history of the South, as well as the set and secure ways of her extended southern family, nourished in her an identity moored in the history of the family, community, and region. The "big, rambling house in Virginia," Justin fondly recalls, not only gave her a happy, secure childhood but also contained her history, fully defined by every object and every corner in the house and reinforced by a comfortable sense of personal-communal identity. Her beloved grandfather, who had taken on the role of father for much of her childhood, introduced her to the uniqueness of the South by taking her on his frequent trips to former slave quarters, encouraging her to participate in the excitement of exploration and discovery. The historical imagination as well as the compassion, eccentricity, and implicit noblesse oblige that marked her grandfather's activities provided Justin with a secure and high place in the southern social order.

23. Barbara A. White, *Growing Up Female: Adolescent Girlhood in American Fiction* (Westport, Conn., 1985), 9. White explains the invention of the concept of adolescence in American culture, including the ideas of psychologist G. Stanley Hall, principal inventor of the concept, who views adolescence "as a time of great possibilities for growth" as well as "a time of turbulence." In transition from "primitive past" to "civilized future," adolescents experience "a variety of contradictions and alternates between 'antithetic impulses'—inertness vs. excitement, self-confidence vs. humility, selfishness vs. altruism, etc."

Her grandmother also shared in shaping Justin's regional and social identity. A "perfect lady" herself, she had tried to raise Justin in her image, training her in the art of southern graciousness. She was harmony and grace incarnated, the only woman, according to Justin's grandfather, "who would behave exactly the same way if nobody were looking" (24). Justin's mother, too, contributed to her sense of the southern social order. Once a "passionate, headstrong young woman," she luxuriated in being the "cherished wife" and "beloved daughter," retaining the old flourishes and "breezy self-assurance" (29) that Justin admired.

This secure, defined existence exploded when, in quick succession, her grandparents and father died, forcing the family to relocate. Against her daughter's desire to stay in the South, Justin's mother decided to go north to live with a relative in an upstate New York suburb. Suddenly, Justin's own childhood became, like the social history of the South, a "gracious past" (6), deprived of everything familiar that would remind her who she was, leaving her with an acute sense of loss, discontinuity, and the emotional disorientation of regional dislocation. She "had lost all the props that defined her" (5), and conflict—"a vital part of the concept of adolescence"[24]—becomes the major key in her life: conflict between her unwelcome present and her cherished past, between individual impulses and societal constraints, between daughter and mother, and between her urgency for self-definition and the powerlessness of her adolescent status.

Accustomed to the distinctive style of southern existence, Justin finds New York's Lucas Meadows subdivision uncongenial to the establishment of a new individual identity. Quickly taking on the social characteristics of the new, post–1945 suburb, their new home strikes Justin with its deadly conformity and uniformity. More than its lack of grace and flourishes, even more than its lack of history, the engulfing sameness of Lucas Meadows threatens to erase Justin's whole personality. "What bothered me most about these houses," she confesses in despair, "was that they seemed designed to make everybody as alike as possible" (21). Nearly everyone in the raw suburb worked for IBM, lived in identical homes, and conformed to everyone's expectations. Worse, they "seemed to conspire" to conform, to revel in their ordinariness:

24. *Ibid.*, 14.

In Lucas Meadows, all mothers seemed to be cooking dinner at the same hour, and all the lights in the children's bedrooms went out at night before the lights in the master bedrooms. Even worse, every single living room had a lamp, its shade still covered with cellophane, on a table squarely in the middle of the picture window. That the mother in every one of these houses had gone out, on her own volition, and bought a lamp to fill her window exactly as her neighbors had done, seemed ominous to me. It was as though Lucas Meadows emanated a germ, and if you caught it, you would become just like everyone else. (21)

Justin's bitter memories evoke the conformity typical of the 1950s suburbs. The mothers by and large stayed home; the men "in gray flannel suits" worked for the archetypal American corporation; everyone was "other-directed," interested only in how to please his bosses and neighbors. In such a conformist environment, teenage rebellion, as critics of "mass culture" never tired of pointing out, was inevitable. But such rebellions were unfocused (like those of James Dean in *Rebel Without a Cause*), sometimes violent, and conformed to the norms of the peer group. Justin's rebellion was far more profound. She experienced a complete crisis of identity, which alienated her from her environment, family, and peer group.

Justin's "most serious thoughts and abiding fears" (89) revolve around the question of identity. She feels submerged in sameness and conformity, trapped in the artificial and unimaginative world of the "Raspberry Ice"— literally the official name for the purplish-pink color on the walls of her bedroom, symbolically the drab, penetrating sameness that imprisons and deprives. "Raspberry Ice" and the identical-looking figures of the milkmaids that decorate the fabric assault Justin's emerging individuality. "Row after row of them, with their wide skirts and pert, beauty-contest smiles," she remembers her younger self complaining, these figures "adorned [her] curtains, the flounce around [her] dressing table, and the dust ruffle of [her] bed" (33). They breed in Justin a profound fear of waking up one morning to find her individuality sucked into their pervading sameness, to forget "what it felt like to be [herself]" (89), and to discover that she is just like everybody else.

Justin's crisis of identity is further compounded by her increasing conflict with her mother. If Justin was once charmed by her mother's role as "cher-

ished wife" and "beloved daughter" (29), she now is distressed at her newly adopted role of "gracious martyr" (32). She misses that carefree and glamorous person of the Fredericksburg days, when "her entrances had been those of the doted-upon star whose affectionate supporting cast has left center stage for her" (29). From Justin's adolescent point of view, her mother is now "determined to make suffering noble and beautiful" (35) and is "purposely trying to transform her whole being as a way of avenging herself on her unhappy fate of losing all her supporters and protectors" (36).

Her mother's renunciation of her old self, of the way she had been, Justin feels, rips out "some vital thread" that had run through her whole childhood. In their "other" life, her mother "had always starred as 'The Daughter,'" whereas Justin played the role of the "sturdy little soul, the companion of the grandparents." As far back as Justin could remember, she always felt "like a prematurely aged little parent [herself], who must exercise self-restraint and empathy" so that her mother "could prolong her life as a girl" (39–40). The death of her grandparents put an end to this adult-child role, leaving her disoriented and feeling "in some kind of limbo, with a lost childhood on either side" (40).

Amid such violent change and emotional dislocation, Justin is seized by two somewhat conflicting impulses. On the one hand, she aches for the lost world of certainty, security, and achieved identity, yearning for ways of rediscovering the beloved world left behind in Virginia. On the other hand, she longs for the freedom of the adult world, wanting to flee the entrapment of the Raspberry Ice world, to grow into a unique individual, "free from petty restraints and clinging baby brothers and hurt looks from mothers and hideous winks from know-it-all aunts" (81). Vaguely understanding the limitations of that lost world, she nevertheless feels deprived to have nothing to replace it. "Gone forever," she reflects, "were the earlier times when I had been conveyed securely along by the cherished traditions of authorities I loved and never thought to question" (102). In her new environment, she can find no one with the wisdom, charm, and inspiration she values to guide her through the turbulent years of adolescent growth—until her chance meeting with Ursula DeVane.

In the forty-four-year-old single woman, brilliant and eccentric, maternal and mercurial, Justin finds a new Fredericksburg, a world beyond the ordi-

nary, tedious existence of Lucas Meadows: music, art, history, imagination, enchantment. Possessing the same kind of beauty and graciousness of traditional southern culture, this new world, richer and more complex, poses demands more challenging than the old world ever did.

As the summer progresses, a profound friendship develops between the forty-four-year-old woman and the fourteen-year-old adolescent, a relationship at once intimately personal, intensely psychological, potently artistic, and mythically filial. Ursula becomes Justin's muse, mentor, and spiritual mother, nurturing and inspiring her artistic and human growth. She draws Justin irresistibly into her world of magic and enchantment, a world filled with complex, often conflicting, impulses and emotions: ambition and obsession, aspiration and defeat, love and betrayal, fantasy and illusion. Overwhelmed by Ursula's captivating presence, Justin struggles to win acceptance from her older friend and feels the thrill of being so deliciously merged into another person. At the same time, however, she feels the need to maintain some psychological distance from her mentor in order to keep intact her personal autonomy. She both suffers from and thrives on the intensity of their relationship, growing, as the summer passes, in knowledge, perception, and artistic ambition.

In the act of "intensely remembering" her summer with Ursula, Justin re-creates the vital character of Ursula and the intense psychological drama that unfolds as she becomes increasingly absorbed by her. Ursula, a woman continually defying prediction and easy, rigid categorization, bewitches Justin throughout the summer with her "mercurial, protean qualities" (172). She shines brilliantly in her originality and defiant difference against the dreary monotony of the "Raspberry Ice" world that envelops Justin. Vibrant and vivacious, she speaks intimately to Justin's yearnings for change and growth, enchanting her with the vitality of her imagination and her dashing personality. To Justin, she is never, from visit to visit, quite the same, transforming and re-creating herself at the "unique demands of the moment" (90) with an admirable dramatic flair. There is always something undefinable about her— an element of surprise—that eludes or shatters all possibilities of judgment or categorization. She never fails to leave Justin a captive audience, never sure of her yet always curious about her.

She charms Justin with tales of her own past, a past wrought with ad-

venture and ambition as well as sacrifice and defeat, so markedly different from Justin's mother's comfortable past existence as "protected wife and daughter" (7). Even her eccentric and economically impoverished present life is charged with the artistic and spiritual energies that Lucas Meadows completely lacks. Living with her brother Julian, a once brilliant pianist attempting a comeback, Ursula maintains the intensity of experience by channeling her thwarted talents toward Julian's artistic fulfillment and staying alert for new, stimulating rhythms of life as a way of coping with the middle-age "danger point" that threatens to congeal her with "the stately rhythms of what [she] knows" (18).

She plants in Justin artistic aspirations, bringing her closer to the life she could then only intuit: "music, art, travel, sensibility, drama, conversations that moved easily into the realms of the imagination" (49). She infuses her with passionate dreams of a future life in the arts. "Your soul," she tells Justin, "craves that constant heightening of reality only art can give" (157–58). Spending time with Ursula always gives Justin an inspiring sense of self-discovery. "She created me as she talked," Justin recalls, "she examined the substance of me and then prophesied, in grand, sweeping strokes, the uses to which I could be put" (157). What Justin only intuitively feels, Ursula beautifully articulates—that art can give shape to lived experience, that the capacity for yearning both torments and stimulates, and that artistic and spiritual vitality lies in feeling that yearning powerfully and "exquisitely." "If you are an artist," Justin remembers her mentor saying, "you learn how to trap the yearning and put it where you want, put it where it goes. That's the secret all true artists come to know" (48).

She challenges the boundaries of Justin's self-perception, forcing her, like "the demanding inquisitor" (94), to formulate her thoughts and "keep track of [her] soul's progress upon a confusing map where adults had already charted their conflicting ideas of reality" (102). She stimulates Justin with the idea of a changing and evolving self, telling her that her androgynous name gives her more room for growth and expansion. She exults in Justin's youth but warns her against congealing into a fixed, final self. She intrigues, fascinates, demands, challenges, and nourishes; she penetrates and absorbs. She expands and enriches Justin: "I found that my brain, my emotions, my imagination needed rest after being with her. She

played me: until I met her, I never knew I had so many tones and vibrations" (176).

Notwithstanding Ursula's recognition and confession of her own defeats and limitations, Justin nonetheless finds her an appealing role model—as a woman who transcends the traditional female roles of wife and mother, as well as the limitations of a narrow existence, and who makes for herself a meaningful life throbbing with spiritual and artistic energies. She becomes Justin's heroine and mentor, awakening and exciting that "lonely, mysterious side" of the adolescent girl who was "just beginning to know" it herself—"a side neither masculine nor feminine but quivering with intimations of mental and spiritual things" (122). Not fully understanding the extent of her preoccupation with her mentor, Justin becomes more and more absorbed in her, letting herself be possessed by her, wanting to be her, and always afraid of losing her.

Justin's memory trip focuses on the intense psychological drama that enters and penetrates the young heroine's friendship with Ursula, delineating adolescent growth as a struggle of balancing the conflicting needs for individuation and subordination. Young Justin recognizes that Ursula dominates her—in the realm of thought, feeling, and imagination. She feels "larger, freer" when she is in Ursula's company, fully absorbed in the reality of being with her. Between visits, in the "less demanding environment of Lucas Meadows" (175), Justin lives with the "constant, straining alertness toward one person and one person only" (46), playing back, through memory and imagination, the questions each visit stirred up and the responses Ursula evoked for her. She would go over her latest visit with Ursula or "cull favorite scenes from the succession of visits and make a gratifying montage of proofs that she liked [her]" (176). She would also "fashion and refashion" Ursula's story, staging in her imagination "various incidents and turning points in her life." "Frequently," she admits, "I became so involved in my productions that the lines of my own individuality became blurred: it seemed as though I were remembering my own past. Sometimes these mental fabrications would carry over into sleep, and I would dream strange concoctions of her life and mine" (176). Indulging her fertile imagination, she sometimes would "feel strange stirrings and almost cease to be [herself]" (157). More than that, she often wanted to be Ursula, "to wake up one morning and find [herself] inside her

body, with her memories, and her duties, and even her disappointments" (47).

Justin's adolescent growth, Godwin suggests, is marked by tension and ambiguity, unfolding itself as a struggle between self-abjuration and self-assertion. Whereas one part of Justin luxuriates in "impersonating" and "belonging" to Ursula, the other part fears losing sight of herself in her whole-hearted preoccupation with, even submergence in, Ursula. "Becoming" Ursula is often ecstatic, making her feel "an agreeable surge of power" (110), but it is sometimes "miserable," sharpening her sense of powerlessness and making her chafe at her "subordinate role in everybody's life" (209). Conscious that Ursula knows that she is "completely in her power" (48), Justin makes every effort to assert her individuality, to separate herself from Ursula, to maintain a desirable distance so as to keep her sense of self distinct. As much as she aches for Ursula's company, she refrains from going to her house too frequently, never, "even in the height of [her] devotion" (176), visiting Ursula more than twice a week. The "calculated frugality" (122) in her careful spacing gives her, she feels, much needed emotional distance from Ursula as well as some psychological control over her mentor: "I didn't want to use up my welcome; I wanted her to miss me a little" (122).

Acts of self-assertion, Godwin shows, measure Justin's growth as an individual. Acutely aware when Ursula relates to her as an equal and when she treats her as a mere child, Justin seizes every opportunity to thrust toward separation and individuation. She grows "bolder than usual in the repeated use of [Ursula's] name" when she excites Ursula with descriptions of her grandmother's garden, feeling she "had something to teach *her,* for a change" (173). And when Ursula corrects her pronunciation, she expresses anger and humiliation in her distinctive, self-assertive way: "For all these weeks, I had been pronouncing her name wrong and she had simply listened to me compounding my mistake, the silent laughter building in her. What was I to her, then: some pet buffoon whose mistakes could be counted on to provide amusement during the dull summer hours when she could not be with her brother? I vowed to myself not to use her name again until she noticed its absence in our conversations and repented of her ridicule" (173–74). Admiring Ursula for always being in command, she stays on guard for opportunities to excel. For instance, seizing control of the situation, perhaps offending Ursula, brings her "a little thrill of superiority" (124), and the deepening tan on her

arms and legs from swimming gives her a competitive edge in relation to her mentor: "A tan was the nearest thing to a transformation I could effect in myself in order to show her I, too, changed from visit to visit" (185).

While she treats adolescent growth as a struggle between separation and merging, individuation and subordination, Godwin also embeds the psychological drama between her two characters in the mother-daughter plot—one of the central themes of her contemporary Bildungsromane. She unfolds, through Justin's memory journey, the complexity of the mother-daughter relationship, delineating the daughter's need for maternal nurturance and her conflicted response to her maternal legacy.

Partially a reaction to her own mother's inadequacy, Justin's friendship with Ursula gradually becomes mythically filial. She "loved Ursula more than she loved [her] mother that summer" (105), and she kept the extent of her preoccupation with the older woman a secret from her mother. She enacted an imaginary mother-daughter scene—the young Ursula in fierce conflict with her own mother—"calling up unacknowledged and potentially dangerous feelings hidden in the depths of [her] psyche and projecting them onto other characters safely removed from [her] personal circumstance" (177). She remained divided between guilt and longing throughout the summer: "commuting between prosaic Lucas Meadows and seductive Old Clove Road, making an effort . . . to render onto the Stokes-Mott world, with its practicalities and family duties, what it required of [her], while secretly preserving [her] highest loyalties for the DeVane kingdom, with its long-standing prides and alienations, its private fantasies, and its obsessive dreams" (104).

Justin's friendship with Ursula brings her into the morally ambivalent world of adult female sexuality, love, and betrayal. At the threshold of womanhood, fourteen-year-old Justin had ambivalent feelings about the transformation and hoped that she would not be "rushed into womanhood with all its distracting appurtenances" (122). Ursula's story of her former student Kitty—a lesbian child in love with her teacher—raises "murky questions and speculations" (224) in Justin about her own sexuality. The even more disturbing story of young Ursula's premeditated betrayal of her own mother at the age of ten sends Justin "tumbling prematurely" to the cusp of "the uncertain abyss of adulthood, where morals, backed up by experience, could never be simple again" (244). Ursula's story implicates Justin in the world

of moral ambivalence, demanding her judgment on such complicated issues as love and betrayal, forcing her to reassess her mentor, to "ask troubling questions" about herself, and to "reestablish where [her] personality stopped and [Ursula's] began" (260).

Justin's painful struggle to cope with the implications of Ursula's story of betrayal captures the confusion and agony of adolescent growth. Despite her troubled feelings about young Ursula's cruel betrayal of her own mother, despite her disappointment at losing the adult Ursula as her "ideal" and "unblemished heroine," Justin feels bound to Ursula through filial loyalty. She wanted to and felt she could forgive her and accept her "with all her strangenesses and faults" (286). As she rides her bicycle toward Ursula's house on that fateful summer evening, she rehearses in elation her pledge to Ursula: "I think I have more in common with you than anybody else. You said I was like your dream daughter. Well, I've decided I want to be your friend for life and your mystical daughter" (284). Avowing her sacred, spiritual bond with her alternate mother, Justin now feels in touch with her best self, secure and blissful in the knowledge of their "solidarity": "Henceforth I would render unto biological motherhood its filial dues and affections, but my secret pact with Ursula would have vaccinated me against losing touch with my best, my imaginative self" (285).

Their enchanting summer friendship, however, ends on a tragic note. Emphasizing the intense, continuous conflict in the mother-daughter plot, Godwin places Justin in the same situation as she did the young Ursula many years ago—catching a maternal figure in a secret tryst with a lover in the stone hut, now designated as Justin's "Finishing School." By making adolescent Justin repeat unwittingly young Ursula's act of betrayal, Godwin illuminates the ongoing drama between the daughters and mothers of the world, with the daughter caught between the conflicting needs to accept and reject the mother, between yearning for maternal guidance and fear of repeating the compromised plot of her mother's story. In agony and bitterness, Justin rejects Ursula as friend, mentor, and alternate mother. To protect her wounded self, she adopts a surface identity, concealing her inner struggle beneath pretended adolescent conformity.

But the summer lives on in memory and imagination, tormenting Justin with confusion, guilt, and pain, haunting her with conflicting images of the

same woman who had taught, nurtured, and inspired her as well as confused, shamed, and hurt her. Too many things—about Ursula, about herself, and about their relationship—need to be sorted out, but it takes the "redemptive power of art" (251) to make something beautiful out of something excruciatingly agonizing.

"To the Ursulas of This World": The Daughter's Continuous Bildung

"What do I want from Ursula now? Why does she again, after twenty-six years, dominate my thoughts?" (148). Midway through her narrative, Justin asks herself this question, intrigued by Ursula's continued power to bewitch her imagination. An established actress and an assured woman, with the defining props of artistic fame, financial security, and all the status of a successful middle-class woman, Justin, herself now almost Ursula's age that summer long ago, stands worlds apart from the adolescent girl of fourteen who had been disoriented by the death of beloved family members and regional dislocation. Fearing that closure which Ursula warned against so many years ago, she wants "to go back and claim the girl [she] was—the girl Ursula DeVane chose for her special friend, that summer in Clove" (106). She wants to "take [herself] through the summer as it unfolded, allowing [herself] no conscious lies or glossings-over, but only the wisdom of retrospect" (106).

Superimposing Justin's adult self on her adolescent self and juxtaposing the narrator-protagonist's backward time travel with her present narrative act as a way of self-renewal, Godwin unfolds simultaneously two processes: adolescent growth movingly recollected by the mature heroine, and continuous adult growth achieved through conscious restructuring of memory and constructive use of internal dialogue.[25] By making memory the action of the novel and by creating a dialogic context for the heroine's continual growth, Godwin brings together Justin's separate strands of existence as an adolescent girl, as an artist, and as a daughter, allowing her narrating heroine to

25. Jane Hill describes *The Finishing School* as a novel "primarily concerned with how perspective is altered by time, how memory adjusts, corrects, forgives much that the younger self cannot." Hill, *Gail Godwin*, 2.

continue her Bildung, to acknowledge her maternal legacy, and to redirect herself toward the possibility of further growth.

Having Justin and Ursula, "mystical" daughter and mother, meet again in the beginning of the novel through the transporting language of the dream world, Godwin reveals the underlying psychological connection between the present, narrating self and the past, remembered self. In that dream, Ursula and Justin are together, "sitting on the crumbling threshold of The Finishing School." A storm suddenly sets in—"the sky turned an ominous color, the pond shivered like a live thing, the old pines hissed and swayed, and hard rain pelted down" (1). Braving crackling skies and pelting rain, Ursula boldly dashes into the storm, challenging a timid Justin with her "tender, teasing" (2) voice and her self-assertive action. As Ursula reaches triumphantly the far side of the pond, Justin huddles in the shelter of The Finishing School, watching Ursula's gradually diminishing figure and seized "with mounting despair": "I knew if I did not jump up and run after her now that I would lose her forever. But I was powerless to move" (1).

The vivid image of an Ursula urging herself to action, taking risks, and testing the boundaries of experience; the profound fear of a Justin losing that image; and the complicated psychological interaction between the two constitute the reverberating strands of Godwin's narrative of double Bildung. As central characters of Godwin's *Künstlerroman,* both in the recollected story of Justin's youthful growth and in the ongoing narrative of her mature development, Ursula and Justin are portrayed as, in Rachel Blau DuPlessis' words, "the emergent daughter artist and the thwarted maternal parent," an important thematic pair in twentieth-century women's *Künstlerromane.* "A specific biographical drama," DuPlessis claims, enters and shapes twentieth-century *Künstlerromane,* engaging a maternal figure who "bequeaths her ambition" to her daughter, who "becomes an artist to extend, reveal, and elaborate her mother's often thwarted talents." The mother figures, DuPlessis explains, are sometimes displaced by generations; the daughter figures sometimes are "not the biological daughters of the mother they seek."[26]

One of Godwin's fullest representations of the mother-daughter plot, *The Finishing School* unfolds movingly, in its dual narrative, the daughter's quest

26. DuPlessis, *Writing Beyond the Ending,* 90–93, 98–99.

for the mother. Muse, mentor, and spiritual mother to adolescent Justin, the Ursula of the recollected story becomes a haunting presence from the past demanding recognition from the mature and successful actress. Becoming the artist Ursula failed to become and producing a moving narrative of their friendship as "a labor of love," "an emotional gift," and "a continuation" of artistic impulses,[27] Justin completes her unfinished task of twenty-six years ago: to acknowledge and affirm "the Ursulas of this world"—mothers who leave their mark on the daughters, whose memories continue to stir, inspire, and nurture the daughters of the world, living in them as long as they live. Making her narrative a gift of love to her alternate mother, Justin speaks for all of Godwin's daughter heroines who are both drawn to and in conflict with their mothers, resentful of their mothers' defeat, ambivalent about motherhood itself, yet deeply in debt to their maternal heritage. With the aid of memory, Justin revives the ardor Ursula once aroused in her, replenishes herself with that youthful power of yearning, and comes in touch again with her best, imaginative self. In her wistful voice, she affirms a daughter's acknowledgment of the mother's nurturing role in her development, celebrates the enduring bond and the continuities between mothers and daughters, and triumphantly claims both female autonomy and sexual identity.

With wonder, bewilderment, and complete honesty, Justin sets out to "attend to what [Ursula's] image, playing its role in last night's dream" (3), comes to tell her. Under the spell of the dream, Justin hears once again Ursula's emphatic statement, made in the summer twenty-six years ago, about congealing. Middle age and adolescence, she remembers Ursula saying, are two turning points in life, when one is in the greatest danger of congealing. Whereas Ursula, in addressing her young friend twenty-six years ago, emphasized adolescence, Justin, as she remembers the statement now, focuses on middle age. She herself has now reached that "traditional danger point" (4) that Ursula was facing when they met. Through the dream world image of Ursula making another tryst with life, Justin makes her first dialogic encounter with her younger self enchanted and possessed by an older woman. Through her remembrance of her mentor's warning against congealing, she makes the initial connection between the act of "intensely remembering" and the continuing process of becoming.

27. *Ibid.*, 104.

"The Ursulas of the world" (4) would know, Justin reflects, if she became congealed, stuck in a role and repeating herself. In the disguise of an imaginary monologue by Ursula, Justin compares her confused yet longing adolescent self with her accomplished adult self. She listens to Ursula's verdict of herself "falling into complacency, that alarming early warning signal of congealment" (5). She hears Ursula's warning as well as her challenge:

> She's done well, of course, but to reach the range and intensity I have seen others capable of, she must tap new sources of feeling. Or old sources which she turned away from at the end of that summer, when she was afraid and confused. Ah, Justin, if you were to come riding over to me again, I would stir up your blood. "Don't you recall," I would say, "how I warned you to be alert for the first signs of jellification? How you must *fight,* the moment you feel its clammy grip. You must hurl yourself into action, take some new risk." (5–6)

Justin is deeply stirred by Ursula's question: "When did you last leave *your* stronghold, Justin? When was the last time you went out alone, forsaking all the props that have come to define you?"(6).

Invoking Ursula as an epic poet invokes his muse, Justin leaves her stronghold of artistic success and, guided by Ursula's rich and compelling voice, goes out alone to "the country of youth" (6) to confront events and feelings she has suppressed since that fateful summer's end. Relying on the vitality and social construction of memory and narrative restructuring, Justin makes her own new pact with life, reaping spiritual returns as she progresses on a journey intensely personal, psychological, social, and dialogic.

Constantly asserting her narrative presence with phrases like "Now I see" or "I understand this now," frequently interrupting the flow of her narrative by digressions, analysis, or interpretations, Justin journeys through the landscape of her youth, trying to grasp the vital connection between present and past, middle age and youth, Ursula and herself. Sometimes "the rebirth of . . . long-suppressed feelings" (49) makes her anticipate her story. Occasionally, "in following the natural flow of [her] memories as they leap forward, then draw back, then leap forward again" (106), she digresses from what she wants to do most. She apologizes for these "literary offenses," yet

she is acutely aware that these digressions, anticipations, and "authorial" assertions express the urgency of narrative self-definition through causality and connection.

Justin's reminiscences of her college acting illustrate brilliantly how memory and internal dialogue can be essential to the heroine's self-definition. After narrating her first meeting with Ursula, Justin briefly turns away from her story to entertain memories of her college acting. She was playing Nina in *The Sea Gull,* "determined to evoke in [her]self the necessary state of enchantment" (44). Though her silent soliloquy—about the world of yearning, illusion, and obsession—evokes the magic and enchantment that enveloped her relationship with Ursula, the twenty-year-old college apprentice actress "purposely" breaks the spell she had invoked, turning away from a then unwelcome confrontation. Narrating that event presently, with "the wisdom of retrospect" (106), Justin is capable of acknowledging now what she already knew but could not acknowledge at the time: "Of *course* I knew what it was like to be enchanted. I had been enchanted the summer I was fourteen and living in that quiet rural village that, after we had left it, seemed a passing dream. I had felt enchantment that summer: the constant, straining alertness toward one person and one person only. All I needed to do in my college room was to remember those feelings and put them into my Nina. I would have been a stunning example of the enchanted girl" (45–46).

But at the time, Justin did not want to acknowledge; she did not want to remember. Six years "had not put enough time and healing distance between the fourteen-year-old who had felt shocked and sick and guilty over what had happened, and the twenty-year-old apprentice actress who might have been able to use those memories for an inspired performance" (46). The unhealed daughter could not yet forgive her mother and acknowledge the bond between them. If she had remembered Ursula then, Justin recollects, she might have despised herself for "trying to be an actress because of her influence" (46) and, in turning away from the pain associated with their broken friendship, she "might have turned away from the thing [she] wanted to become, the thing [she] most wanted to do" (47).

By breaking narrative sequence to include a later event and engage in causal analysis, Justin asserts her power as the narrating "I" in organizing experience and giving it shape and meaning. Again, the freedom of the character

here reflects an aspect of authorial design. As in *Violet Clay,* Godwin creates a dialogic context, with multiple time schemes and multiple versions of the self encountering and interacting with one another—a possessed adolescent self twenty-six years ago, an apprehensive apprentice actress self twenty years ago, and a present, narrating self trying fiercely to understand and claim those past selves. In superimposing Justin's three selves one on the other and demonstrating their connections, Godwin asserts not only the authority of her female speaking subject but also the self-defining value of memory, narration, and internal dialogue. Whereas the twenty-year-old apprentice actress refused to remember for fear of self-denial, the forty-year-old successful artist now chooses to use her long-suppressed memories for renewed self-definition. She can remember now Ursula's absorbing presence; she can remember "the continual charged consciousness" (46) she had of her. She can remember both wanting to be Ursula and not wanting to be her for the reason that Ursula's life "had been foreclosed" whereas her own life "was still unfolding" (47). Of most importance, she can now acknowledge, without fear of losing herself, that in becoming what Ursula wanted to become, she is, in a sense, her creature.

The double Bildung of *The Finishing School* links Justin's adolescent struggle for self-identity and her adult striving for continuous growth, bringing the remembered story and remembering act into continual interaction with each other to yield new self-perceptions and self-definitions. The "connective tissue" (20) that binds the two together is "a special kind of love" (48) that Ursula once defined for Justin—"a powerful and constant state of yearning" (48) at once tormenting, alluring, and inspiring. The secret and enduring strength of an artist, Ursula insists, lies in her continued capacity to feel this yearning intensely and exquisitely.

When she heard these words, Justin recalls, she was "so full of the things" (48) Ursula was describing. Remembering them now, so vividly and so powerfully, she attempts to feel and vibrate to them again. The further back she journeys into "the country of youth," the deeper she enters into a dialogic relationship with her past, with Ursula as her alternate mother, and with the younger versions of herself. Ursula's words about congealment, revived in the beginning of her narrative through the spell of her dream, had set memory in motion. Now she recalls these words again, midway through her nar-

rative, asking herself penetrating questions about her fierce attachment to that past world of yearning she and Ursula shared many years ago. "Is it because," she asks herself, "I am reaching that dangerous age, the 'traditional danger point' that Ursula spoke of so warily, when people must either take some new risk or congeal?" (149). She bombards herself with questions, makes propositions, and arrives at tentative conclusions, affirming once more the defining power of remembering: "In allowing myself full recall of the power [Ursula] had over the girl Justin, I am trying to *take on* that power, to beam it back onto myself as an adult and as an actress, until it infuses me and I become bright with it" (149).

More and more consciously, more and more urgently, Justin uses memory and internal dialogue to locate the source of her spiritual energy, to find and reclaim the self that she once was, a self that, for all its confusion and disappointment, possessed the power of yearning. The more fiercely she remembers Ursula's world of enchantment, the more firmly she grasps the connection between the narrated self—the adolescent Justin struggling to define herself from scratch—and the narrating self—the mature actress increasingly "encumbered" with the defining props of success.

Ursula, connecting the world of striving and the world of success, continually dominates both strands of the narrative. Deeply drawn into the past, Justin can now think and feel as her mentor must have thought and felt in speaking about "unrequited yearnings" (49). When she recalls for the second time Ursula's words about yearning, spoken on that faraway afternoon to a spellbound girl of fourteen, she has come to a full understanding of Ursula's significance in relation to the urgency of her narrated self-definition. Looking back on that afternoon and seeing that young girl vibrant with intense desire and yearning, she can empathize with Ursula in envying "the taut drama of youth, strung with all its erotic and spiritual demands" (211). She now speaks directly to that young, aching girl she once was, inviting her back through dialogue as she has invited Ursula back through dream images and memory:

Oh, young Justin, what would I say to you if I could penetrate the time barrier and murmur in your ear? I am so much more certain of myself than you were; I am probably happier, as the world defines happi-

ness. Yet you draw me, you awaken me, as I watch you sitting there, surrounded by your treasures of so many intense desires and fears. Exult in your riches—though of course you won't—because the day will come when you will look back enviously on your longings. The day will come when you understand . . . that the act of longing for something will always be more intense than the requiting of it. (211–12)

Speaking as Ursula would have spoken to young Justin, the narrator-protagonist absorbs the "thematic pair" of mother and daughter into one person, emphasizing generational bond and the connection between an enduring capacity for yearning and the unending process of becoming. Authentic self-definition, she recognizes, does not end with the achievement of a goal. Those content with previously achieved self-definitions are more dead than alive because evolving selfhood is a continuous process rather than an end product.

No nostalgic mourning for a state of being forever lost, Justin's backward journey in time involves "a forward motion to yearning" (256). By using memory and internal dialogue consciously and actively to reconstruct her younger, longing self, she reengages her mature self with yearning and becoming. Remembering and narrating, for Justin, is starting to yearn again, and, in Ursula's words, "as long as you yearn, you can't congeal" (256). The narrated story and the narrating act converge to reinforce the idea that the self finds its greatest vitality in the act of yearning and striving, that coherence lies in the state of becoming.

Constantly feeling "a lusty surge of renewal" pulsating from the remembered world of enchantment, Justin vigorously continues her journey of inner growth. In vivid, selective detail, she recollects and restructures the progress of her friendship with Ursula, tracing its psychological pattern and reexperiencing the intensity of balancing the desire for closeness and the fear of immersion. Toward the end of her narrative, she relives the tragic ending of her friendship with Ursula, remembering, with painful vividness, not only what happened on the scene but also her hurtful rejection of Ursula: "The great fascination with her was gone. Evaporated. And with it, the 'love' I had believed would last forever. I could *remember* feeling it, but that was in the past. It was as though she had died, too" (307). With Ursula's sym-

bolic death and Justin's bare survival from a "fatal illness" (307), the summer of their enchanting friendship ended, leaving Justin struggling with conflicted feelings: pity, regret, disgust, betrayal, shame, guilt, disillusionment, and pain. Despite everything, she was glad to be rid of Ursula's possession, to be able to get on with her life, to become the heroine of her own story.

Narrating the climax of her recollected story, Justin brings her time travel to conclusion, making it the climax of her narrating act. Now her narrative has come full circle, returning to the mystical mother and daughter, the inseparable pair in the protagonist's double Bildung. Juxtaposing the evocative dream world of the beginning that had set memory in motion is the wistful reflection of the ending, informed with love, understanding, and wisdom. Having gone through again the stages of "adoring," "despising," and "forgiving" Ursula through memory, Justin can now accept Ursula as part of herself, honoring her role as nurturing mother, offering her the enduring love and respect of a daughter, and celebrating the strengths of their "bond of womanhood" (256). "[It] has taken me this long," she concludes, "to understand that I lose nothing by acknowledging her influences on me" (322). At forty, she can "willingly" be the girl she was at fourteen, "ride back and forth on that yellow school bus now, and stare steadily at the windows of that house, eager for clues that will tell [her] how [Ursula] is going on" (322). More than that, she has added and enriched Ursula's memory, making it part of her own continuing growth. The thwarted maternal parent, in Justin's renewed world of yearning and becoming, has transcended her "wasted existence" and taken on new roles of her own. Now Justin's thoughts freely "go forward to meet hers" (322), and Justin and Ursula meet in spirit, sharing the sacred knowledge that "as long as you can go on creating new roles for yourself, you are not vanquished" (322).

In the "Notes" section of "My Personal Life"—a teen record book with "pre-organized compartments" that Aunt Mona gave her for her fourteenth birthday—the adolescent Justin had written: "I have made a new friend this summer who I admire a lot because she is sweet, interesting, and funny." Looking at this sentence, Justin cheerfully anticipates the success of her narrative self-definition: "I stare at that commonplace sentence written by yesterday's teenager. I will it to render up all the passions and fears I know lie waiting

for me in the silt of the reclaimed past" (147). Out of the confusion and pain of the past, Godwin's mature artist-heroine has made a coherent story—a story at once of her adolescent struggles and her adult, ongoing Bildung. "Memory," she asserts confidently, "lives in the brain of the rememberer" (154). The essence of her Bildung, memory has enabled Justin to revitalize herself and to claim triumphantly a continuous, vibrant, and evolving selfhood that embraces past and present, mother and daughter, experience and consciousness, and, above all, yearning, striving, and becoming.

4

Toward a Dialogic Imagination
A Mother and Two Daughters

Godwin's ongoing exploration of an evolving self takes a new and exciting turn in the first of her "major-key" novels, *A Mother and Two Daughters.* She shifts from fictional portrayals of a single protagonist—the wedded young woman attempting to build an independent identity or the solitary academic/artist seeking coherent self-definition—to construction of multiple characters, each with a distinct voice and each in search of a unique self. With three major protagonists, Godwin in *A Mother and Two Daughters* explores in greater depth generational and familial conflicts and the ways they shape individual growth.

Prior to *A Mother and Two Daughters,* Godwin worked hard to make the best of a single point of view, stretching, as she describes in an essay published in the same year as *A Mother and Two Daughters,* "each heroine as far as [she] could" to make her a complex and fascinating character engaged in a continuous struggle for self-definition. She made her heroine "travel far from home, get involved with complex or unusual people"; she made her "suffer, think and grow." She successfully created vibrant heroines who are immersed in memory, interested in history as identity, and capable of constructing a mature, coherent, and evolving identity through an internal process of self-definition. By depicting the complex interplay between past and present, between earlier and later selves, and by emphasizing the role of memory and internal dialogue, Godwin has made the single point of view remarkably

multiple, dramatizing the concept of self as plural, continuous, and in-process.

"But something in me," Godwin confesses in the same essay, "was longing to leap that point-of-view barrier and be more than one person at a time."[1] However important memory and internal dialogue are to growth, however significantly a single consciousness is multiplied, the single point of view limited Godwin's exploration of an evolving self to what Bakhtin calls the "internal sovereign territory"—individual consciousness, solitary quest, and internal means of self-definition. She has brilliantly embedded her heroines' personal struggle in family, region, and culture, never lapsing into what Bakhtin terms an "enclosure within the self."[2] But she realizes that, to expand her novelistic horizons, to represent in greater depth the complexity of the contemporary self and the dynamic process of growth, she must "escape that terribly limiting enclosure of one point of view" and explore individual consciousness in the context of "the strata of society."[3]

A Mother and Two Daughters, Godwin explains, "demanded three points of view, if I were to show the subjective reality of each character, complete with her history, her style of behavior and speech and thought, the important people in her life, and—most crucial, perhaps—the mysterious way in which she had shaped and been shaped by the other two heroines."[4] Using three protagonists and three points of view enables Godwin to portray radically different characters and examine diverse processes of female growth over the life cycle. In delineating three heroines' separate journeys of self-discovery, Godwin not only shifts from one heroine to another in each of their diverging paths of self-search but also switches between their solitary pursuits and their interactive dialogues, intense conflicts, and converging consciousnesses. In so doing, Godwin gives herself the opportunity to examine

1. Gail Godwin, "Becoming the Characters in Your Novel," *Writer,* XCV (June, 1982), 12.
2. Bakhtin emphasizes the "impossibility of the existence of a single consciousness." For him, "the most important acts constituting self-consciousness are determined by a relationship toward another consciousness (toward a *thou*)." In a fully dialogized novelistic world, he maintains, one "has no internal sovereign territory"; "every internal experience ends up on the boundary, encounters another." Solitude is of an illusory nature: "Looking inside himself, he looks *into the eyes of another* or *with the eyes of another.*" See *Problems of Dostoevsky's Poetics,* 287.
3. Godwin, interview with *Contemporary Authors,* 159.
4. Godwin, "Becoming the Characters in Your Novel," 12.

the dynamics of family drama as it shapes and defines the individual and to reach out to the broader society of the newest South, of modern women, white and—for the first time in her fiction—black.

Of most importance, however, breaking out of the single point of view provides Godwin with new thematic as well as narrative possibilities for her continuing explorations of the concept of the self. In significant ways, the story of "three strong and different women bound in the closest of ties" accentuates the idea of multiplicity.[5] Centering on the present, ongoing family drama in the contemporary South, Godwin moves region and family to center stage and situates solitary quest, individual consciousness, and the psychological process of memory in the larger phenomenon of human interconnectedness. Self, in *A Mother and Two Daughters,* is multiple not only in the internal, solitary, and retrospective process of memory but also in the interactive, ongoing process of communication. Self-definition, therefore, takes on a new dimension, becoming an intensely dialogic encounter, both inward with the varied voices of one's own self and outward with the voices of other individuals.

Godwin's shift from single to multiple characters and points of view can be seen as a movement toward a Bakhtinian vision of the world, real as well as fictional. Speaking of Dostoevsky's novels, Bakhtin points to the centrality of dialogue in the making of novels. He persuasively argues that a single consciousness does not exist, that an individual does not achieve a full identity except in a dialogic context. The thoroughly dialogized world, both of Dostoevsky's fiction and of human life at large, is characterized, Bakhtin explains, by the multiplicity of voices and consciousnesses interacting with one another, each "independent," "unmerged," "fully valid," asserting its own right, its own world, and its "rigorous," "irrevocable *multi-voicedness* and *vari-voicedness.*" Consciousness, he asserts, "is in essence multiple," and "life by its very nature is dialogic." To be "means to communicate dialogically," and an "open-ended dialogue with an evolving multi-voiced meaning" lies at the center of human experience. The dialogic encounter of individual voices and consciousnesses, Bakhtin maintains, is ultimately crucial to an individual's sense of self and his understanding of the relationship and opposition between "I" and "the other."[6]

5. *Ibid.*
6. Bakhtin, *Problems of Dostoevsky's Poetics,* 6, 252, 265, 288, 293, 298, 299.

Rich and resounding in its multiple voices and consciousnesses, revealing in its complex dialogues, Godwin's first "major-key" novel partakes of Bakhtin's dialogic imagination. In this novel, each of the three individual consciousnesses is inseparable from the consciousnesses of the other two individuals, and growth and self-definition result from painful, dialogic encounters, through the "*surplus* of vision and understanding," expressed variedly through "love," "confession," "forgiveness," and "an active (not a duplicating) understanding, a willingness to listen."[7]

Individual Growth

Godwin's compelling portrayal of "three very strong, and very different women"[8] marks a full development of her long-standing interest in different types of heroines and in the role of female networks. The four novels preceding *A Mother and Two Daughters* have featured a variety of heroines: mothers, daughters, wives, domestic and professional women, single intellectuals and artists. Moreover, the heroine in each novel always meets, is related to, or establishes friendship with other female characters, seeing their lives as alternative cultural expressions of femaleness and consciously measuring and assessing her own experience against theirs.

In *A Mother and Two Daughters,* Godwin continues to explore the dimensions of her characteristic heroine—the single intellectual or artist with her fierce intensity and her existential angst of search. At the same time, she turns back to two familiar figures in her previous novels: the married young woman yearning for a space of her own and the mother resigned to the premature ending of her story. But her use of these two characters is pro-

7. In his notes for the original edition of *Problems of Dostoevsky's Poetics*, Bakhtin writes about the multiplicity and interdependence of consciousnesses in terms of Dostoevsky's use of a "surplus" of vision—"open" and "honest" communication "dissolved in dialogue, positioned face to face," through "love . . . and then, confession, forgiveness, finally, simply an active (not a duplicating) understanding, a willingness to listen." See *Problems of Dostoevsky's Poetics*, 299.

8. Gail Godwin, *A Mother and Two Daughters* (New York, 1982), 56. Subsequent references will be indicated in parentheses within the text.

foundly transformed in her first major-key novel. Groping for vision and struggling with craft, Godwin made her two married protagonists in *The Perfectionists* and *Glass People* more the victims of patriarchal oppression than heroines of feminist self-definition. On the other hand, she has, prior to *A Mother and Two Daughters,* invariably placed the mother/grandmother figure in the background of the heroine's story, seen by the heroine as disappointing role models or retrieved by her from memory as nostalgic images for solace or self-pity.

In sharp contrast, Godwin portrays in *A Mother and Two Daughters* three women from the same family growing together, perceiving in their experiences three positive modes of self-definition—through existential questing, social striving, and spiritual self-regeneration. Each is distinctly different from the other two; each is a valid and unique expression of evolving selfhood. Cate Strickland, a single, forty-year-old professor of English, persists in her struggle against escaping her own history, truncating her identity, and losing the will to resist "compromise" and "cowardice" (66) in order to stay fluid, to continually become, and to retain her freedom and mobility to meet the challenges of the future. Lydia Strickland, a thirty-six-year-old young wife and mother, succeeds in breaking out of her constraining marriage, returns to college (like so many women of her age in the 1980s), and becomes successful in her profession, furnishing an appealing role model hitherto nonexistent in Godwin's fiction. Nell Strickland, a widow of sixty-three, becomes a heroine in the foreground of her own story, confronting her particular problems of identity with as much courage and perseverance as her two daughters confront theirs. Treating the three heroines equally allows Godwin, for the first time, to examine her crucial themes of female growth and self-definition within a context of women maturing to and beyond middle age.

Godwin's characterization of Cate centers on the vital idea of existential self-search. Older than Jane Clifford and Violet Clay, without the reassurance of successful self-definition through work that allows Violet and Justin to reclaim their past selves with "the wisdom of retrospect,"[9] Cate is portrayed as a heroine thick with self-doubt, deploring fast shrinking opportunities and battling the constant "erosion" of self-confidence, as "Old Father Time [is] chip-chipping away at the cherished edifice of self" (73). In delin-

---

9. Godwin, *The Finishing School,* 106.

eating Cate's struggle not to give up striving for the self she believes in, Godwin creates a heroine who conceives of herself as "an *existential process*,"[10] projective, creative, and evolving. Cate has lived "for seeing things and feeling them honestly" (76), plunging herself daringly into radical causes, pitting herself against "jagged" challenges, zestfully moving forward "to meet the advance of the unpredictable" (26). She envisions her life as moving in an evolutionary pattern, seeing past mistakes as constructive to present understanding and future decisions. Self-realization, in her judgment, is a concept of process and movement, constantly regenerated by renewed belief in one's future and growing capacities to make new discoveries.

In contrast to the narrative patterns of *Violet Clay* and *The Finishing School,* which center on the mature, accomplished heroine's interior journey into the past as a joyful continuation of growth, Godwin now juxtaposes the internal process of self-renewal with the external process of aging. She portrays Cate, reaching her fortieth birthday, without "accomplishing" anything definite in the eyes of the world, as a heroine seized by middle-age despair, especially fearing the loss of her will to resist "compromise," "cowardice," and "the sucking pull of the Status Quo" (66).

At a moment when Cate's life is stalled in a temporary job in a small Iowa college, "when her self-esteem was ailing and her defenses were low" (203), Roger Jernigan, the millionaire pesticide king, enters her life, testing the strengths of her ideal of existential self-search. Jernigan stands for everything Cate's socialist beliefs have led her to reject, but she is physically attracted to him, to his energy and entrepreneurial bravado. She is, at the same time, dangerously in need of him, tortured by self-doubt about the good of "trying to be herself" (205) and yearning "to collapse into the protective embrace of someone else's responsibility" (36), to "give up on keeping her stubborn, weary balance and just sink" (205).

In the protective shelter of Jernigan's "solid warmth," Cate wages an in-

10. Ferguson's "aspect theory of self" provides an alternative to both the liberal humanist idea of self as "an unchanging, unified consciousness" (which she terms the "national maximizer theory of self") and the psychoanalytic/feminist theory of self that emphasizes sexual differences (which she terms "difference theory"). In contrast, she perceives the self as "an ongoing process in which both unique individual priorities and social constraints vie in limiting and defining one's self-identity." See "A Feminist Aspect Theory of the Self," 93–107.

tense inner struggle, caught between opposing roles from which she develops her self-perceptions. Her weary, middle-aged, culturally scripted self finds it "all too easy to abandon her modernity," to "sign away all [her] troublesome, thought-provoking rights to [her] unclear and insecure future," and to seal "her fate as a happy woman" cared for by a male creature "who is reducing [her] to [her] essential female creatureness" (239–40). On the other hand, her feminist, existential, vigilantly resisting self clings for dear life to the integrity of her personal history, past as well as future, and to an evolving identity defined by feminist endeavor, not the cultural text of femininity. In declining Jernigan's marriage proposal, in forgoing comfort, security, and passion in favor of "keeping a space ready" (245) for what one does want when it comes, Cate affirms her existential belief in self-identity as an ongoing process of struggle, an inward search for potential, and a forward motion toward the future.

In her portrayal of Cate's existential struggle for self-renewal, Godwin suggests that rebellious southern daughters who flee the region to seek feminist self-definition may be fleeing from part of their own history. Ultimately, Cate must confront her growing middle-age anxiety about self-identity in the very place she had started from—the region she rejected in fleeing away and the room in which her teenage self dreamed "arrogant young dreams" and "made bold and sweeping plans for the romance of her future" (479–80). There, she enters into a naked confrontation with herself, coming to grips with the knowledge of her inescapable rootedness in her own history. School, books, region, family—the "great conspiracy" (38) she has been fleeing from since girlhood to protect her individual identity—are all "ingredients of her own history—those she could control and those she could not" (480). Without rejecting her past endeavors, she comes to realize that honest, authentic self-search entails accepting and understanding the whole of her history.

With this self-liberating knowledge, Cate resurrects herself from the depths of despair. Continuing to strike out into new territories of self-fulfillment, she "returns at the end to her roots in the hills of North Carolina, as a base from which she travels to earn her venturesome living."[11] By committing her vibrant, questing heroine to the fullest exploration of herself, dramatizing

11. Rhodes, "Gail Godwin and the Ideal of Southern Womanhood," 63.

her struggle to persist in a projective, creative mode of living, Godwin makes her grow, expand, cohere, and become.

If Cate's characterization adds to the "dramas of psychological progress featuring the growth" of the "questing daughters" who flee from the South, Lydia's points to a significant change in Godwin's fictional portrayal of southern daughters. Until *A Mother and Two Daughters,* Godwin "held out little hope for daughters who stayed at home."[12] In a region where a young female finds, in Godwin's own words, "an image of womanhood already cut out for her, stitched securely by the practiced hands of tradition," too many docile daughters have succumbed to the cultural script of southern womanhood "without ever having once strained toward what Jung called 'the task of personality'; without ever having once confronted her true reflection beyond the quicksilver image of what her heritage has prepared her to be."[13]

Lydia—a docile daughter who stays in the South; a young mother with child-caring responsibilities; a proper, prudent, conventional, and practical woman—has little in common with Godwin's venturous southern daughters who flee the constraints of family and region in solitary quest of selfhood. By making Lydia her first heroine who wrestles with the "task of personality" in the region that has shaped her growth as a female, Godwin explores a different process of mature self-definition from that of existential questing.

Whereas she makes Cate respond to internally generated criteria in her existential self-search, Godwin emphasizes Lydia's commitment to "accomplishment" as a yardstick for judging the success or failure of self-definition. As a dutiful southern daughter of the 1950s steeped in an idealized traditional South, Lydia attained her most remarkable accomplishment in finding a good husband, her own Prince Charming, a feat she achieved by mustering the skills that are quintessential expressions of the ideal of southern womanhood—impeccable manners, graciousness, elegance, self-effacement, modesty, and tact.[14] She deftly "handles" Max Mansfield, who in her eyes possesses all the good assets a southern young woman seeks in a man, exciting his interest in her through feminine charm while exercising

12. *Ibid.,* 61–62.
13. Gail Godwin, "The Southern Belle," *Ms,* July, 1975, p. 51.
14. *Ibid.,* 49–52.

care not to "frighten him off." By looking at him "the way girls do who have
no intention of growing up yet" (125), she maps out for herself, at eighteen,
a future of truncated growth, marked by the fulfillment of cultural expectations of female lives—marriage, pregnancies, "wifely response" (132), and
motherly duties.

Godwin, however, makes her heroine face the troublesome question of
"Who am I?" when she turns thirty-six. She sets Lydia out, in her own words,
"on her course of cautious, but ardent, self-emancipation,"[15] awakened on
the one hand to the realities of her constraining marriage and on the other
to the increasing possibilities for women as independent workers in a
world of ideological change. No less driven by her need to accomplish, Lydia comes to redefine proper southern womanhood, seeking "quiet, free spaciousness" in which to "structure activities that would express" herself (133).
Whereas her past accomplishments were self-obliterating, she now aims at a
balanced approach, emphasizing self-development while reaching out for
possibilities of social achievement, continuing to serve others' needs at the
same time as she carefully and ardently attends to her own.

In Lydia's growth, Godwin makes the drive toward social achievement
and the quest for a fulfilling self-identity converge and mutually reinforce as
a basis for the heroine's self-assessment. Lydia leaves her husband and returns to school, expanding herself in various directions: studying sociology,
exploring feminism, developing a sisterly friendship with her black professor, and taking up a half-Jewish lover. Despite radical changes in her life, she
continues to rely on careful planning to accomplish all the tasks that she considers important to her sense of self. Thriving in her new roles as student,
lover, and feminist friend, she awakens to a totally new self—animated; energetic; developing at once intellectually, socially, and sexually; fully absorbed
in the present and vitally interested in the future. In her continuing role as
mother, she becomes more conscious of her own role as a shaping force in
her children's development, hence making motherhood an inspiring, self-
enlightening task conducive to the growth of both mother and children.

While delineating Lydia's personal growth, Godwin also evokes a sense
of social change that makes the characterization of Lydia possible, exploring, for the first time in her fiction, a newer South and the possibilities it opens

15. Godwin, "Becoming the Characters in Your Novel," 13.

up for feminist subversion of old cultural texts. Before the success of the Civil Rights Movement had opened the South to northern and feminist influences, Lydia could have made these changes only by abandoning the South. By the late 1970s, during which period most of the novel's action occurs, a questing woman could remain true to the new, liberalized South but become an independent career woman, taking a forbidden lover and befriending a strong and radical black woman.

Lydia, for instance, embraces new developments in her life but keeps intact the compartment that reads "STILL A LADY" (253), rejecting, in Carolyn Rhodes's words, its "central demand for a selflessness that precludes self-discovery" but cherishing the beauty of order and gracious living.[16] Lydia's successful self-definition is a direct result of her immersion in southern culture and her feminist redefinition of its ideal of grace and tact. Armed with new self-confidence and the endearing virtues of charm and poise, Lydia becomes a social success as well as an inspiration to female self-discovery, having her own weekly television show, which is "a sort of continuing education itself" (559); making money; gaining influence, respect, and admiration. Without abandoning the South but integrating her new feminist self into a new version of the Southern Lady, Lydia achieves a positive integration of self and region, fulfilling Godwin's best hopes that "Southern grace in its best sense can be cherished, can still enhance the old South's new daughters."[17]

Until *A Mother and Two Daughters,* Godwin's fiction was daughter-centered, portraying the daughter's struggle for selfhood in the context of contemporary reality and her southern, maternal heritage. She granted the maternal figure a continually important role in the daughter's psychological and gendered development but never made her an evolving character on her own account. Instead, she emphasized the premature ending of her story, when marriage, followed by motherhood, gives her the definitive identity, truncating her growth and terminating her personal history. Although she invariably included the maternal figure in her novels (with the single exception of *The Perfectionists*), Godwin sometimes made her a totally muted character, as in the case of Violet's suicidal mother, who leaves the daughter feel-

16. Rhodes, "Gail Godwin and the Ideal of Southern Womanhood," 64.
17. *Ibid.,* 55, 65.

ing abandoned and deprived. Often she emphasized the estrangement between mother and daughter, as in *Glass People* and *The Odd Woman*, depicting the daughter's longing for a lost sisterly intimacy with the mother. Occasionally, she used the maternal figure as a nostalgic haven for the daughter, as in the case of Jane's dead grandmother, retrieved from memory for the comforting simplicity of her life, "where no dangerous questions are broached and the troublesome self is negated."[18] Whatever the case might be, Godwin emphasized the daughter's perspective, pushing the maternal figure to the background of the daughter's story, without a voice of her own, found wanting and inadequate, rejected as a desirable role model.

In marked contrast to her treatment of the maternal figure in earlier novels, Godwin gives Nell Strickland a voice of her own, making her one of the three major protagonists constructing her own story. Examining the psychological process of aging and the loneliness of widowhood, Godwin extends her fictional exploration of female growth beyond middle age, covering the life cycle of female experience. Her portrayal of a sixty-three-year-old widow struggling for self-understanding as she journeys through grief and the "pains of memory" (152) offers, in Kathleen Woodward's words, "a vision of aging as a possible positive experience" entailing a special kind of growth.[19]

Conceiving widowhood as a psychological process of shedding secondary identities[20] and old age as an important phase of continuous self-definition, Godwin explores the meditative, creative, and regenerative energies of widowhood "devoted to the composing . . . of the self."[21] Reduced to "half of a whole that no longer exists" (425), her aging heroine strives to create her own wholeness by discovering the pleasure of solitude. But Nell's search for the self extends beyond what Kathleen Woodward calls "a policy of detachment"[22] and what Annis Pratt defines as spiritual quest.[23] Instead of spiri-

18. Godwin, "The Southern Belle," 85.

19. Kathleen Woodward, "May Sarton and Fictions of Old Age," in *Gender and Literary Voice*, ed. Janet Todd (New York, 1980), 108.

20. Pratt, with White *et al.*, *Archetypal Patterns in Women's Fiction*, 128.

21. Woodward, "May Sarton and Fictions of Old Age," 108.

22. Examining May Sarton's fiction of old age, Woodward emphasizes Sarton's fictional celebration of detachment as a "spiritual exercise" necessary to the growth of older heroines toward wholeness. See "May Sarton and Fictons of Old Age," 108–27.

23. Pratt distinguishes between novels of spiritual quest and social quest: "In women's fic-

tual detachment or unity with nature, Godwin emphasizes Nell's gradual movement from detachment to reengagement, a shifting from personal to social space. Depicting Nell's emergence from solitary grief, reentrance into society, and discovery of a new life, Godwin perceives yet another process of successful self-definition, one that embraces at once spiritual self-regeneration, personal friendship, social engagement, and love.

Making grief the center of Nell's consciousness, Godwin explores her heroine's complex experience of widowhood, juxtaposing the remembrance of a secure, fulfilled past with the "anxiety about the future" (152) of frightening solitude. As Nell recollects her life with Leonard, she sees a gentle, loving man, who "held things together" (43), protecting her from the public world and harsh self-judgment. His death, Nell realizes, leaves her one of "the long-lived females of the race, the proverbial 'survivors'" (155), facing old age alone with "its ugliness and helplessness" (160). "But what am I supposed to do with my 'life'?" Nell asks in anguishing despair. "I'm sixty-three years old. It would have been simpler and neater for everybody if I'd died in that accident, too" (69).

To survive as a full human being, to live beyond her husband's death, Nell must redefine herself. The urgency of self-redefinition becomes the driving force behind Nell's reminiscences of her past experience. In recalling how she assisted Leonard in making their first meeting into a "romantic narrative" (167) for their daughters, Nell gains a poignant understanding of the long-standing process of self-suppression.[24] "She had lived in Leonard's story until it became more true than her own suppressed version. The lonely, self-defensive, sharp-tongued nurse with her young appetites all a-jangle seemed more like a younger sister who aroused Nell's dutiful attachment,

tion social quests are usually found in the bildungsroman and spiritual quests in novels whose heroes are over thirty, most often in middle or old age." She defines older heroines' spiritual quest as "a transformation of the personality, a centering upon personal, rather than patriarchal, space." Their goal is "to integrate her self with herself," often through unity with nature. See *Archetypal Patterns in Women's Fiction*, 135–36.

24. Westerlund also comments on Nell's complex feelings about her marriage to Leonard, the "family patriarch." In part, Westerlund argues, Nell's marriage has functioned as "a cover story silencing her own voice," and her husband's death allows her to "find greater freedom and affirmation of her self." She "reconnects with past, denied parts of herself, and finally finds her own voice again." Westerlund, *Escaping the Castle of Patriarchy*, 15, 31.

but also her impatience. That young woman . . . had become encased in a smoother, wiser, rounder version of herself—made possible by Leonard's belief in her as a woman of temperament, but also a good and capable woman" (168–69). Dissecting what has become a "family myth" (166), Nell comes to grasp the pattern of self-suppression that dominated her relationship with Leonard. Committing an act of self-silencing from the beginning of their relationship, Nell lived through her married life surrendering to Leonard's domination "by leisure," curbing her "shrillness," losing "her savor for arguing with him," and accepting his gentle restraints (169).

Such critical self-perception is vital to Nell's growth as a heroine-in-progress, who gradually moves away from detachment to reengagement. Initially, Nell's new self-definition does take the form of detachment, concentrating intensely on living as a solitary being. Immersing herself in the small tasks of housekeeping, tuning herself to the rhythms of natural growth, and attending to "the demanding and arduous discipline" of solitude,[25] Nell discovers the joy of being fully herself:

> There was a sort of mellow ecstasy in just letting yourself go in the sun, contemplating the shifts of light in a day, or the wind in the trees, or the life of a bird family. When the struggle to "be yourself," and "hold your own"—and hold on to the people you thought you could not lose and still live without—was over, you could actually find pleasure in being nobody. Or you could *be* yourself, but without all that unnecessary pain of assertion, and simply sit and possess all the moments in your life that a certain sunlight or a particular wind reminded you of. (328)

Lost moments are recovered in this "time of pure presence,"[26] entirely at her disposal and devoted to meditative self-composition. Finding harmony within herself, Nell achieves what Annis Pratt describes as a spiritual self-integration in her discussion of novels of "rebirth" and "transformation."[27]

Emphasizing on the one hand continuing grief and the inevitable approach of death and on the other the newly found joy of solitary living, Godwin

25. Woodward, "May Sarton and the Fictions of Old Age," 116.
26. *Ibid.,* 111.
27. Pratt, with White *et al., Archetypal Patterns in Women's Fiction,* 135–36.

vividly juxtaposes the definitive state of completion that only death can bring and the continuing capacity for change and evolution that life embraces. Bringing Nell back to the family's island cottage, where she experiences the renewal of sharp grief and encounters vicariously, through her sick school friend Merle, the battle against death, Godwin puts her aging heroine to a special test of what Jung calls "the task of personality."[28] Deeply moved by Merle's ardent desire for life, even when it means "just getting up in the morning" and "looking out to see what kind of day it's going to be" (432), Nell takes up nursing her dying friend. "Trained to put duty before pleasure, or peace, or 'self-realization'" (473), Nell comes to redefine cultural conceptions of a woman's duty by asserting "the privilege of the living" (474) through caring for a dying person, finding harmony between duty and self-actualization. The encounter with death ultimately inspires Nell to move beyond her "self-contained existence" (520) and reengage with society. Reeducating herself, she finds a job teaching emergency techniques at a rescue center, redefining herself as an independent worker while finding emotional fulfillment in marrying Merle's widowed husband, enjoying, to her great amazement, "a side of life she had thought was over forever" (563).

Godwin's portrayal of Cate, Lydia, and Nell as distinct heroines, each with her own goal, gives both consistency and variety to her pursuit of an evolving self. Envisioning an ending she wants for her heroine, Godwin writes in "Towards a Fully Human Heroine": "No channels to drain away her full nature. No hidden life, no unvisited tomb for her. I want her to have a name, a face, an occupation and a future."[29] In delineating the three Stricklands' separate journeys toward self-definition, respectively through conquering middle-age despair, cultural scripts of womanhood, and the grief and loneliness of widowhood, Godwin affirms the continuity of growth and an individual's capacity for evolving. As long as she accepts the "task of personality," a heroine, as Godwin perceives her, continually embraces the possibility of making "it into the future" (333), beyond middle age, into old age, with a renewing capacity to write her story of becoming.

28. Godwin, "The Southern Belle," 51.
29. Godwin, "Towards a Fully Human Heroine," 28.

The Potency of Relatedness

"Why in God's name did people form families? What made them imprison themselves in the separate pressure cookers referred to as 'nuclear families'?" Cate asks this question in a moment of despair after yet another intense, lacerating family dialogue. Recalling her teenage alienation from family, Cate delivers a vehement attack on the destructive power of the nuclear family: "First the smug exclusion of all others, of the 'outside world'; then the grim multiplication of oneself and one's partner behind closed doors; then the nauseating, unclean moiling about of all the family members in their 'nuclear' caldron, bumping against one another, everyone knowing all too well everyone else's worst faults—all of them *stewing* themselves in one another's juices" (440). Viewing family as antagonistic to personal development, Cate concludes fiercely that "nobody who is, first and foremost, a 'family member' has a hope in hell of becoming a whole person" (441).

Cate's bitter accusation reveals a complete alienation from family and a profound distrust of familial relationships. Yet the story of a mother and two daughters is not one of despair and disintegration. It is concurrently a story of individual growth and a story of extended, intensely emotional dialogue between sisters and among mother and daughters, with "its intimacy and distance, passion and violence."[30] Portraying three heroines "bound in the closest of ties,"[31] Godwin accentuates the theme of family dialogue by placing them amid familial and personal changes—Nell's widowhood, Lydia's separation and social endeavor, Cate's loss of job and abortion, the family's forced togetherness in their summer cottage. She depicts their response to and interaction with each other, exploring each heroine's participation in what Bakhtin would describe as "dialogic activities"—the act of engaging oneself in "a continuous and open-ended interior dialogue" while at the same time carrying on a dialogue with others. The dyadic and triadic relationships among the Stricklands constitute a communicative experience that, as Bakhtin writes, "takes place on the *boundary* between one's own and someone else's consciousness, on the *threshold*."[32] Each heroine's struggle for self becomes

30. Hirsch, "Mothers and Daughters," 204.
31. Godwin, "Becoming the Characters in Your Novel," 12.
32. Bakhtin, *Problems of Dostoevsky's Poetics*, 251, 287.

embedded in the complex family dialogues—intense, vehement, hateful, and loving, illuminating the relationship between family and self, the potency of relatedness, and the power of family as it bears on an individual's identity and development.

Sisters: Embracing Differences

In "Becoming the Characters in Your Novel," Godwin outlines her conceptions of Cate and Lydia as protagonists:

> Concerning Cate, the older daughter, I knew what it feels like to rail against complacency and rebel against the status quo; I have never been particularly brave, or even very much of a rebel, but I could start Cate on her way to being one, with the basis of those feelings rooted in my own experience. Concerning Lydia, the proper younger daughter, so nervous with her sense of responsibility, so aching with her need to accomplish something for herself, I could bond myself to her with those shared feelings and set her on her course of cautious, but ardent, self-emancipation.

In the same essay, Godwin emphasizes that the most crucial aspect of her novelistic representation in *A Mother and Two Daughters* is to show "the mysterious way in which" each heroine "had shaped and been shaped" by the other two heroines.[33]

Setting Lydia and Cate—the "good" and the rebel daughter of the family—in mutual antagonism and bringing them into close contact with one another through sisterly rivalry, contention, and reconciliation, Godwin creates a dialogic context for the development of evolving selfhood. In constructing the extended dialogue between the sisters, marked by an intense interplay of voices, she explores the mutually painful but ultimately revealing process of "coming to know another's word,"[34] illuminating that *boundary* experience "between one's own and someone else's

33. Godwin, "Becoming the Characters in Your Novel," 12–13.
34. Bakhtin, *The Dialogic Imagination*, 353.

consciousness" that Bakhtın deems essential to self-understanding and growth.[35]

The two sisters are markedly different in personality and outlook. Lydia, the "good" daughter of the family, stays within the safe bounds of parental and societal approval; Cate, the rebel, flees from everything—school, family, and region—that threatens to impinge on her individuality. Prudent and self-protective, the younger sister refrains from the intensity of experience: she prefers to stand in the shallows of the sea, or enter the water without "hurl[ing] at the might of the waves" and submerge herself "gradually in this chancy element, at her own secure style and pace" (398). Reckless and daring, the older sister flings herself against the world, plunging fearlessly into "the angriest-looking part of a wave," each time emerging "triumphantly battered from her defeat," only to "head out for the next beating" (398).

Since adolescence, abrasion and mutual rejection have characterized the relationship between the sisters. To Cate, Lydia is a coward, complacent in her "safe, circumscribed, orderly little kingdom," never "taking a real chance or making a real choice" (459–60). To Lydia, Cate is a dangerous trouble-maker feeding on "an endless capacity to criticize" others (459). Neither feels she could comfortably be herself in the presence of the other without creating tension or causing conflict. However, not standing on an equal footing, they relate to each other differently. Cate, the rebellious daughter of the South, has nothing but contempt for Lydia's neatly compartmentalized life, her complacency, her obsession with other people's images of her, and her lack of courage to live imaginatively. Lydia, on the other hand, has since adolescence suffered from "the taunting urge to compete with the Cates of the world" (399), constantly subjecting herself to the "torturous indecision" of whether to respond boldly to her sister's "invitation to the fray," against her own better judgment, or to act cautiously and "be thought a coward" (398).

Dominating their girlhoods and persisting into their adult years, rivalry and antagonism have shaped not only their perception of each other but also their sense of self. The rebellious older sister thrives on her adventurous living, fully confident of its infinite possibilities; the conventional younger sister contently fulfills her wifely and motherly duties in her culturally correct marriage, insecure in her claim to authentic experience. Taking this long-

35. Bakhtin, *Problems of Dostoevsky's Poetics,* 287.

established pattern of sisterly contention as a point of departure, Godwin unfolds a process of change and growth. She brings new circumstances—Lydia's invigorating self-exploration and Cate's growing despair over continually shrinking possibilities as she reaches forty—into the old patterns of sisterly relationship, forcing the sisters into a fierce dialogue, sometimes handled with caution and restraint on the part of each, sometimes erupting into violent confrontation.

In a dialogic context, Godwin's family drama shows, individual growth becomes a complex interplay of voices: resurging voices of the past, speaking voices of the present, and internal voices, addressed to oneself or imaginarily heard by another. For each heroine, encountering and communicating with each other concur with encountering and communicating with herself, leading each toward new perceptions, toward fuller consciousness of herself through revealing herself "for another, through another, and with the help of another."[36] Portraying this dialogue between the sisters as intense, disturbing, sometimes angry and humiliating, Godwin nonetheless affirms the gradual movement—at once painful and liberating—away from self-destructive antagonism toward mutual understanding and reconciliation.

Three times in the novel, Godwin brings the sisters together, unfolding a continuous dialogue that evokes many distinctive voices. The brief encounter between them at their father's funeral in the beginning of the novel sets the dialogue in motion. Godwin emphasizes the depth of antagonism between the two by manipulating the interplay of voices. For instance, Cate's cynical voice protesting the ways of the world is juxtaposed with Lydia's internal voice questioning her sister's sanity, and distinct voices of their teenage conflict surface as an undercurrent of their present dialogue. With an innocent report, Lydia effortlessly elicits Cate's ironic voice, which ostensibly praises Lydia's efficiency but internally expresses a disdain for a mode of living she sees as predicated on spurious accomplishment. When Lydia, in a gesture of sisterly solidarity, confides in Cate about her separation from her husband, Cate readily adopts her relentlessly critical voice, hurting Lydia with a "neat interpretation of her decision" to leave her husband, "over which she had agonized for months" (32).

While replaying the old antagonistic voices, Godwin introduces into the

36. *Ibid.*

sisterly dialogue a new voice destined to change their relationship. She gives Lydia, the South's docile, conventional daughter standing at the threshold of a new life, a voice of an emerging heroine. When Lydia tells Cate about her separation from her husband, for instance, she speaks consciously, even approvingly, of herself as a "troublemaker," claiming for herself a "privileged" position that plays against expectations and has hitherto been reserved only for her audacious and rebellious sister. By appropriating Cate's persona, Lydia embraces a new, dialogic mode of self-perception, envisioning herself through another person. Although she wants to "love" and "admire" her sister and continues to feel fascinated by Cate's capacity for self-renewal, Lydia nevertheless asserts her new voice, inventing two new personae for each of them: Cate in need of assistance as she moves "each year a bit closer to the precarious edge" and herself in service to Cate, kindly helping her "put the pieces of her back together" if she happens to fall (35).

The restrained interplay of old and new voices erupts into a violently emotional confrontation and an intensely psychological warfare in a scene set on an island, where the two sisters are forced into abrasive proximity. The vehement, hateful accusations they direct against each other ultimately become, in the dialogic context Godwin creates for her novelistic world, psychologically liberating, enabling each sister to communicate on the "boundary" between the consciousness of each. For Lydia, coping with Cate's criticism brings her face to face with that flinching, insecure, baby-sister self that has tormented her since adolescence, whose timid, resentful voice collaborates with Cate's superior, accusing voice to negate her claim to successful self-definition. For Cate, suffering through the worst of her fights with Lydia finally leads her to penetrating self-examination, permitting her to acknowledge the validity of modes of living other than her own.

"We're the same blood, but we're a different species of soul" (428), says Cate, and her pronouncement ruthlessly points to the insurmountable distance, philosophical as well as psychological, between the two sisters. Despite change, each sister remains true to her vision of self-fulfillment. Lydia, who has always been obsessed with other people's images of her, aptly phrases her most desired goal of self-realization as becoming a "widely admired and influential woman" (399). In contrast to Lydia's adherence to external criteria as measurement of her success, Cate searches inward for the

meaning of her existence, placing emphasis on subjective self-evaluation of her personal history. Cherishing more than anything else her "freedom and mobility" to "conduct [her] own sustained inquiry" into the world, to "investigate things as they are, and maybe call a few truths as [she] see[s] them" (368), Cate persists in a deeply existential quest for a self of becoming, a self as an internal process of developing consciousness.

Although Lydia invariably equates Cate's higher intensity with eccentricity, even madness, she nonetheless despairs at the tremendous disparity between them. On the other hand, Cate never fails to attack Lydia's "elegant management of trivia" (374), openly acknowledging the near-pleasure of shocking Lydia "out of her complacency" (428). They have, with each other's help, established a communicative pattern between them, with Lydia habitually on the defensive and Cate on the offensive, each feeding on the other. The balance, however, is finally disrupted by a reversal of positions. Lydia, the baby sister long held in contempt, is now blossoming in her newly found freedom. In contrast, the older sister who has in the past intimidated Lydia with many an "invitation to the fray" (398) finds herself on the brink of defeat, suffering "middle-aged panic" (367) and subjecting herself to images of decay and disintegration. Old patterns of relationship are called into question, but new ones have yet to emerge.

Shifting the point of view from one sister to the other and documenting their intensely dialogic encounters, during which they grasp themselves and their relationship to each other by forming new judgments, interpreting concealed subtexts, and probing their own consciousnesses, Godwin reveals a process of painful yet necessary growth. Upon meeting Cate, Lydia, "in the pink of health and success and self-approval" (372), becomes nervously conscious of her Cate-induced feelings of inadequacy. Closely observant, she catches "a touch of too much mirth" (373) in Cate's compliment on her careful planning. Resentment of that hidden voice of deprecation and disapproval from her sister immediately seizes Lydia: "With a simple tone of voice," Cate could easily revert things "instantly to the way they had always been," making her own setbacks an accomplishment while rendering Lydia's carefully monitored achievements "wanting" and "slightly ludicrous" (372–73).

Overcoming that crippling sense of inferiority is crucial to Lydia's growth, and the most useful means to achieve that end is through fruitful interplay

of voices. In an interior dialogue, Lydia conducts a constructive self-inquiry, documenting one by one her accomplishments—successful motherhood, academic progress, career prospects, and satisfying love life—and resolving to outgrow her Cate-related feelings of inferiority. Confronting these feelings and affirming her own progress, Lydia finally grasps a revelation that liberates her from the destructive dynamic between Cate and herself. As Lydia watches her older sister dramatize with accelerating intensity her own failure, she hears not only her present internal voice pronouncing Cate's "madness" but all her past indicting voices making the same verdict, and "a sharp sense of déjà vu" (377) leads to a new perception. "How many times before," Lydia reflects, "had she . . . gone through just this sequence of thought?" Challenged by Cate's higher intensity, she "became confused, lost control of the situation, and projected her confusion back on Cate in the form of 'madness.'" For the first time, Lydia analyzes her own self-destructive posture toward Cate and the role it has played in sustaining the unbalanced, antagonistic relationship between them. For the first time, she feels "strong enough to blame herself a little in order to protect Cate" (377), finally outgrowing her fearful, insecure baby-sister self and gaining in self-respect and confidence.

Dialogue is equally essential in Cate's effort to cope with a part of herself in order to grow in self-perception. Like Lydia, Cate engages herself both in an external, social dialogue with her sister and an intensely private dialogue with herself. Despite genuine curiosity about, even a degree of admiration for, her sister's progress, Cate is tormented by complicated feelings about Lydia's success and by the disheartening thought of herself "fading into the morning light of somebody else's day" (367). Jealousy, contempt, and despair reduce Cate to outright cynicism, leading her to a savage attack on Lydia and her black friends, in which she contemptuously dismisses all their striving for success as inauthentic, trivial, a mere surrender to the "sucking pull of the Status Quo" (66). Her vehement, ruthless words invite an equally lethal attack from Lydia on her failure.

The sisterly dialogue ends in anger, disgust, and hatred. The painful confrontations, however, are ultimately conducive to Cate's growth, liberating her from her exclusive world of self-searching. With anguish and difficulty, Cate comes to grips with a chastening self-knowledge. For the first time, she

sees the "destroyer" in herself, recognizing her "proclivity toward belit-
tling others" and holding herself contemptible for "exert[ing] her entire intellectual force toward making Lydia acknowledge that she was trivial, insignificant, banal—no matter what she could or would do with her life" (466).
Her intense capacity to criticize, she realizes, has the dangerous potential
of undermining other people's endeavors, different from her own but perhaps equally valid and authentic.

Bringing the sisters together once again in the novel's epilogue, five
years after their disastrous vacation on the island, Godwin provides the ground
for them to acknowledge to each other what has come out of their hostile
contention and painful self-search. She emphasizes that the psychological
drama between them continues, letting Cate choose the territory for their
meeting and Lydia the time for them to be alone together. Furthermore, she
shows that Lydia is as irresistibly curious as usual about Cate's venturesome
living and that Cate has as much difficulty as always in refraining from bait-
ing her younger sister in the old way. Yet she movingly portrays the two
sisters engaging each other dialogically, reaching out, cautiously but warmly,
to embrace each other's difference and to begin a new dialogue. She brings
them to communicate on two planes: present voices evoke past voices, and
each sister hears not only the mutually accusing voices of the two five years
ago but also the present, internal voice of the other. Mutually aware of
each other and deeply conscious of the "threshold" they must cross in order
to begin any constructive dialogue, the two sisters regain a moment of intimacy, "cautiously trying out each other's viewpoints" and "replaying the
fight, but each from the other's side" (555).

Through such dialogic encounters, each of the sisters learns to encompass
a world different from her own, thereby making her own world larger. With
one of them reaping professional recognition, money, and popularity and the
other subsisting on itinerant teaching—"an insecure series of self-created
'courses'"—the two sisters now feel more respect, even admiration, for each
other than ever. Continuing to cherish her own self-of-becoming, Cate now
can speak approvingly of Lydia's achievements, reassuring her of the validity of a world she ruthlessly repudiated as petty and contemptible five
years earlier. And she can delight in, rather than resent, Lydia's continued curiosity about her life, seeing it not as a repugnantly vicarious sampling of her

experience but as a form of support, approval, and esteem. Lydia, too, experiences an eye-opening revelation, "up here in Cate's kingdom," finding Cate's world alluring rather than shocking. Basking "in the sunshine of her accomplishments," Lydia nonetheless is seized by a "sudden yearning, profound and unfulfillable." Her wonder-filled response to this intense yearning marks the beginning of her understanding and appreciation of Cate's existential questing. What is missing in her own life? For what or whom does she yearn? Lydia asks herself. What is it that "made it seem as if all the windows and doors of her own carefully appointed house had blown open, and a capricious wind had come whooshing through, and then, just as she had got over her fear that it might break or upset something, had gone blowing out again, bound for somewhere else, leaving her wistfully behind to watch it disappear into the unexplored distance?" (558–59).

Mothers and Daughters: An Ongoing Dialogue

Women's role as mothers of daughters and daughters of mothers, Marianne Hirsch observes, has become a key issue in feminist investigations of female subject-formation.[37] She points out that, despite their differences in perspective and methodology, various schools of psychoanalytic feminism have emphasized the "multiplicity, plurality, and continuity" of female identity, seeing it as in-process and connected, in Jung's words, "backwards" to the mother and "forwards" to the daughter.[38]

Godwin's profound interest in the mother-daughter plot evolves, in her first major-key novel, into a full exploration of the ongoing dialogue between mother and daughter. As in *The Odd Woman,* Godwin perceives the mother-daughter conflict as at once generational, social, cultural, and psychological, rather than predominantly psychosexual, where feminist psychoanalysts tend to focus in their investigation of the subject. Nonetheless, feminist emphasis upon the multiplicity and continuity of female identity and the centrality of the mother-daughter dyad to female self-definition illuminates Godwin's com-

---

37. See Hirsch's review essay "Mothers and Daughters" and her book *The Mother/Daughter Plot,* 12–13.

38. Hirsch, "Mothers and Daughters," 209.

pelling depiction of the complex interaction between Nell and her two daughters, and Bakhtin's dialogic vision again provides an interpretive tool for examining Godwin's fictional world of mothers and daughters.

In distinct contrast to her depiction of the mother-daughter dyad in earlier novels, where the daughter's monologic voice speaks ambivalently about her maternal legacy, Godwin's development of this complex, conflicting relationship in *A Mother and Two Daughters* foregrounds the "complicated interaction of maternal and daughterly voices."[39] Alongside the daughterly discourse of disappointment and demand, Godwin places the maternal discourse of frustration, love, and anger. Furthermore, by incorporating sisterly discord into the mother-daughter discourse and delineating each daughter's unique response to the maternal voice, she adds yet another psychological dimension to the complexity of the primal, bonding mother-daughter relationship. Vying for their mother's attention, Lydia yearns for maternal closeness and recognition, and Cate despairs of maternal understanding. Loving both daughters but loving them better from a distance, Nell relies on the "good" daughter's practicality and dutifulness, yet she finds in the rebel daughter a continuous source of stimulation. Among the three, an intense, complex set of dyadic and triadic dialogues develops. With their own distinct and fully valid voices, mother and daughters each "speak for themselves as well as for and with one another."[40] Their open-ended dialogue, multivoiced and multicentered, dramatizes the cross-generational continuity of female identity, both in its fierce attachment and intense conflict, illuminating the relationship between familial structure and individual development.

In the daughters' deep-seated need for the mother as well as the mother's connectedness to her daughters, Godwin portrays the enduring strengths of the mother-daughter bonding. Persistently, daughters yearn for maternal understanding, approval, guidance, and emotional nurturance. Nell, for instance, remembers how powerfully, as a confused young woman going through a crisis of conscience, she yearned for a mother to confide in, an "Ideal Mother, an all-wise female whose advice would be based on far-reaching principles of benevolence" (168). Lydia, the "good" daughter of the family, is jealous of the "curious, taut fascination" (257) in her parents' raised voices when

39. Hirsch, *The Mother/Daughter Plot*, 178.
40. *Ibid.*, 16.

they discuss her sister, painfully aware that her docility and dependability have only led, paradoxically, to reduced parental attention. A mother herself and a satisfied lover, Lydia passionately yearns for closeness to Nell, seeking time alone with her to talk about "old times" and reinforce "their bonds" (290). Notwithstanding her alienation from family, Cate invariably turns to her mother in times of distress, both "demanding and on the defensive" (323), sometimes feeling like "bursting into blubbery, childish tears and dumping the whole problem in Nell's lap" (205), as passionately in need of maternal support as Nell was while a young woman.

Side by side with the daughterly voice of need and longing, Godwin inserts the distinctly maternal voice speaking of the joy and frustration of motherhood. Taking Nell backward in time through the prism of memory to the symbiotic state of pregnancy and the uniquely maternal experience of giving birth, Godwin unfolds the experience of motherhood over the life course, from the infant-mother bond through the rebellious teenagers' arrogant rejection of maternal guidance to the grownup daughters' "frenzied, passionate demands" (326) for maternal intimacy and wisdom. In Godwin's representation, both daughterly and maternal voices articulate the potent connection between mothers and daughters. Particularly, Godwin emphasizes that a mother speaks with two voices, functioning, in Hirsch's words, both as the "object" in her daughter's "process of subject-formation" and as the speaking subject with her own story to tell.[41] By representing the mother's dual perspective, Godwin connects the experience of motherhood and daughterhood, making a powerful claim to the continuity and multiplicity of female identity—cross-generational, in-process, inevitably changing, yet eternally enduring.

While Godwin emphasizes the individual struggle for both mother and daughters to make their own identities, she also links their lives together by way of mother-daughter identification. Nell, for example, identifies in her older daughter's alienation from southern culture a version of her own self she feels obligated to suppress. Always conscious of "the innermost kernel of herself, that unsocialized observer who had masqueraded adequately since puberty as a 'Southern Lady'" (6), Nell remains critically detached from traditional southernness. But, as Carolyn Rhodes argues, her "conscious pride"

41. *Ibid.*, 12.

in her own freedom from it is coupled with "a lasting distress at Cate's greater freedom from it."[42] Cherishing her own unsocialized self, she nevertheless cannot forgive Cate "for not making more of an effort to blend gracefully into the landscape" (6), as she herself has done. Conversely, Cate makes her own negative identification with Nell, seeing maternal disapproval connected to her mother's own suppressed "unruly instincts" (6) and rooted in her distress at the daughter's rebellious behavior. "Mother stifles me," Cate reflects. "I can just glance at her and see her expecting some kind of excessive behavior from me; it's as if she predicts it, knows what it's going to be before it comes. Now, why is that? Because she's got the same seeds in herself and is piqued with me for not stifling them as well as she has?" (428).

Furthermore, Godwin adds a dialogic dimension to this mother-daughter identification, bringing the internal voice of one heroine into contact with other voices: the voices of tradition, modernity, her other selves, and other heroines. Consider, for example, her portrayal of Lydia's fantasy about visiting her mother with Stanley, her half-Jewish lover. In this imaginary encounter, Lydia sees Nell "wearing that unsettling smile she could get on her face when one part of her found something amusing but the other part told her she must behave" (261). What she imagines hearing is her mother's graceful, ladylike voice, making pleasant social talk with Stanley. Beneath that smoothly toned voice, Lydia also "hears" a hidden voice, skeptical and a little critical. Particularly, Lydia flinches as she "hears" Nell's internal, embarrassingly flattering voice speaking about sexual attraction and passionate lovers, a voice unsettling in its association with her image of her mother as a lady, with her mother's image of her daughter as dutiful and proper, and with female sexuality, a part of herself she is still discovering.

In documenting Cate's penetrating perception of the triadic familial structure upon which the lives of the three Stricklands are patterned, Godwin provides another example of the dialogic encounter that binds mother and daughters together. Conscious of her own upbeat, "everything's-under-control" voice addressing Jernigan to cover up her bitterness during a lovers' quarrel, Cate suddenly "hears" the "smooth hostess" voice her young mother adopted the moment her father entered the house. Distant in time yet intimately together through an act of dialogic activity, the daughterly voice and motherly

42. Rhodes, "Gail Godwin and the Ideal of Southern Womanhood," 64.

voice blend into one another, impinging upon the daughter's consciousness of both herself and her mother and of their connectedness: "How funny that her own 'hostess' voice a few moments ago had been an exact duplication of Mother's, even though she, Cate, hadn't been sincere. Maybe, all those years ago, Mother hadn't been sincere, either. They had both been acting out the old scene of getting their man from the outside world to the kitchen, sparing him the household battleground in between." Cate's negative identification with her mother in the novel's present time in turn opens a dialogue with the past, leading to revelation and interpretation of the mother-daughter continuity: "But it had confused her and Lydia, as little girls, when their mother suddenly became smaller and smoother when Daddy came home. Cate's way of steadying herself against the sudden chemical change in the family mixture had been to assume the more ferocious properties of the vanished mother, while Lydia, the baby, had retreated into the quiet, neat shell of herself. Which, Cate saw now, not only kept Lydia from being noticed (i.e., punished) but made Lydia resemble a small copy of the 'tamed' mother" (210). Thus, far away in her Iowa apartment or in her lover's home, Cate enters a dialogue with herself, her mother, and their shared past, gaining perspectives on gender, culture, and family, and the ways they interrelate with one another in the development of personal identity.

As in the relationship between the sisters, dialogue between mother and daughters is both internal and external, one inseparably fused with the other. Locked in what Cate labels the crippling pressure cooker of the nuclear family, without the restraining presence of father/husband, the three heroines participate in an intense mutual-triadic scrutiny, each conducting an interior dialogue while engaging the other two interactively. Sometimes censoring what they say, often simulating appropriate reactions, almost always knowing what to expect, but seldom confident of full mutual understanding, mother and daughters are always in what Bakhtin describes as a "tension-filled encounter," where "every internal experience ends up on the boundary, encounters another"[43] in an open-ended dialogue.

With each daughter's particular relationship to her mother, Nell's separate relationship to each daughter, and the conflict between the two sisters, the triadic relationship of the three heroines becomes extremely complicated.

43. Bakhtin, *Problems of Dostoevsky's Poetics*, 287.

Cate and Lydia both vie for their mother's attention, but each has a particular set of problems with the mother-daughter relationship. Despite frequent sisterly rifts, they occasionally find common ground against their mother. Exercising the balancing act required of a mother, Nell sometimes finds it necessary to "inject some humanity" into one daughter in defense of the other, but generally she prefers to "let the sisters tend to each other" (391), touched when they show rapport and distressed when they fight, wanting them to be friends so that there will be two people knowing her "better than anyone else alive" (325). The complex, "ambivalent dynamics" (210) of the family establishes certain delicate, mutually held bounds each tries not to overstep, whereas the internal and external voices of all three contend in a cacophony of conflict that seems unresolvable for most of the novel.

Lydia's relationship with her mother is intimately linked to her relationship with Cate and her insecure sense of self. Jealous of Cate's privileged status with Nell and yearning for maternal attention, she feels punished by being the "good" daughter of the family. Every time she tries to get close to her mother—planning a trip to the island cottage alone with her, for example—Cate intervenes to destroy the moment. Consciously or unconsciously, Lydia uses Cate as a mediator between Nell and herself. Sometimes she feels obligated to ask her mother about Cate's well-being and simulate a sincere response; other times she chooses to bring up the subject of Cate to provoke an interesting conversation with her mother. When she succeeds, however, as she does while driving with Nell to the island, she subjects herself to more conflicting feelings, with her heart "divided between jealousy at how *animated* Mother had become since the discussion had turned to Cate, and fascination at Cate's latest adventure" (383). Even her promised public success cannot alleviate her sense of insecurity and bitterness about her place in the family. Rather, she projects her fear of failure on her sister and mother, and is distressed at the thought that no matter what she accomplishes in the world, she may never be a success to each of them.

If Godwin allows the daughterly voice to dominate in her depiction of the relationship between Lydia and Nell, she makes maternal voice prevail in her portrayal of the relationship between Nell and Cate. Focusing on Nell's reaction to Cate's behavior, she unfolds the difficult yet rewarding process of maternal understanding. Disapproving of Cate's intransigence, intensity,

extremity, and her "steamroller judgments on everything and everybody" (350), Nell nonetheless continues to be drawn to her rebellious older daughter. She finds stimulation in her audacious, unconventional behavior but feels frustrated that the extra attention she gives Cate only accentuates the conflicts between the two but rarely leads to understanding. In every phone conversation they have, tension builds as Nell finds herself anticipating Cate's contradictory response and trying to figure out her motives. Often provoked by Cate's intransigence into a response she subsequently judges unfair or mean, Nell traps herself in an emotionally vicious circle: first feeling guilty at being unfair or mean to Cate, then feeling "angry at Cate for making her feel guilty" (44). Underlying her complicated, mixed emotions toward Cate— anger, pity, love, frustration, hate, guilt—is the desire to understand her. "Wanting to understand Cate," she admits, "had been the frustrated project of her life" (350).

Again, Godwin gives dialogue a crucial role in Nell's painstaking effort to understand her daughter. As the two meet in Nell's house, before Lydia joins them for the family trip to the island, an intense dialogue begins—externally and internally—bringing mother and daughter alternately into tension and solidarity. Documenting their casual exchanges and carefully chosen utterances, intransigent statements and guarded responses, offenses and apologies, cheerful mutuality and repellent negation, Godwin shows how tension and solidarity short-circuit each other in the mother-daughter dynamics and explores how dialogic encounters might help a mother understand a daughter.

In Nell's struggle to solve the "Cate problem" (350), the maternal voice of frustration and desire comes into contact with other voices that impinge on her perceptions of her daughter and their relationship. Trying to sort out her own divided feelings about Cate, Nell hears a cacophony of voices, all interacting with her own internal voice: Theodora's muted rejection of Cate, Lydia's angry accusations against Cate's style, Leonard's fascinated speculations about Cate's next adventure. Loudest of all, Nell hears Cate's stubborn voice of refusal to compromise—powerfully transmuted into her childhood "unrepentant little chant" (352) that Nell now recollects—and her own angry resentment of that "incorrigible . . . Cate-ness" (350). By encountering and questioning all these voices, especially her own voice of rejection,

Nell prepares herself for a new dialogue with her daughter. Was she, she asks herself, responsible for the strained mother-daughter relationship? Though she could not solve "the riddle of her firstborn" (367), the internal dialogue marks the beginning steps toward understanding, reconciliation, and a more satisfying mode of relating to her daughter.

Nell's dream image of swimming is most revealing of the complexity of the mother-daughter bond. In a dream, Nell swims with Cate "in a curious body of water," with Cate having the body of a little baby but her adult face. Cate "swam on ahead, with thrashing, determined stroke." Nell fears that, as a baby, Cate should not "be out that far." She wanted to stop her, but "she was afraid to enlighten Cate with the fact, because she knew that if Cate were to look down and see that she had the body of a little baby, she would panic and drown" (354). With its potent womb imagery, Nell's dream evokes a sense of what feminist psychoanalysts describe as the "fluctuations of symbiosis and separation from the mother."[44] In contrast to the daughterly perspective usually adopted by feminist psychoanalysts, however, Nell's dream reveals the difficult process of a daughter's development from the maternal perspective: Nell must accept her daughter's "incorrigible . . . Cate-ness," trying to understand her rather than criticizing and rejecting her.

Like the sisterly contention between Cate and Lydia, the complex dyadic-triadic conflicts of the three heroines are not fully resolved at the end of the novel. But, partially because Cate and Lydia are able to establish a new truce in their relationship, a truce that both asserts and embraces the differences between them, the family tension subsides. Lydia comes to accept the fact that her mother perhaps will always respond to Cate with greater verve and fascination, and this acceptance is achieved and communicated "on the boundary," through the perception of another person—Lydia's own "good" child Leo. Watching his mother run out to welcome his younger brother Dickie with an ecstatic expression on her face, Leo reflects: "She admires me and approves of my character, she knows she can depend on me to do what I say I will, but it's Dickie, secretly, who makes her happiest" (560). This scene resonates with an earlier episode, when Lydia realizes that both Leo and she herself are the "good" children of the family and achieves the conviction that she *can* reinforce her bond with the "good" child of the fam-

44. Abel, Hirsch, and Langland, Introduction to *The Voyage In*, 10.

ily through love and understanding. Dialogically, through cross-generational dialogue, Lydia gains a more balanced perspective on her relationship with her mother.

Cate and Nell also arrive at some mutual understanding and acceptance, achieved through Nell's honest, touching account of Cate's birth and Cate's appreciative response. "You were a seven-pound bundle of aching, miserable *questions*," Nell tells Cate. She describes her "awesome helplessness" with that "screaming," inconsolable baby: "I was your *mother* and there was no language, no way I could get the message across. You broke my heart." In acknowledging the differences between her two daughters' births, Nell communicates to Cate her perceptions of her relationship to each daughter: "It was as if I had conveyed my certainty to her, the certainty I didn't have with you. You missed the certainty, but in a way, Lydia got shortchanged, too. I was so busy doing what I knew to do that I skipped over the awe." In response to her mother's candor, Cate says: "I'd rather have had the awe. Too much certainty, right there at the beginning, might have cramped my style" (521). The laugh from both mother and daughter after Cate's remark captures a rare moment of "dialogic communion,"[45] a mutual understanding and acceptance of their singular relationship.

Beyond Family

A "hybrid party," with participants from various families and socioeconomic, age, and ethnic groups, ends *A Mother and Two Daughters* on a sunny note of harmony. The ending in itself is perhaps too perfect, too neatly wrapped up, with virtually every character reaching some sort of resolution, variedly in death, birth, marriage, new families, success, recovery, reconciliation, new friendships, fleeing daughter's return, and lovers' reunion.[46] By evoking a sense of multiplicity, however, Godwin makes the ending into an image of a fully dialogized world that goes beyond family to encompass the whole of southern society.

45. Bakhtin, *Problems of Dostoevsky's Poetics*, 300.

46. Hill sees something new to Godwin's heroines indicated by the family party at the end of the novel—the "joyous acceptance of one's sexuality" that, she argues, "demonstrates a new sense of peace and affirmation in Godwin's female characters." See *Gail Godwin*, 72.

The ending contrasts with the beginning of the novel—where Theodora's annual Christmas party is taking place—both structurally and thematically. The opening party is closed and exclusive, held in a room with "not even a piece of furniture rearranged since 1938" (3), hosting mostly Nell's "social set" in Mountain City. The only exceptions are subservient dependents: Wickie Lee, a pregnant, homeless hillbilly country cousin whom Theodora has brought into her residence, and Azalea, Theodora's black maid. The closing party, on the other hand, is open and inclusive in every sense— social, ethnic, regional, and cross-generational, held in the open, beautiful landscape of Big Sandy Mountain. The opening party is observed exclusively from Nell's point of view, whose ironic stance provides a mental commentary on the society she is both a part of and alienated from. The closing party, in purposeful contrast, is multicentered and multivoiced, unfolding itself through many consciousnesses, each participating in a dialogic communion, each adding to the potency of relatedness.

In constructing the experiences, memories, and social worlds of her three heroines, Godwin also creates a society populated by "multiple and varied characters," each "with a need to express himself or herself."[47] She delineates, first of all, the new social order of the contemporary South of the late 1970s, a society where for the first time educated blacks are welcomed in corporate offices, professional women join the labor force in increasing numbers, and research parks employ thousands of educated adults. While the voices of tradition persist, expressed in racial bigotry, in the ideal of southern womanhood, and in the perpetuation of southern poverty, white and black, the voices of modernity, in their various pitches and accents, dominate the society: black southern politicians and professionals, southern feminists both white and black, middle-class migrants from the North.

While Godwin concentrates on this modern new South, she also represents an older, more traditional South through her description of the Mountain City Book Club, with Theodora as the "undisputed leader" (3). Founded in 1886, the club consists of middle-class women, a large number of them widows, including Nell, whose ironic and critical perspective provides illuminating commentaries upon its activities. Like similar women's clubs, the Book Club conserves traditional southern-style bourgeois values, sustains

47. Godwin, "Becoming the Characters in Your Novel," 12–13.

the moral authority of an elite group of women, and provides a public identity for women who are supposedly limited to the private sphere.[48] With its "stress on the refinements of culture" (180), the club has served as a citadel for the traditional ideal of southern womanhood, perpetuating the "set of values bent toward restraining Southern belles to narrow notions of grace and duty."[49]

Although the portrayal of the Book Club is only a small part of the novel, it serves as a metonymy for traditional southern culture. Each member of Nell's club takes turns hosting its monthly meeting. "Though each hostess operated under the illusion of freedom, she was bound by a great number of strictures and traditions regarding menu, decoration, and order of events" (179). A dramatic embodiment of the quintessential southern belle that Godwin describes in her essay on the subject, the hostess thus puts herself to the test of southern style, trying to maintain "the appearance of congeniality."[50] She agonizes "for months ahead of time about menu and centerpiece and cake" (158) and exercises fully her "skills for keeping the surface of life smooth." Each member, too, contributes her own share to the appearance of culture, congeniality, and smoothness, putting on her best social self, passing as a "lovely person," and protecting her image as a "gracious" woman, even if it means faking enthusiasm or suffering a "martyrdom of discomfort herself."[51] Despite her disdain for some of the club's traditions, Nell cannot help feeling a keen interest in her social set as "amusing anachronisms" of southern manners and grace.[52]

Alongside the smooth, gracious social voice of Mountain City Book Club, Godwin places the "twangy mountain voice" (7) of Theodora's country cousin, Wickie Lee—unwed teenage mother, victim of sexual abuse, poverty, and exploitation. Discovered by Theodora at New Hope House for unwed mothers, Wickie Lee is taken in by the Maiden Queen as a houseguest and a protégée. A social underdog, she dazzles "a bunch of privileged, middle-class

48. Nancy Press, "Private Faces, Public Lives: The Women of the Downtown Group of Charleston, South Carolina," in Women in the South: An Anthropological Perspective, ed. Holly F. Mathews (Athens, Ga., 1989), 95–109.

49. Rhodes, "Gail Godwin and the Ideal of Southern Womanhood," 55.

50. Godwin, "The Southern Belle," 49.

51. Ibid., 49, 51.

52. Rhodes, "Gail Godwin and the Ideal of Southern Womanhood," 63.

ladies with her stark, womanly drama" (507), furnishing them with an animating subject for gossip: speculations about her origin, warnings of her cunning ingratiation, curiosity about her mountain ways and crafts, and reports
of her rift with Theodora. Much of her experience is reported indirectly
through the observations of and discussions within Nell's social set and
through Nell's phone conversations with her daughters. Toward the end of
the novel, however, Godwin gives her hillbilly character a self-assertive voice.
In a meeting with Cate, Wickie Lee bitterly accuses her protectress of taking
control of her life and shortchanging her identity. "I'm who I am" (514), she
ardently affirms. One seeking existential freedom of inquiry, the other
seeking freedom "in its simplest and most fundamental aspects" (516), Cate
and Wickie Lee, Theodora's two failed protégées, share a moment of mutuality when they both assert the sovereignty of the individual soul, their voices
different but, Godwin seems to imply, equally valid.

Godwin's delineation of upward achieving black professionals also juxtaposes powerfully the voice of tradition and the voice of modernity. Renee,
Lydia's black sociology professor, received her degree from Harvard and
returns to North Carolina to teach. Ambitious, successful, and dedicated,
she is an inspiring role model for Lydia, who enrolls in her class "History
of Female Consciousness" and develops an intimate, sisterly friendship with
her. Calvin, Renee's friend and "a fellow pilgrim on the upwardly mobile
trip" (304), turned down an offer as assistant director at NBC and returns
to his home state, dreaming of establishing a cultural network, "to be beamed
from North Carolina and financed completely by private subscriptions" (456).
Though Cate bitterly accuses Renee and Calvin of trying to build "bourgeois
castles" (553) on the rubble of the "old oppressive society" (459), Lydia admires them for wanting "to claim their share of what Cate calls the 'dying
world' because they haven't *had* their share yet" (464). Representing the new
South of the 1970s, they nevertheless cannot escape the old, traditional South.
Forced out of his southern job by racial intimidation, Calvin returns to work
in New York; determined to redress social injustice, Renee enters law school
to become a civil rights lawyer.

Although Godwin does not treat any of the above characters extensively
in *A Mother and Two Daughters*, their presence in the novel is significant
because it not only constitutes a dimension of what Godwin calls major-key

novels but also presages the direction Godwin seems to be heading—toward diversity, multiplicity, and social heteroglossia—in her exploration of an evolving self. This movement toward greater multi- and vari-centeredness is brilliantly illustrated in the image of a "hybrid" party that concludes the novel. Under the open sky, music "draws people together" while each person has his or her own "reveries," each "looking through the landscape as if it were a veil" and, behind it, seeing "other landscapes, other faces, certain ghosts" (562). In the spaciousness of the party, sisters reconcile, parents and children reinforce their bond, lovers reunite and augment their happiness, and people relate to each other across generations, classes, regions, and races. Everybody sees new faces and hears old voices, remembering the past and partaking of the present, experiencing changes and reformulating responses. In such dialogic engagement, "the world is enlarged for us, not by new objects, but by finding more affinities and potencies in those we have."[53]

53. Godwin uses Emerson's words from "Success" for the Epilogue of *A Mother and Two Daughters.*

5

Social Heteroglossia and the Bildungsroman
A Southern Family

"I had a vision—from half-sleep—," Godwin writes in her journal, "of people in a crowded place, milling around in some vast place like Penn Station. I have been brought up to believe that each person is *alone* in that crowd, but I now saw how, one day, they might all be connected and *know themselves connected.*" When individuals are connected and "mutually aware of this connection," she asks, "would they be able to influence anything as a *group,* as well as changing something as an individual? An individual can walk across the floor and purchase a magazine. What kind of thing-activity would a group-mind, a group-body be capable of?"[1]

Written in 1987, the year in which *A Southern Family* appeared, Godwin's journal entry illuminates a further novelistic development that marks her second major-key novel. In *A Southern Family,* her most expansive and innovative novel to date, Godwin explores in depth and breadth the reality of human interconnectedness—its complexity and multidimensionality; its intense emotional entanglement; its debilitating constraints on individual development; and its potential for growth of self-perception and understanding. While she continues to develop potent themes found in *A Mother and Two Daughters*—self, family, and society; multiple and interactive voices; dialogic processes—Godwin in *A Southern Family* transcends her thematic fo-

1. Gail Godwin, "Journals: 1982–1987," in *Our Private Lives,* ed. Daniel Halpern (New York, 1990), 194.

cus on female growth and invents a more complex fictional form to accentuate the underlying dialogic principle and bring social heteroglossia into the novel. In place of a nuclear family of three middle-class females, Godwin unfolds the deeply entangled life of an extended family, where male and female characters claim equal thematic significance, familial strife is embedded in class conflict, and success in self-definition is painfully set off by failure. Instead of using multiple main characters, as she did in *A Mother and Two Daughters,* Godwin now dispenses entirely with main characters, emphasizing a multitude of perspectives, voices, and consciousnesses, distinctly differing from one another and often conflicting or contradictory with each other.[2] In her richly diversified fictional world, no single voice or consciousness is privileged; all voices and consciousnesses are presented as equally authentic and valid.

In *A Southern Family,* Godwin realizes fully the artistic possibilities of what Bakhtin calls a "hybrid" novel.[3] Nearly every chapter of the novel is "assigned" to a single character (on occasion deliberately to two characters) presented as the center of consciousness in that chapter, providing his or her unique version of the family story from his or her particular perspective, in his or her particular language. The entire novel, then, becomes a cacophony of vastly different voices, languages, and consciousnesses, vying in turn for recognition and significance. Three of these chapters have stylistic distinctions that set them apart from the others: Snow Mullins' first-person narrative assertion of her mountain identity and accent; Rafe Quick's painful confession to the school psychiatrist; and Clare Campion's anguished communion with her dead brother Theo in the form of a letter. Incorporating multiple perspectives into one single chapter, the "family" chapter toward the end of the novel stands in vivid contrast to all other chapters. Within each individual chapter, internal dialogue, narrated stories, and remembered utterances are fused together to enlarge further the sense of multiplicity and diversity.

2. In a recent interview, Godwin speaks of the difficulty and the enlarging experience of doing different points of view. She admits that to be fair to all characters, "even the ones that were alien to [her]"—Ralph and Snow, for instance—is an enormous challenge. She "had to make every effort to write from the way they felt it." See Pearlman and Henderson, eds., "Gail Godwin," 36–37.

3. Bakhtin, *The Dialogic Imagination,* 366.

With conscious and careful manipulation, Godwin achieves Bakhtin's definition of authorial goals: the novelistic orchestration of voices, *"the passing of a theme through many and various voices,* its rigorous and . . . irrevocable *multi-voicedness* and *vari-voicedness."*[4] She creates a multitude of characters—kindred and friends—speaking in a collage of diverse voices, with "a wide range of their links and inter-relationships."[5] Furthermore, she gives a southern family the character of a little southern society, one of great diversity—across borders of class, gender, region, race, and generation, one that juxtaposes aspiring middle-class professionals with poor mountain hillbillies, compromised mothers with questing daughters, the fleeing heroine with the returning one, tragic failure with hard-won success, at the meeting place of old and new Souths.

In emphasizing the social dimensions as well as the interrelatedness of individual identity, Godwin broadens and deepens her explorations of an evolving self. In depicting the complex interplay of conflicting ideas, belief systems, and voices but giving privilege to none, she transcends not only the limitations of a single point of view but also those of a privileged discourse that permeates her earlier novels: the middle-class, questing heroine's successful self-definition. Growth and self-definition, as Godwin's vision and art mature, become an increasingly complex, dialogic process, encompassing both the internal route of memory as well as the interpersonal and social act of "coming to know" another's language.[6]

Who Is Telling the Truth? A Decentered World

Felix, Clare's European lover, tells Clare, the writer-protagonist of the novel, that knowing her family is "like being inside a drama in which good influences and bad influences are being played out through the family members." Unlike "the old morality plays where the saint or the villain was cut out of whole cloth," in Clare's family, "the good and bad, the true and the false

---

4. Bakhtin, *Problems of Dostoevsky's Poetics,* 265.
5. Bakhtin, *The Dialogic Imagination,* 263, 366.
6. *Ibid.,* 353.

show up in everybody." The complex dynamics of the Quick family, Felix admits, makes it impossible for him "ever to affix *blame* for very long," ever to feel sure "who's telling the truth or even if there is any one truth when it comes to Quick matters."[7]

Felix's observations on the Quick family serve as a poignant summary of the central themes of the novel: family entanglement, conflicting voices, social heteroglossia. Orchestrating her themes through a multitude of voices, Godwin makes almost every character in the novel pass a verdict similar in spirit to Felix's on the Quick family, each in his or her unique individual voice. For Theo Quick, Clare's stepbrother, whose violent and mysterious death occurs in the first pages of the novel, what dooms his family is "that we haven't been able to be ourselves. Every one of us has wasted too much time being ashamed of the wrong things" (300). Lily Quick, Clare's mother, bitterly concludes at her son's funeral that "if guns don't kill you, families will" (162). Snow Mullins, Theo's estranged hillbilly wife, pronounces sharply the character of the family to which she never really belonged: "It's like they are all acting in a play or something. Each one's got themself a part and they have to stay in that part as long as they're around the other" (236). Julia Richardson Lowndes, Clare's close friend, observes from the outside the "unpleasant thrust of Quick personalities" that sometimes hopelessly infects her childhood friend Clare, who left home at sixteen and comes back to visit only once or twice a year. To Julia, the Quick family has lived amidst "layer upon layer of debilitating resentments and intrigues that over the years had sapped the family members of their individual strengths, and yet bathed them, as a unit, in a certain sinister charm" (14–15). Clare Campion, who kept her own father's name in order to maintain a psychological distance from the family she fled from, at times painfully admits her own share of that confusing, debilitating "Quick murk" (443).

The emotional crosscurrents that flow in the Quick family and underlie each member's unique responses to other family members and to the family as a whole unfold themselves through Godwin's deft handling of multiple voices. Fully aware of the narrative challenges she was facing in writing a novel without main characters (or with many main characters), a novel that

7. Godwin, *A Southern Family*, 440. Subsequent references will be indicated in parentheses within the text.

meanders through the consciousnesses of a large number of characters diverse in class, age, gender, and ideology, Godwin resolved to "find some kind of interweaving process so that the reader never minds leaving one character for another because s/he knows that there will be more (and perhaps contradictory) things to be learned *about that character* through switching to another character's mind."[8]

That "interweaving process" is profoundly dialogic, one of diverse voices coming into contact with, interanimating, and contesting one another. Using a family death as the catalyst for the unfolding events of the novel, Godwin turns what begins as a detective's question—"What happened at Theo's death?"—into an in-depth social inquiry into the experiences that shaped each member of the family, their relationship to and perceptions of each other, and their sense of their own identity. She portrays at once the inward journey each member of the family takes in search of some answer to the irrevocable loss experienced in Theo's death, and their interactive, dialogic activities that reveal not only strands of experience that contributed to the making of a particular individual but also the complex interrelationships of the individual members of the family, accounting for the choices they have made and the lives they choose to live.

Out of the diverse experiences of individual characters, Godwin builds a rich, complex novelistic world, a world in which no one knows the whole truth but each character has his or her own part of it. With each character telling markedly different, often contradictory, versions of the same story, each vying for articulation, authority, and significance, Godwin's fictional world of southern men and women becomes distinctively decentered, leaving no room for what Bakhtin terms "the absolutism of a single and unitary language." Instead, it is a "vast plenitude" of "social languages—all of which are equally capable of being 'languages of truth'" and "all of which are equally relative, reified and limited, as they are merely the languages of social groups, professions and other cross-sections of everyday life." It is a world without a single language center, where a "lively play" of diverse languages takes ascendance, where "no language could claim to be an authentic, incontestable face."[9]

8. Godwin, "Journals: 1982–1987," 191.
9. Bakhtin, *The Dialogic Imagination,* 366–67, 273.

The occasion for Felix's observation about Quick "murk" provides a revealing example of the war of languages that characterizes the familial conflicts of the Quicks. In this instance, a small change in Ralph's plan—bringing Lily to Clare's beach cottage two days ahead of schedule—leads to a chain of events that once more locks the family in its hopelessly complex entanglement, making accuracy, truthfulness, and the allocation of blame out of the question. Clare had planned her guest schedule "with the meticulousness of a hostess determined to see all the people she wanted to see without subjecting enemies or rivals to unbearable proximity" (409). She especially wanted to see Snow, with whom she had slowly and tentatively begun a dialogue—part of her inward journey toward self-understanding and outward reach toward a constructive relationship with her dead brother's estranged wife. As she originally planned it, Snow was to bring her child Jason to the beach, stay for three days, and leave before Lily and Ralph arrived.

But Clare's carefully planned family gathering quickly fell apart: Lily called to inform Clare of their early arrival and Snow's refusal to come. Clare tries to reconstruct the circumstances of Snow's decision and grasp the truth of the occasion, only to encounter great frustration about the seeming impossibility of her endeavor. Instead of answers, she besieges herself with questions. Did Ralph or Lily or both of them insinuatingly prevent Snow from coming by telling her of their earlier arrival? Or had Snow already decided against coming—for a number of possible reasons—before Ralph's call? Or did Snow ever plan to come in the first place? Did she use Ralph's call as an excuse to back out? Or did Clare herself "subliminally" keep Snow from coming by not phoning her earlier to confirm the invitation, causing her to read Ralph's call as an indirect message of unwelcome from Clare?

As Clare tries to explain to Felix her understanding of the situation from her phone conversation with Lily, she realizes how difficult it is to grasp the truth of a Quick family transaction. First, Ralph calls Snow, not Clare the hostess, about the change in his schedule. "'And then [Snow] says, or rather Lily says she said . . . or, to be perfectly accurate, which this family's lost the ability to be, *Ralph* tells Lily that Snow said she isn't coming to the beach'" (439). Here, by documenting the complex process of linguistic transmission and making us aware of the range of positions various speakers assume in an act of communication, Godwin shows how language constructs

one's perceptions of reality and sense of his or her relationship to that reality.

The confusion that stems from such linguistic transmission plunges Clare, from whose center of consciousness the event is seen, deep into "the maelstrom of family cross-purposes" (444). An episode like this, she confesses to Felix, "sets [her] back *years*" in her hard struggle to "grow up and be a straightforward, responsible adult" (442), pulling her back into the family drama she disentangled herself from at sixteen. Despite herself, Clare contributes her own share to that Quick murk and its perpetuation. When she calls Snow to find the "truth" from her, she fails to be truthful herself because "the whole premise of [her] call [is] a lie" (442). Instead of telling Snow the true purpose of her call, Clare pretends that she does not know anything contrary to Snow's coming and is "just innocently calling to confirm" (441) her arrival the next day.

The chapter in which the above episode occurs is a microcosm of the entire novel, reverberating in its multivoicedness and multicenteredness. In this chapter, Godwin brings to Clare's beach cottage every member of the Quick family, including, dialogically, the absent Snow and the dead Theo. Though not physically present, these two silent voices emerge as equally valid as all other, present voices: Snow's very absence gives her a distinct, powerful voice that speaks a certain truth about the Quick family; Theo's death, on the other hand, grants him an "irrecoverable presence" that makes "the silent centerpiece" (409) of the year's gathering. Against the backdrop of their silent voices, Godwin ushers in the other family members, letting each take turns as center of consciousness, perceiving, interpreting, and reacting from his or her own particular, limited angle of truth. In so doing, she orchestrates the novelistic process of, in Bakhtin's words, "decentering the ideological world."[10]

Godwin uses the episode of Snow's abortive visit to illustrate that process of decentering. From her angle of truth, Clare has every reason to suspect foul play, knowing her family's hatred of Snow and their ability to "screw things up" (443). From Ralph's point of view, however, what mandates his return to Mountain City on Monday is separate from the family's hatred of their former daughter-in-law: the hospital has scheduled his eye operation on Monday, which makes it impossible for him to send Jason back to Snow on

10. *Ibid.*, 332, 367.

Tuesday as planned. This may not convincingly diffuse Clare's suspicion of his foul play, but in Godwin's skillful handling of voices, Ralph's presentation of his views is as "truthful" and authentic as Clare's presentation of hers.

Clare's reaction to the Quick foul play is, at least partially, rooted in her perception of her mother's marriage to Ralph. Infuriated at her family's intervention in her plans, Clare brands Ralph and Lily's marriage as a sinister union, with one deciding and the other colluding or vice versa, like "a can of worms" that writhe around together "till you can't tell where one stops and the other begins" (439). Clare's picture of vicious collaboration between Ralph and Lily stands in direct contrast to Ralph's vision of fierce antagonism between the two. From Ralph's perspective, his decision about when to have the operation, saturated in bitterness about the irreparable decay of their marriage, is an act of angry provocation against Lily rather than one of deliberate collaboration with her. Such juxtaposition highlights the fact that there is no unitary, undeniable truth, only versions of truth, each of which is invariably disputable.

This contest of truths, by which different and contradictory voices compete against each other, is characteristic of Godwin's thematic development in *A Southern Family*. As her handling of Snow's abortive visit shows, she often makes characters narrate and evaluate the key events of the novel alternately, turning each incident into a many-sided prism that reveals the narrators' individual, often disparate, attitudes, perspectives, and languages. The story of Snow's first meeting with Theo at a working-class club, for example, is told by Ralph, Lily, and Rafe in their respective chapters. Ralph sees the event as an ill-fated occurrence, making Snow into a despicable piece of white trash and deploring Theo's foolishness in rescuing her. "You and Rafe found your way into that ill-fated dance," he says in a long interior monologue addressed to his dead son, "where Rafe took it into his head to dance with a little piece of pure trouble named Snow Mullins and managed to insult her, and then you, going too far as always, had to set things right by doing nothing less than marrying her" (133).

Sharing Ralph's disgust with Snow but telling the story with bourgeois-tinted glasses, Lily couches her narrative in romantic language, contrasting Theo's gentlemanly behavior with the ferocity of "the local rowdies." After Rafe had danced with Snow and said something "to make her fly out at him,"

Lily reminisces, "Theo had gone over to smooth things over before they both got clobbered by the local rowdies." In her version of the story, Snow cursed Theo, too, "but just like a gentleman in an old script bent on placating a lady's wounded pride, he had found out where she lived and asked if he could come and see her the next day" (204). Rafe, talking about the event to his school psychiatrist, paints himself as a naïve innocent but makes Snow into a sexually manipulative woman. "While we were dancing," he tells his psychiatrist, "she said I was making fun of the way she talked, and we almost had hell to pay, Theo and I. Her redneck friends surrounded us like goons and I had to do some fancy talking to get us out of there. But Theo finds out where she lives and goes to see her the next day. To apologize for *me*. And that's when the little spider started spinning her web for him" (264).

Despite variations, these three versions all derive from what Snow calls the "official" story, with class hostility couched respectively in paternal, romantic, and sexual terms. Against this collective, official discourse, Godwin sets Snow's marginal, contesting voice that tells her own version of the story, brings out the class antagonism of the occasion, and defends herself against what she considers unjust accusations. Not only does Snow give a detailed, poignant account of the event retrieved from memory and filtered through her interpreting consciousness, but the angry hillbilly character relates in her own voice what she bitterly calls the "official" story. "The 'official' story," Snow begins, "the one out of the Queen Mother's book of family fairy tales, goes like this: . . ." (219). Juxtaposing Snow's version with the official ones and making hers a caustic comment on the Quicks' class prejudice, Godwin gives the marginal voice as much validity as she gives to the authoritative bourgeois word.

Snow's chapter reveals the complex level of heteroglossia in Godwin's fictional world. First, Godwin makes the "official story" Snow's rendition of another voice, juxtaposed with the three versions articulated directly by Ralph, Lily, and Rafe respectively. Furthermore, she sets Snow's mimicry of Clare's voice of bourgeois tolerance and condescension against her rendition of the outright hostile voice that the narrating hillbilly character captures in the "official" story. Clare's voice, however, is twice removed, as Godwin makes it a voice of Snow's imagination, rendered through her interpreting consciousness. Mimicking what she perceives to be surface tolerance but

deep-seated disdain, Snow protests against being turned into an object—"quaint" and "romantic"—of anthropological curiosity. "I could just hear her," Snow begins, "hearing" Clare's voice telling stories about her family to her New York friends. "Yes, that's the family my brother has married into. But he always was the strange brother. He's never done things the way anybody else does. . . . He's always wanting to befriend the needy, to rescue people. . . . So when you look at it in that light, it's not so surprising he married Snow. It was right in character. He has always been attracted to people he could help" (240). For Snow, this condescending voice is as infuriating as the hostile voice because it shows no respect for the truth: "It didn't make a bit of difference what the truth was, why Theo really married me, why I married him. Clare is just like the rest of them in that respect. No, she's worse. Because she makes up lies about real people and writes them down in books and makes a lot of money off the lies" (240).

Godwin's dramatization of each character's equal preoccupation with "truth" (the literal truth of Theo's death and the symbolic truth of his life and his family) and their conflicting, often contradictory, perceptions of reality reveals an understanding and an insistence on her part—that there are only competing individual truths, rather than a single, unitary, and universal truth. Godwin shows these discrete truths to be equally limited by emphasizing that each is colored by the experiences, values, and beliefs of the individual who articulates it. She also shows them, on the other hand, to be equally valid and authentic by making them "truthful" expressions of each individual consciousness. Through her manipulation of diverse characters and voices, Godwin creates what Bakhtin would call "languages of heteroglossia," which, in Bakhtin's description, "like mirrors that face each other, each reflecting in its own way . . . a tiny corner of the world, force us to guess at and grasp for a world behind their mutually reflecting aspects that is broader, more multi-leveled, containing more and varied horizons than would be available to a single language or a single mirror."[11]

More than any other event in the novel, Godwin uses Theo's death as a fertile ground for creating and interpreting "languages of heteroglossia." The shocking reality of suicide wrenches apart everyone's carefully structured little kingdom and forces each to confront and grasp the unsaid behind the ob-

11. *Ibid.*, 414–15.

vious. In delineating each character's internal search for clues that might have explained the misery of Theo's life and for answers to whatever disturbing questions Theo's death raises for them, Godwin constructs for us, from the fragments filtered through the consciousnesses of discrete characters, multiple images of Theo, at once decentered and cohesive.

Ralph, for instance, remembers a particular night when Theo walked down to the basement, where he was preparing to sort out bills, and asked to do the accounting for him. At the time Ralph felt Theo was "exuding an expectation of intimacy that was ill timed and downright oppressive" (131). Unable to open himself up to his son for a moment of "father-son confidences" (135), Ralph sent Theo away feeling rejected. As Ralph relives this episode, he hears his own past voice of indifference and callous rejection, which now fills him with pain and remorse. With passionate longing to recover that moment when he could have tried to help Theo by confiding in him his own disappointment in love and work and attending to his son's emotional needs, Ralph now talks to Theo, in a long interior monologue addressed to him, as he might have done that evening.

Lily, too, speaks about Theo in her frustrated maternal voice as she searches back for an image of her son that she failed to see when he was alive. In a warm letter she received after Theo's death, a woman who had once worked with Theo praised him for his integrity, tenderheartedness, and trustworthiness. For Lily, reading and rereading this letter is like "reading a new chapter in the biography of someone you very much wanted to understand" (184). As she drives from one nursing home to another, visiting elderly women and thinking about the humiliations of old age, she is seized by a sudden revelation, a truth about Theo that came to her only after his death: "It was Theo, I realize, now that it is too late to lay my head against his neck and whisper it to him (and how happy it would have made him!) . . . it was Theo whom I trusted most to always love me" (177).

Clare, Rafe, Julia, and Felix, each in turn, attempt to reconstruct parts of Theo's life that might carry special yet unacknowledged meanings to each of them. Clare recollects Theo's effort to impress her and her failure to respond as a good sister. Rafe confronts his own rejection of Theo because he felt Theo, in his outright antibourgeois behavior, was pulling himself down. Julia remembers Theo as her once problematic student, challenging

her with "that daunting combination of insolence and *need*" (26). For her, Theo "was a troubled young man growing up in a society that wasn't much help to him" (97). Felix finds Theo both fascinating and exasperating; at the same time he is the only person who sees in Theo a kind of psychic energy and intensity resembling Clare at her creative best. Finally, Snow paints a picture of Theo caught between middle-class snobbery and the hillbilly earthiness she represents. This reconstruction of different aspects of Theo's life produces a more comprehensive biography of Theo's life and flashes of insight into the mystery of his suicide. At the same time, it serves as a narrative device for bringing diverse individual consciousnesses into dialogic contact.

By delineating the impact of Theo's death on each character's self-perception and his or her perceptions of family relations through the use of diverse centers of consciousness, Godwin explores the dialogic process of human interaction. In her decentered novelistic world, all utterances have equal urgency and significance. Emotionally involved family members or relatively detached outsiders, intellectually sophisticated high achievers or complacent mountain hillbillies, elegantly mannered middle-class matron or bluntly forthright hillbilly daughter-in-law—all are granted a language of truth, equally limited, equally authentic, and equally contestable. Frequently, as we have seen, voices from diverse characters are conflicting and contradictory; but occasionally they join together to reveal a consenting truth, as in the case of Theo's compassion and his antibourgeois ambition to be a highway patrol man. Often, one character's word is confirmed by another character's or by what has been revealed in the course of the novel. For instance, Snow's conviction of Rafe's hatred of her is proven by Rafe's own confession in his chapter and by his ferocious curses of Snow and her family recollected by Lily in her "private movie" (164). Similarly, Snow's speculation after a visit from Rafe that his report back on the Quick's Hill would add "one more entry on the wrong side of [her] ledger" (245) carries conviction because of what we learn in the course of the novel about his role in originating the "official" story of Snow's first meeting with Theo.

Sometimes class provides a basis for judgment, as shown in the Quicks' attitudes toward Snow. Other times, however, class lines give way to personal observation, as illustrated in various characters' consenting verdict on the

emotional cross-purposes of the Quick family and its debilitating dynamics. Snow, Clare, and Felix all compare the family to a play; Julia, Snow, Clare, and Theo all find the air on the Quick's Hill suffocating. Looking at Theo's dead face, both Ralph and Snow see someone purged of all his miseries, someone Theo was meant to be or should have become. All utterances and voices, whether conflicting or consenting, gain credibility precisely by being tested and contested among shifting perspectives in Godwin's decentered fictional world. Ultimately, the reader, too, becomes deeply engaged with all the voices, responding to the dialogue among the characters, establishing his or her own dialogic relationship with each, and testing and contesting each individual truth and his or her own perceptions of that truth.

Class, Ideology, and Self-Identity

In *A Southern Family*, Godwin gives her first full representation of class conflict. This thematic expansion reveals on Godwin's part a sharpened perception of social-linguistic differentiations and a further movement toward, in Bakhtin's words, the "broadening and deepening of the language horizon" of the novel. Whereas her inclusion of the character Wickie Lee in *A Mother and Two Daughters* touches upon the theme of class differentiation, her in-depth representation of the theme in *A Southern Family* provides an illuminating example of a highly developed, intensely differentiated speaking community, where the act of attaching one's own word to another's word assumes crucial importance. As Bakhtin explains, "another's word will be the subject of passionate communication, an object of interpretation, discussion, evaluation, rebuttal, support, [and] further development." In creating a decentered novelistic world throbbing with "many worlds of language, all equal in their ability to conceptualize and to be expressive,"[12] Godwin makes two voices stand out in stark contrast to each other: the voice of middle-class respectability or aspiration and the voice of hillbilly mountain culture, juxtaposing them as authoritative, "official" language and marginal, rebellious language, one overpowering with the threat of exclusion and the other proudly thriving on resistance.

12. *Ibid.*, 366, 337, 286.

Godwin's representation of class conflict transforms her continuing exploration of self-definition and growth. In novels prior to *A Southern Family,* the heroines must resist the cultural script of bourgeois womanhood in order to write their own stories of growth. Although Godwin embeds their struggle for selfhood in family, region, and culture, she presents growth as a largely solitary, personal experience in *The Odd Woman, Violet Clay,* and *The Finishing School,* and as a concurrently personal and interpersonal one in *A Mother and Two Daughters.* By focusing on family drama in southern culture and society and by emphasizing the interconnection of self, family, region, class, and culture in *A Southern Family,* Godwin brings a new dimension to her contemporary Bildungsromane. She shows that an individual's struggle for selfhood becomes further compounded when class conflict intersects with cultural ideology and when identity becomes ensnared in complicated social relations. The process of growth, as it emerges in *A Southern Family,* becomes simultaneously personal, interpersonal, and social, yielding a more complex notion of the formation of self.

Breaking through the "terribly limiting enclosure of one point of view"[13] embodied by the rebellious middle-class heroine in solitary search of an identity outside marriage and motherhood, Godwin in *A Mother and Two Daughters* expands the domain of female self-search, affirming different modes of positive self-definition. Taking it a step further in *A Southern Family,* she leaps the boundaries of middle-class experience, portraying a collage of individuals from different socioeconomic and cultural groups seeking in their own ways self-definition and personal growth. She presents with equal credibility a number of diverse discourses—the middle-class discourse of ambition and success, the feminist discourse of existential search, the antibourgeois discourse of personal freedom, and the collective familial discourse of mountain culture, each with its own characteristic notion of identity and success. These diverse, conflicting voices, Godwin shows, compete against one another, generating a battle of languages.

The marriage of middle-class Theo Quick and hillbilly Snow Mullins and the ensuing social relations between the Quick and Mullins families lie at the center of the class conflict in *A Southern Family,* implicating members of both families but exacting their heaviest toll on Snow and Theo. The Quicks, only

---

13. Godwin, "Becoming the Characters in Your Novel," 14.

one generation removed from the white working class or (in Lily's case) the poor, if "respectable," lower-middle class, keep moving into bigger, costlier houses until they station themselves at the top of the Quick's Hill, with a private road leading to their spacious house. With its "acres of privacy" (390) and "unobstructed view of valley, hills, town, and mountain ranges all the way to the Tennessee border" (70), the house symbolizes the Quicks' successful upward mobility and attainment of the American Dream. Lily and Ralph sent their sons to private boys' schools, adopted tolerant racial attitudes, joined the highbrow Episcopal Church, and participated in bourgeois volunteerism. Their children all attend college, seeking professional occupations in business, accounting, or writing. However much and however variously all three children rebel, they begin with middle-class values.

For members of the Quick family, personal identity is first and foremost embedded in an ethic of bourgeois individualism, one that privileges financial and professional success on the one hand and a quest for a distinct self-identity on the other. Yet Ralph and Lily, their sons Rafe and Theo, and Lily's daughter Clare each have varied experiences within that bourgeois discourse, with different degrees of assimilation into and rebellion from that bourgeois identity. Each family member's perspective on that identity has a major impact upon his or her relations with the Mullins family.

Proud of his upward climb from poverty and racism, Ralph derives his sense of self directly from his success as a self-made man and his entry into middle-class respectability. At the pinnacle of his success, he enjoyed being a man "in charge of a family, in charge of a business, in charge of the men who worked for him" (131). A series of personal and familial failures—tension with Lily, hostility from Clare, Rafe's expulsion from an elite high school, and a disastrous business transaction—progressively erode the bourgeois identity he has built for himself, leaving him confused and lethargic. His sense of identity becomes reconnected with his humble origin—his Cherokee blood and penniless youth—both as a self-comforting recognition of his success and as a reassertion of his difference and detachment from "the enclave of bourgeois pretensions" (125) with which he has become bitterly disillusioned. His relationship to Snow is predicated on his own experience; he is critical of her lack of ambition while empathic about her alienation from the bourgeois identity his family attempts to impose on her.

For Lily Quick, the question of identity is embedded in a cluster of personal experiences that she tries to suppress. Her smooth, beautifully evasive style only slightly disguises a private life story painfully locked in memory—"that bewildering *molting* period of her life" (167), during which strands of her life became hopelessly knotted together and "probably could never be separated again" (447). She had, in those years, "watched herself metamorphose from a woman used to earning a living and making decisions for herself and others into a female 'dependent' in thrall to an increasing number of small, debasing tyrannies that had succeeded at last in sapping all her ambition to overcome them" (167–68). Lacking courage to look back with honest, self-questioning scrutiny and confront the "essence of her life story" (447), Lily chooses to immerse herself in religious piety and charitable activities, both a form of self-effacement. But she still adheres to the ideal of southern ladyhood, which dictates her social relations and her disdain of the Mullinses.

Rafe Quick, the younger son of the family, perhaps best illustrates the ambiguities and limitations of the middle-class discourse of ambition. At twenty-six, Rafe "was still sheltering beneath the umbrella of college life at Chapel Hill" (26), sometimes self-destructively alcoholic and pleasure-loving. Yet he receives from everyone the love and attention denied to his brother, for no better reason than his easy disposition. No one is worried about his future because, smart and ambitious, he will eventually make it to middle-class success and respectability. Though he "would have used up a decade to meander through college towards a profession, he was certainly not a failure according to the world's standards or even his own" (481). Only Clare, from her existential vantage point, feels her heart clench for him because of an "emptiness" or "untapped level" in him: "She was afraid he might never be called upon, or might never call upon himself, to use his intelligence to its fullest" (482). To Clare, no material and professional success could compensate for the fact that "on some deeply imaginative level" (482), Rafe has not really lived.

Clare Campion, the rebellious southern daughter, the fleeing heroine from family and region, successfully integrates the bourgeois discourse of ambition and the feminist discourse of self-definition. Escaping at sixteen from domestic tyranny and male dominance, she eventually finds her home in New

York, a successful writer with financial security, national fame, and a satisfying relationship with a man. With "consuming ambition" (57) and little tolerance for failure, self-delusion, and petty family squabbles, Clare has long established the central themes of her story—getting on with her own life and living it to its fullest potential. For her, successful self-definition is not a matter of meeting socially approved standards but a process of tapping her own inner energies to achieve the self-identity as a heroine-in-the-becoming. Her carefully structured world and her powerfully stimulating sense of self are challenged by Theo, and it takes his death for her to recognize that Theo's failure is a whole story in itself, a story of someone stubbornly rebelling against bourgeois ambition and painfully seeking individual selfhood.

If Rafe's identity is inextricably embedded in the middle-class ideal of material and professional success and Clare's is firmly rooted in the existential process of becoming, Theo seeks the simple pleasure of becoming a highway patrol man: working in the rescue profession is his heart's desire, regardless of the middle-class voice of respectability. Despite his death in the first pages of the novel, Theo's presence hovers over the novel, his anguished voice heard persistently and refractedly through other characters' remembrances, stories, silent grieving, and direct addresses.

Theo's life story, retold from many different angles, unfolds itself, throbbing with misery, pain, anger, and desperation. Not unlike Godwin's searching heroines, Theo is a rebel against authority and cultural imperatives, against any force that constrains or debilitates his individual development. His story, furthermore, bespeaks the tremendous gap between what Bakhtin perceives as two profoundly different categories of discourse: "authoritative discourse"—the word of religion, politics, morality, father, adults, teachers, and the like; and "an internally persuasive discourse"—one that is not externally authoritative but is "tightly interwoven with 'one's own word.'" An individual's becoming, in Bakhtin's view, is an ideological process "characterized precisely by a sharp gap between these two categories."[14]

Alienated from any self-identity within the authoritative bourgeois mold yet lacking a strong, resisting, "internally persuasive discourse" that sustains Godwin's heroines in their search, Theo surrenders his own vision of self-fulfillment to the authoritative discourse of middle-class respectability. But

14. Bakhtin, *The Dialogic Imagination*, 342, 345.

internal resistance obstructs his passage to success: he does not enjoy the accounting work he is trained to do and fails part of his CPA examination. In the meantime, he is continually drawn to the rescue profession, attempting to find a job in the Internal Revenue Service—collecting taxes from fraudulent wealthy men—where, as Clare comes to recognize, "[he] would have been able to combine the excitement of the police work [he] hankered after with the tedious checking over columns of figures that [he] despised" (388).

In a sense, Theo's rebellion against the "authoritative discourse" is more difficult than Clare's because the gap between the authoritative discourse of middle-class reason and the internally persuasive discourse of individual impulse is greater in his case than in Clare's. For Clare, her gendered, internally persuasive voice of feminist self-search is both a resistance to and a subversive redefinition of male-centered bourgeois discourse, opening up for her new possibilities of self-definition. For Theo, trying to make the authoritative discourse his own yet unable to give it his "unconditional allegiance"[15] dooms him to failure. By the standards of his family and society, Theo's failure is one of middle-class ambition; by the standards of existential becoming, it is a failure to develop an internally persuasive voice in order to resist the power of the authoritative discourse.

The role of class and ideology in shaping one's sense of self, Godwin shows, assumes greater magnitude when marriage between Theo and Snow establishes new social relations and makes class conflict a daily occurrence within the family. Though Ralph and Lily's marriage itself was shockingly unconventional at the time, they adamantly opposed their son's marriage to Snow. To the Quick family, the Mullinses represent all that they have left behind in their struggle for upward mobility and middle-class respectability; everywhere they look, they see poverty, ignorance, laziness, a lack of middle-class ambition, and viscerally racist attitudes. Contrary to middle-class aspirations, the Mullinses, especially Snow, seek to retain what is positive in their centuries-old culture: its respect for family, its subsistence ethic, its opposition to oppression by the wealthy, and its peculiar seventeenth-century

15. Bakhtin writes: "The authoritative word demands that we acknowledge it, that we make it our own; it binds us, quite independent of any power it might have to persuade us internally; we encounter it with its authority already fused to it. . . . It is a *prior* discourse. . . . [It] demands our unconditional allegiance." See *The Dialogic Imagination*, 342–43.

language. The chasm between two ideological points of view and value systems is compounded by marriage and intensified by the ensuing separation and pending divorce of Theo and Snow, threatening the self-identity of both.

In the chapter she assigns to Snow, Godwin deliberately uses language as a device for illuminating the construction of subjectivity. She shows, through Snow's angry, impassioned first-person narrative, that language is essential to Snow's conceptions of identity. Giving Snow a distinctly individual voice—a revealing mixture of her original mountain language and the "standard" English she partially assimilated as the Quicks' daughter-in-law—Godwin unfolds Snow's individual becoming as another example of a battle of languages, between Snow's "internally persuasive" voice, vividly expressed in her mountain accent, and the authoritative discourse of bourgeois respectability the Quick family tries to impose on her. Unlike Theo, who compromises his identity by capitulating to the authoritative discourse from which he is alienated, Snow succeeds in reasserting her identity through powerful resistance, affirming her own marginal language against the official language of middle-class authority.

Godwin highlights the centrality of language in Snow's conceptions of herself in the very beginning of her narrative. Opening her story with an account of her first meeting with Theo, Snow quickly superimposes her present narrating self upon her past, experiencing self, informing experience with an interpreting consciousness. As she narrates how she became aware of Rafe's mimicking of her mountain accent, she merges present and past, using the matter of language as both a means of protest against middle-class encroachment on her identity and a means of self-reassertion. She admits that now she talks differently, after "the Queen Mother and Theo between them took it on themselves to launder [her] grammar." Nonetheless, she proudly asserts her difference: "I'm not like I was but I'm not like the Quicks, either. I hope I will never be like them" (216). Although she has made the best of her enforced bourgeois education, gaining through resistance to the authoritative discourse a more informed perspective on her own identity, she revels in her son's reimmersion in mountain language and mores, seeing in it an ultimate form of self-reassertion.

Articulating *her* "truth" about the family she married into and grieving over Theo's tragic death—literal as well as spiritual—Snow reasserts her iden-

tity as a mountain hillbilly, an identity loathed by the Quick family, especially Lily Quick. Growing up in Granny Squirrel—where most people not only
know each other but are related way back in history—and nurtured by the collective consciousness of mountain culture, Snow derives her identity from a
pride in her culture and an awareness of her individuality, particularly of her
unique mountain language. Her argument with Rafe at the Teen Center—the
first instance of class conflict between the two families—is, significantly enough,
a battle of languages between Rafe's ridicule and Snow's ardent defense of her
peculiar mountain accent, an important component of Snow's identity and personal dignity. Her initial attraction to Theo, too, is embedded in language, and
remembering and narrating her story allows her to become conscious of the
truth of her experience. As she recalls Theo's words: "I'd like to get to know
you better, Snow, I really would" (229), she grasps the meaning embedded in
these words, meaning that she might have grasped only intuitively at the time
of the experience. She repeats Theo's words, now italicized for emphasis, and
sees in these words Theo's genuine interest in her as a unique person and in her
own reaction to these words an affirmation of her uniqueness.

A self-assertive voice and a controlling sense of individual identity characterize Snow's passionate outcries against the Quick family's powerfully "authoritative discourse." Retrieving past events through memory but allowing
free thought associations to interrupt narrative chronology, Snow reconstructs
in vivid detail the bittersweet story of her marriage to and separation from
Theo, a story of a personal relationship deeply enmeshed in class relations. Recollecting and interpreting a series of events ranging from her first meeting with
Theo to her victory in the custody battle, Snow evokes in her narrative various
Quick voices of antagonism, suppression, and denial. From Snow's perspective, these voices (Rafe's taunting imitation of her mountain twang, Lily's poorly
disguised solicitation, Ralph's firm demands, and Theo's brutal dismissal) are
all, as Bakhtin would put it, "alien words," part of that privileged, "prior" discourse of authority[16] demanding her to surrender her difference and enter the
bourgeois mold. Even Clare's genuine curiosity about mountain people (an
imagined discourse rather than actual utterances), in Snow's perception, amounts
to an offensive cultural reduction of individuals to types.

For Snow, narrating and interpreting her experience of enforced bourgeois

16. *Ibid.*, 276, 342.

growth that Lily took it upon herself to administer (correcting her English, criticizing her housekeeping, developing her taste in clothes, and trying to broaden her horizon of interest) becomes the crucial means for reasserting her self-identity. Refusing to be intimidated, silenced, "erased," made into an object, assigned a part in the family play, or reduced to a type, Snow assumes the authority of the speaking "I," a voice that does not "reflect" the Quicks but asserts her resistance, "internally persuasive" and affirmatively self-reinforcing. In responding to the Quick languages of opposition ("a no-count piece of trash" [226], "poor ignorant lazy hillbilly" [228], "common little hillbilly slut" [245]) with her own language of resistance, Snow achieves what Bakhtin would call "an active and engaged understanding." She comes, in Bakhtin's words, "to know [her] own language as it is perceived in someone else's language,"[17] entering a dialogic process that heightens her consciousness of her own mountain identity, one that has nurtured her sense of self and continues in the next generation.

Just as every member of the Quick family speculates about Theo's life and death out of personal knowledge and perspective, Snow gives her own interpretations. Veering between resentment against a man she became estranged from and anguish over his torturous life and violent death, Snow at times aligns Theo with his family in opposition to herself and at other times aligns him with herself in protest against the Quicks' repression. In her spontaneous outpourings of emotion, she captures the essence of Theo's dilemma. Caught between the two sides in a war of languages, Theo both participated in and resisted the Quicks' "authoritative discourse," trying both to escape and please his family: "he didn't like them finding fault with me, but at the same time he was always wanting to go back up there. It was like he was afraid of missing something, even though he knew they was going to hurt him or make him mad the minute he walked in the door" (237). His entrapment in bourgeois discourse augmented Snow's alienation and contributed to the breaking up of their marriage. By adopting the taunting voice of his family, despising Snow for not bettering herself and calling her a "vessel" who gave birth to Jason, Theo realigned himself with his family in the war of languages, denying Snow the dignity and individual identity she proudly adheres to.

17. *Ibid.*, 282, 365.

Despite her resentment against Theo, Snow articulates movingly her anguish over the life and death of a man she once shared life with and came to understand in ways she claims no one in his family ever did: "I done him the courtesy of seeing who he really was and not what they wanted to make him into or keep him from being" (235). Looking at Theo's tranquil face in the casket, she sees "the man Theo was meant to be": "I saw the way he would of looked if he could of just been himself and not so intent on pleasing and escaping them, both at the same time" (235). For Snow, watching Theo's "beautiful" and "dignified" face, stripped of its living knots, is receiving a painful revelation: "It was like seeing the husband I could have had, only they'd taken him away from me before I ever even met him. I could of loved this one" (235). In Snow's verdict, Theo's family killed him by taking away "his natural joy in himself" (236), and Theo, lacking in self-trust, "let them do it," never living "his own life," never being "his own self" (238).

The Dialogic Process of Becoming

The internal dialogism of the novel form, with its capacity for representing "an era's many and diverse languages," Bakhtin cogently argues, is of special significance to the Bildungsroman, "where the very idea of a man's becoming and developing—based on his own choices—makes necessary a generous and full representation of the social worlds, voices, languages of the era, among which the hero's becoming—the result of his testing and his choices—is accomplished."[18]

The idea of Bildung and the image of a heroine in the process of becoming have been crucial components of Godwin's contemporary Bildungsromane. From Jane Clifford's act of writing beyond the prescribed endings of female lives, through Violet Clay and Justin Stokes's triumphant assertions of the female speaking "I," to the three Stricklands' intertwined struggles for self-actualization, Godwin has constructed increasingly complex images of a heroine-in-progress, moving determinedly toward a maturer, deepening vision of the plurality of female identity.

Experimenting with multiple characters and multiple points of view in *A*

18. *Ibid.*, 411.

Mother and Two Daughters, Godwin explores the dynamic process of individual voices coming into contact with each other, of radically different heroines embracing each other's kingdom through active understanding. In *A Southern Family,* Godwin not only continues to examine the possibilities of growth through the dialogic process of "coming to know another's word" but she weaves new, more complex patterns of human interconnectedness into her novelistic world by crossing gender and class lines. Juxtaposing striving middle-class heroines with complacent (but assertive) poor mountain hillbillies and contrasting their markedly different modes of self-definition, Godwin broadens the language horizon of her contemporary Bildungsromane and embeds the crucial concept of an evolving self within social and class conflict. Accentuating male characters—no longer abstractions of concepts or secondary, background figures in the heroines' lives but significant, dramatized individual characters—Godwin creates a more diverse and stratified novelistic world, with vital, distinctive voices from various protagonists and antagonists, both male and female, contributing to social heteroglossia in the novel.

In the richer, broader, and deeply differentiated fictional world of *A Southern Family,* nothing occurs in isolation; no one has access to any single, incontestable truth. Instead, a great many truths, often more contradictory than consenting, coexist and interact. More than any of Godwin's previous novels, *A Southern Family* is rich in speaking voices that relay another's utterances. Its characters frequently, as Bakhtin puts it, "transmit, recall, weigh and pass judgment on other people's words, opinions, assertions, information"; they "agree with them, contest them, refer to them."[19]

The convoluted lives of the Quick family are rife with a multiplicity of possible dialogues among various sets of characters, and the entire novel revolves around the successes and failures of engaging another in constructive dialogue. Ralph and Lily, for example, are locked in a deadly destructive pattern of communication, each hearing the other's antagonistic voice yet unable to reach a minimal level of understanding. Ralph and Clare, on the other hand, partially regain a long-lost level of mutuality when Clare, responding to Ralph's persistent, painful attempt to understand his own life, bursts into one of their old songs and Ralph joins in with "aching heart," knowing

19. *Ibid.,* 338.

that they have blissfully crossed the threshold of consciousness. Snow and Clare, through active acts of communication, also come closer in knowing each other's language. Even Lily, learning tolerance from her young grandson, somewhat overcomes her deep-seated class hostility. In referring to Snow as Mother, rather than "vessel," in the end of the novel, Lily embraces the one common ground between the two of them. In allowing the "hideous green pot with plastic lilies in it" (521)—a tribute from the Mullinses—to remain in "its prominent center space" (521) at Theo's grave, Lily responds with a little understanding to the mutually held feelings of grief.

Two of the novel's many sets of characters engaged in dialogic encounters, Clare and Julia and Clare and Theo, especially merit examination. Through her depiction of these two sets of characters, Godwin marshals two aspects of the dialogic process: mutual development through "active and engaged understanding" and individual becoming through anguished internal dialogue.[20] Clare and Julia exemplify one, and Clare and Theo the other.

Godwin has previously created heroines who form constructive relationships with other female characters, as in the case of Jane and her colleague Sonia, Lydia and her black professor Renee, and Justin and her mentor Ursula. Her portrayal of female friendship in *A Southern Family*, however, is significantly more comprehensive and revealing. Here, she develops the vital, long-standing friendship between two southern women, one who permanently flees the South and the other who returns. Not only does Godwin continue to explore some of the central themes of her fiction—the concept of a heroine-in-progress, struggle for successful self-definition, a southern daughter's internal conflict (feminist rebellion against traditional southern culture and psychological embeddedness in the region)—but she creates a unique dialogic context for the further development of these themes. In the mutual becoming of Clare and Julia, Godwin makes her quintessential heroine as questing southern daughter into two characters, seeking self-definition in two different roles. From their separate fields of vision, they provide each other with alternative perspectives and frames of reference and use each other's example to sustain their own continuous struggle for mature selfhood. They thrive on their need for and support from each other, and mutual growth comes out of a fruitfully dialogic relationship through response and understanding.

20. *Ibid.*, 282.

A southern daughter, Clare flees from family and region to escape the debilitating family drama and embrace freedom and mobility. Geographical distance, however, does not sever her psychological ties with the South. She "felt the spasm of homesickness" (417) when she selected a new vacation spot for Felix and herself on a North Carolina beach. Each year, she takes back to New York several bottles of the local lotion from the beach cottage, whose smell "represented her victory over her ambivalent feeling about the 'Old South'" (434). She comes back to Mountain City year after year despite her knowledge that, once up on the Quick's Hill, she would lose "all capacity for independent mobility" (14). She tells Felix that Theo exasperates her because she sees too much of herself in him, "the kind of person [she] might have turned into" (309) if she had not escaped at sixteen. Yet sometimes she has the "dismal sensation of never having left home," admitting that "no amount of love or distance or success" has been able to free her from that core part of herself which remains stuck in "a place at once provoking and sorrowful and treacherous and vengeful and duplicitous and miasmic—yet perversely compelling" (109).

Julia, on the other hand, experiences the internal conflict of a southern daughter from the opposite end. She cherishes her adventurous and self-fulfilling past—those "gloriously invigorating days when she had dared to live purely for herself" (30), when "her destinations [were] still ahead of her somewhere on the vast and diversified map of possibilities" (332). Yet affirming her decision to come back to Mountain City at the call of "Duty to Family," she finds ways of using her past constructively to make her present a healthy, balanced existence. She writes doggerel lines—"vehement, satirical, angry, or mournful outbursts" (43), using them as "a balancing stratagem, a private and necessary outlet for her mixed feelings about being home again and all that it might augur" (43). She makes it a "self-imposed commission" to find a different and new place in the mountains for her annual hiking and picnic with Clare, making it "a way of reassuring herself that the old and familiar harbored special revelations for those who hung around faithfully and stayed alert" (45).

As questing heroines, both Clare and Julia strive for self-fulfillment and try their best to grow and become, but they each take a different approach. Clare thrives on a consuming drive for success, "quivering from head to foot

with ambition" (52) and "striving for self-improvement to the very end . . . beyond" (373). She has become, as Julia observes, the writer she "had wanted to be since she was twelve" and "achieved an enviable combination of artistic and popular success, yet she was still tensed . . . for a crushing defeat" (16). Julia, in contrast, absorbs herself quietly into teaching at a small southern liberal arts college, determined to be "a force in the lives of her students" (332) and use history to "locate (and then better understand) aspects of self"— the personal self as well as "the vast, extended Self that used history to become conscious of what it was . . . and could be" (40). Yet she does not escape from a feeling of being closed in and is acutely aware that "the crux of her frustration" lies in her knowledge that "there [are] whole areas of herself nobody [is] using" (333). Despite her acceptance and defense of her own decision, she sometimes fantasizes about what her academic reputations would have been if she "had gone on with [her] research into black slave family life instead of rushing home to [her] family's call of distress" (342).

Symbolically, too, Clare and Julia represent two roles in a single heroine. Clare steps outside to become the novelist who writes about the South— southern families and its questing heroines; Julia remains a character in the novel but also becomes the critic who comments upon her friend's writing. Shaken by Theo's scathing criticism of her fiction, Clare turns to Julia for clarification and perspective. In her role as loyal friend and perceptive critic, Julia always has to tread carefully, sometimes verbalizing her criticism with force, other times silently weighing her judgment and keeping it to herself until she has strong evidence to support it, always balancing her reservations about her friend's writing with her determination to protect her from destructive self-doubt and self-criticism.

Different yet in many ways revealingly similar, Clare and Julia need each other. Together, they represent the complex and ambivalent reality of a southern daughter's search for mature, fulfilled selfhood. Each affirms her own decisions; each also lives vicariously in the choice the other made, sometimes gently criticizing the other's approach but always seeing the other's perspective as a healthy contrast to her own. Despite her frequent nervous anticipation of defeat, Clare has "provided Julia with much-needed doses of confidence and courage" (16). Though slightly critical of Julia's lack of ambition, Clare nevertheless finds "this very attitude of hers" comforting,

even inspiring. Clare admires Julia for "being the good daughter," but frequently takes it upon herself to "warn Julia of the temptations of 'burying herself' in such a role" (335). Julia sees in Clare the typical Quick quality of "shortchanging reality" (35) but determinedly argues her friend out of self-destructive negation of her writing. They acknowledge the circumstances out of which they each made their own decisions and recognize the hardships inherent in each.

Of most importance, they see possibilities of growth in the lives they each choose to live. As long as they stay alert, as long as they keep developing the capacity to create challenges for themselves, Clare will continue her fictional explorations of self from her creative power base of New York, and Julia will always try to find ways to remind "her old friend that there were rewards for those who returned to live in the place where they were born" (45). They will continue to grow together, always "comparing notes" on the completed parts of their lives and "plotting strategies and attitudes to meet" (473) the next one. Each heroine's individual process of becoming is an inseparable part of a mutuality on which both depend for a reinforcing sense of selfhood.

If Godwin uses the mutually enhancing friendship of Clare and Julia to illustrate one aspect of the dialogic process of growth—mutual development through creative acts of understanding, she uses the troubled relationship between Clare and Theo to illuminate the other—individual becoming through anguished internal dialogue. Unlike the long-standing dialogue between Clare and Julia, Clare begins her dialogue with Theo in a real sense only after his death. Ironically, Clare's last, agonized conversation with Theo, hours before his suicide, sets in motion an intense dialogue that Clare failed to develop while her brother was alive. Theo's vehement accusation—that Clare's fiction is uniformly, deceptively optimistic and affirmative—demands a reply, but only Theo's suicide gives an immediate urgency to the response. In the agony of her struggle to cope with the truth of Theo's death, to cope with "the real meaning of Theo's last afternoon" and "the essence of what Theo— who could never explain himself again—had been" (86), Clare begins the long-delayed process of responding to someone she has until now shut out of her consciousness.

Understanding and growth, in light of Bakhtin's dialogic theory, take place on the boundary—when one comes into contact with his or her own various

voices and the voices of other persons and responds to them. Placing Clare on just such a boundary, Godwin traces the process of Clare's becoming by showing how the heroine comes to reverse her initial response to Theo's criticism of her work. Through memory, intense self-questioning, discussions with Felix and Julia, contacts with Snow, and a postmortem letter written to Theo, Clare moves away from her impatient dismissal of Theo as a failure toward a profound self-reevaluation of her fiction and her ways of seeing and being.

"You take care of [your characters] so nicely," Theo had said to Clare. "You let them suffer a little, just enough to improve their characters, but you always rescue them from the abyss at the last minute and reward them with love or money or the perfect job—or sometimes all three" (49). Rejecting Clare's world in which "everything gets wrapped up at the end," Theo had demanded: "Why don't you write a book about something that can *never* be wrapped up? What if you came across something like that in life? Would you want to write about it?" (50). Despite the momentary self-doubt Theo's criticism instills in her, Clare silently, almost contemptuously, brushes him aside as a near middle-aged failure who has done nothing to make himself a main character in anybody's book, let alone her own carefully constructed fictional world of courageous, heroic striving that demands persistent struggle but does not admit failure. Affirming her vision of life, she tells Theo that "a lot of the unwrappable chaos and meaninglessness and dreariness that goes on in the world doesn't excite [her] curiosity at all" (50).

The "unsavory realities" (92) of Theo's death—its mystery, violence, and horror—challenge Clare "to deal with something that resisted shapely or logical exposition" (86). After her return to New York, the full force of the tragedy hits her, tormenting her with guilt, rage, pain, and self-hate. She throws out the draft of a novel she has worked on for almost a year, unable to sustain her hopeful vision of the world in face of Theo's powerful personal statement of despair. Hearing from Snow that Theo loved her only deepens her anguish and guilt. She searches, through recollection and Theo's letters to her, for revelations of sisterly compassion, only to find evidence of her blatant neglect of her brother. "Whole months of my life went by without my thinking of him. Maybe some whole *years*" (340), she admits to Julia. Painfully, Clare begins to make connections between Theo's world and her own, see-

ing a kind of failure in her carefully administered success. "I won't let things be themselves," she confesses to Julia, "I arrange things around the way I want them . . . the way I need them to be . . . and shut the rest out." Her flawed artistic vision, she believes, parallels her flawed relationship with Theo: at sixteen she wanted to flee "the family caldron" (371), not to nurture a baby brother; at thirty-two, she was too busy building her career even to write him, to respond to his need for sisterly understanding. She put Theo out of her mind, she realizes, with the same impatience and disdain with which she cuts losers from her fiction.

At Julia's suggestion, Clare writes Theo a long, confessional letter in response to his modest request many years ago for a letter that tells about "what a sister's day is like" (372). In Snow's chapter, Godwin has used the first-person narrative, with the narrator's assertive speaking voice articulating her peculiarly mixed language, to illuminate how subjectivity—conditions of selfhood—is constructed in language. Now, in the same spirit, Godwin gives Clare's chapter the form of a letter, seeing the writer/heroine's growth partially in terms of writing, an act of manipulating language and at the same time one of constructing and contesting one's self-conceptions.

Relentless and powerful in its self-revelation, Clare's letter constitutes her fresh response to Theo's criticism of her work, a dialogue outwardly with Theo and inwardly with herself. Writing about a day in her life and retrieving past events through memory, Clare weaves into impassioned pages various strands of her life and evokes multiple voices of herself from moments of the past, as remote as her visit home more than a decade ago and as recent as the immediately past moment. Even as Clare proceeds, her self-examination and confession reveal a dialogic process at work, one that illuminates Godwin's deliberate use of the role of writer as a device to accentuate the interconnection between language and subjectivity. In Clare's written account of those segments of her experience important to her self-perception, different voices join each other to inform the writer's consciousness of herself—the young, questing heroine/writer-to-be in face of her first ordeal in New York; the mature, successful writer deploring her brother's failure and affirming her belief; the bereft sister mourning Theo's death; and the earnest confessor struggling to be true to herself. As she proceeds in the act of writing, telling Theo her response to his criticism, Clare becomes conscious of

the unexpected need to respond to her retelling, even to revise herself in order to give an accurate, truthful self-representation. Such dialogic activities give her confession and response a double-voicedness that Bakhtin considers essential to the act of writing.

Thus Clare uses writing as re-vision, constructing new conceptions of herself as she contests and revises old, self-deluding ones. Reviewing her whole life in light of Theo's death, Clare comes to grips with what she now sees as an embarrassingly self-satisfied "Campion tone" that characterizes her conceptions of life as well as her writing: "the wry, self-deprecating recounting of the fears, the setbacks, so as to make it acceptable when . . . 'everything gets wrapped up'" (382). This revelation forces Clare to reevaluate her writing and the vision behind it, ultimately allowing her to form a new response to Theo as a person and to his criticism of her fiction. She admits to Theo that he did not "mean enough to [her] at that moment to have the power to hurt" her (383), a painful confession of her disregard for Theo, connected to an equally revealing confession of her tendency to "pad an experience with more significance, and wisdom" and to "heroinize [herself] in retrospect" (383).

By spending most of the day with Theo through writing—"more consecutive hours than [she] ever gave to [him] in [his] lifetime" (396)—Clare finds her own way of engaging Theo in a dialogue and responding to him. Haunted by the image of Theo falling off a ladder outside the window, with the rapturous expression of a young brother mischievously spying on his sister, she aches for the lost opportunities to be a good sister. Through her dream of "pure, vivid emotion"—of "the giant, unbearable reality of not being loved and wanting to kill/die to avenge [herself] and put an end to the anguish" (378)—she comes to relate to Theo in the way she never did before, feeling vicariously his pain and responding to it with compassion and understanding.

Growing out of her initial negative perception of Theo as a failure, Clare now hears her brother's voice of anguish and yearning beneath his voice of cynical accusation. She connects his failure to grow with her own failure—not only failure of understanding in the role of sister but also failure of creative vision in the role of writer. As a sister, she must take full responsibility for not loving Theo enough to give him the help he needed to grow into a

strong, mature person. As a writer, she must confront the "profoundly troubling specters" Theo's criticism of her writing raises, answering for herself
"what ugly truths of human existence" she had been "regularly avoiding in
[her] life and work in order to maintain [her] vision of life and [her] belief in
[herself]" (383).

Crossing the boundary of Theo's consciousness and coming to know his
language, Clare not only achieves an "active and engaged understanding"[21]
of her brother but also grasps and constructs new conceptions of herself, thus
making the crucial step in the dialogic process of becoming.

But the process itself continues, for Clare as well as for other characters
in the novel. In contrast to the sunny epilogue of *A Mother and Two Daughters,* where each of the three heroines enjoys a happy ending—if only to that
particular phase of her struggle—in an atmosphere of general harmony
and content, *A Southern Family* ends on the first anniversary of Theo's death,
evoking tragic memories and painful implications. The legacy of Theo's death
allows various sets of characters only to begin, not to end, healing dialogues.
Conflict between Clare and Ralph is only partially eased, not fully resolved.
Rafe and Snow remain as intensely antagonistic to each other as ever. Clare
and Snow have started a dialogue but still have a long way to go toward
achieving mutual understanding. Ralph and Lily have yet to begin any
honest communication. Dialogue between various voices continues, beyond
the ending, "pregnant with an endless multitude of dialogic confrontations, . . . forever dying, living, being born."[22]

21. *Ibid.*
22. *Ibid.,* 365.

A Journey Beyond Who We Are
Father Melancholy's Daughter

"What of me is singularly *mine,* and would be so regardless of whom I was born to and how or where I grew up? What of anybody's was purely her own or his own, if you took away family and region and upbringing and social class?"[1] Near the chronological end of *A Southern Family,* writer-protagonist Clare Campion asks once again, with no less perplexity and with equal urgency, the questions that have preoccupied most of Godwin's heroines. For all their in-depth self-exploration, they refuse to take any achieved identity for granted; constantly on guard against complacency, they journey farther on the road of self-discovery, making and remaking their personal identities, probing deeper and deeper into their social and psychological grounding.

Father Melancholy's Daughter (1991) continues to explore the idea of an evolving self through the portrayal of Margaret Gower, another southern heroine in search of her maternal heritage, as in *The Odd Woman,* another narrator-protagonist telling once again the story of a mother and a daughter, as in *The Finishing School.* Working with familiar themes and narrative techniques, however, Godwin creates a novel markedly different from her previous work. Most of Godwin's earlier heroines, growing up in the 1950s, begin their struggle for self-identity by fleeing their southern birthplaces, escaping from the lives of their mothers, and pursuing an independent ca-

1. Godwin, *A Southern Family,* 424.

reer far away from home. Their solitary struggle ultimately takes them back
to the South, with fuller understanding of the intricate ways in which their
heritage—family, region, class—continues to shape their lives and their self-
identity, no matter how far they have escaped from the South geographically.

In *Father Melancholy's Daughter,* however, the mother flees and the daughter remains behind. Growing up in a more enlightened era than any of Godwin's previous heroines, when greater opportunities were available to women,
Margaret learns to embrace both tradition and modernity. Like the title character of *Violet Clay* and Justin Stokes of *The Finishing School,* she makes
creative use of memory and narration to write her own mother-daughter
story, seeking to understand the effect of her mother's absence on her own
psychological and sexual identity. At the same time, she fulfills the maternal
role in the Gower household, becoming her father's caretaker and, as Father
Gower's daughter, linking her search for identity with her father's religious
calling. The life she shares with her father, the rector of St. Cuthbert's, is as
important in the novel as her intense search for her mother; coping with
the absence of one and the presence of the other is the dual challenge to her
self-becoming. On the one hand, she must come to terms with her mother's
abandonment in order to embrace her legacy; on the other hand, she must
struggle with her ambivalences about the nurturing role, traditionally seen
as constraining female development, in order to make it a positive part of
her social and psychological growth in the enlightened 1980s.

The religious framework of *Father Melancholy's Daughter* further distinguishes Godwin's latest novel from her other work. Set in Romulus, a town
in Virginia's Shenandoah Valley Godwin made up for the novel (and a
place much like the Asheville, North Carolina, of Godwin's youth),[2] the novel
depicts the life of a religious community and its spiritual leader, Father Gower.
Family and region—the essential social bases for the growth of gender identity in Godwin's earlier work—remain unequivocally important in this novel,
but the "explicitly Christian character of both the inherited script" the heroine attempts to outgrow and the "revision" she undertakes in writing her
own life adds a theological dimension to the heroine's becoming.[3] For Mar-

2. See Lihong Xie and Allan Kulikoff, "A Dialogue with Gail Godwin," *Mississippi Quarterly,* XLVI (1993), 176.

3. Peter S. Hawkins, Review of Gail Godwin's *Father Melancholy's Daughter,* in *Christian
Century,* CVIII (1991), 1037–38.

garet Gower, personal growth is inseparably linked to larger issues of faith and destiny, and the mundane details of everyday living assume a special "grace of daily obligation"[4] when placed in their spiritual contexts. The Christ story—with its birth and baptism, death and resurrection—and the annual cycle of the church calendar provide a spiritual center for Margaret's daily responsibilities; the story of Easter, with its promise of redemption, plays a critical role in Margaret's personal growth and struggle to discover her own identity.

Father Melancholy's Daughter, then, tells a mother-daughter story as well as a father-daughter story, the former in the form of a memory journey, the latter embedded in the religious structure of the novel. Growing up motherless, Margaret searches intensely throughout the novel for the meaning of her mother's life and death in relation to her own development; taking care of a charming but melancholy father, she gropes her way ahead, navigating between the responsibilities of a traditional caretaker and the possibilities of modern feminist self-definition, that open-ended, evolving process that characterizes an individual's becoming. Unfolding within the liturgical year, Margaret's story links the intensely personal search characteristic of Godwin's fiction and the highly spiritual quest unique to *Father Melancholy's Daughter*.[5] Where her narrative journey concludes, through spiritual reunion with her mother and the redeeming death of her father, a new journey begins for her. In Godwin's own words, having finished knowing who her parents were and who she is, a heroine "must go on to discover what [she is]: a seer, a doer, a helper, a savior, an instigator, an explicator, a pollinator, one of those bigger categories of human activity than just the personal who."[6]

4. Gail Godwin, *Father Melancholy's Daughter* (New York, 1991), 199. Subsequent references will be indicated in parentheses within the text.

5. Godwin describes *Father Melancholy's Daughter* as "less of a social novel, although there's much about society in it." It is "more a novel about the making of a soul, a soul discovering itself, and discovering how other people are components of your own soul." See Xie and Kulikoff, "A Dialogue with Gail Godwin," 168–69.

6. *Ibid.,* 169.

Her Mother's Daughter: The Many Faces of Ruth Gower

Godwin has made the mother-daughter relationship a central theme of her fiction, depicting its complexity and celebrating its endurance. She has juxtaposed recurring conflict and achieved mutual understanding between mother and daughter, balanced the daughter's perspective with the mother's, and affirmed the strengths of generational continuity. In *Father Melancholy's Daughter,* she further develops this theme. The mother figure, unable to reconcile her social role, which requires mastery of the art of pleasing others, with her artistic aspirations, which require the freedom to please oneself, leaves home to seek a life of her own, in the company of a female artist-friend, an agent provocateur whose feminism suggests an alternative to her traditional "womanly" role. Nurturing, art, female friendship, self-identity—all of these contribute to the dilemma of the questing daughter as she reconstructs and interprets her mother's story, seeking to reject or transcend it.

In her struggle to recover her long-absent mother, Margaret embarks on a psychological journey of multiple, interactive memory sequences. She begins her narrative by recounting the events of the day on which her "life of unpremeditated childhood ended" (7). A precocious six-year-old, young Margaret had entered a stage crucial in the psycho-social development of children. By age six, according to psychoanalyst Erik Erikson, a child has begun to identify intensely with the parent of his or her own sex as a way of forming a mature sexual and social identity. Moreover, the child begins school at that time, making friends outside the family circle for the first time.[7] It is at this crucial period in Margaret's development, just after mother and daughter have formed a close relationship and begun the process of acculturation, that Ruth Gower leaves her.

Margaret vividly recalls the details of her learning process in the months before her mother left. Ruth always had time for her. She gave her swimming lessons and began to teach her how to behave by example, precept, and word. Mother and daughter shared jokes and secrets about the witch that Margaret believed lurked behind her closet. They walked together to the school-bus stop every morning and, "swinging hands" beside the carved Christ figure at the bottom of the church property, made plans for the afternoon. Just

7. Erik H. Erikson, *Identity: Youth and Crisis* (New York, 1968), 122–28.

before Ruth left, they concocted a Wednesday morning game for themselves on the way to the school-bus stop—a contest of impersonations of parishioners attending Wednesday mass. It was, Margaret remembers, their "closest time together," and it was theirs alone, with Ruth in the role of an older sister leading Margaret "willingly into rebellion against Daddy's Wednesday flock" (28).

Margaret also remembers the special emotional closeness mother and daughter had formed early in her life. She liked the way Ruth kissed her, "snarling like an animal and nuzzling [her] throat" (26). She let Ruth "cuff [her] affectionately" while telling her stories. In particular, she remembers her mother's enigmatic way of talking to her, using "simple" and "harmless" (8) words with undercurrents too complicated for the child to grasp or comprehend. Reciprocally, young Margaret loved to do things to please her mother, trying to be brave and daring because her "dread of losing [Ruth's] respect turned out to be greater" (25) than her fear of danger. Such shared experiences between mother and daughter were central to the very young Margaret's emotional security and sense of self.

The intensity of the relationship between Ruth and Margaret shows how thoroughly both are embedded in the traditions of femininity, womanhood, and domesticity that have defined southern ladies for more than a century. Ruth crafts her identity within the social circle of her husband's congregation (where she plays the role of rector's wife to perfection) and in nurturing and educating her daughter; Margaret enjoys the attention, bonds closely with her mother, and builds a world centered around daily rituals between mother and daughter. Ruth's domestic and social responsibilities and her exemplary behavior give young Margaret her earliest understanding of the role of traditional womanhood; yet for Ruth, the role of the rector's wife, with its rounds of sociability—teas, meetings, services, and Easter egg hunts—thrusts her into the worst of webs that entrap women. Just beneath the surface of the placid female world mother and daughter have built lie the embers of Ruth's desire for a more fulfilling life as an achieving individual, apart from her husband and child.

The visit of Madelyn Farley, Ruth's close friend from boarding school and at the time a struggling stage designer, changes the cozy domestic scene forever, disrupting the emotional balance of the Gower household and robbing

young Margaret of "the luxury of being so sure of her mother that [she] could afford to forget all about her" (31). Madelyn's visit clearly serves as a catalyst for all the deep-seated frustration Ruth has tried to suppress in her married life—her own thwarted artistic ambition, the emotional roller-coaster of her husband's depression, and the social demands to which her role as the rector's wife subjects her, all of which encroach on her personal identity. Sensitive and observant, young Margaret feels the undercurrents of tension— "sudden shifts in alliances, eddies of resentment, gusts of unsuppressed yearning" (22)—beneath the controlled surface of hospitality and propriety that surround the evening of Madelyn's visit.

More than faithfully recording her childhood impressions and observations, Margaret, in her role as a conscious narrator, learns to use these impressions and reflections as a tool for understanding others and herself. As her memory journey continues through time, Margaret's intensive reflections lead her to shape and reshape that understanding. At the beginning of her narrative, for example, Margaret chooses to use a child's point of view, with its characteristic fixation on external and physical details; yet superimposed upon the child's seemingly innocent impressions are analytical observations or interpretations filtered through a mature narrative consciousness. To six-year-old Margaret, Ruth looks "fresh and lovely" (9); she is "a collection of pleasing colors, with her honey-smooth tan, aquamarine eyes, and the silky hair with its red and gold and even some bluish lights" (9). The child's perceptions of her mother are physical and sensual and, in her idealized memory picture, Ruth is in perfect harmony with nature: "With the bright fall sunshine upon her, she seemed partly made out of silky, liquid light herself" (9). Culled from memory, that "vivid instant" (9) of a child's genuine appreciation of what her mother is to her has become a means to preserve for her some feel for the "essential Ruth-ness" (9).

In equally vivid detail, young Margaret paints a viscerally negative picture of their overnight guest Madelyn Farley. "The same morning sun that glorified my mother," Margaret recalls, "shone cruelly through the visitor's short, wispy, tinsel-colored hair" (10). A "pale, lanky person" (13), her eyes "a hard metallic gray" (11), Madelyn wears unattractive, even "preposterous" (16) clothes and delivers "brusque sallies and jabs" (22) in a "flat, clipped voice" (12). She is, Margaret remembers herself observing, "differ-

ent from the grown-up women" she knew, like "another species altogether from [the] church ladies with their constricted, mincing walks and their soft-spoken pleasantries" (13). Audacious and deviant, Madelyn gives the young child "the stirrings of a profound uneasiness" (14). Remembering her feelings now, the narrator wonders whether she then suspected the "demonic" powers Madelyn seems to possess.

Since the day Ruth leaves home with Madelyn, her brief vacation stretching into a prolonged absence followed by the eternal silence of death, Margaret has engaged herself in a deeply psychological drama, where she plays out the many possible versions of her mother's story—her motives for leaving, her intentions of return, the circumstances of her life and death—and the relationship between that story and her own. As she journeys through childhood and adolescence into young adulthood, with ambiguous and conflicted self-perceptions, Margaret returns again and again to her mother's story, examining its subtexts, looking for connections, and threading her own life through the story of her mother's life as she reconstructs it. Understanding the nature of female identity, as her narrative shows, lies at the center of Margaret's search.

Juxtaposing the bold, immediate impressions of a child and the subtler observations of a young adult, Margaret the narrator recognizes the polarity that characterizes her childhood perceptions of Ruth's and Madelyn's gendered identities. For young Margaret, Ruth was the embodiment of feminine loveliness and refinement, whereas Madelyn seemed unnatural precisely because of her lack of grace and femininity. Southern upbringing, particularly the careful tending of a mother entrapped in the most constraining of "womanly" roles, inculcated in young Margaret the value of traditional womanhood, predisposing her against what Madelyn exemplifies—the feminist urge for female equality and self-realization, a choice that would potentially destroy the feminine difference at the center of young Margaret's relationship with Ruth. When Ruth left home with Madelyn, she might not have consciously chosen feminist equality over motherly difference, but her action reflects the heated debates among contemporary feminists about the relative importance of equality and difference in female identity. Only through her memory journey, stretching from age six to college graduation, can Margaret come to understand why her mother made such a baffling choice, and nav-

igate herself between the opposite poles of traditional womanhood and feminist self-actualization.

Ruth's absence causes tremendous psychological difficulties for young Margaret. In contrast to the total emotional security she has enjoyed, she becomes increasingly baffled by her mother's "double messages of connection and separation."[8] Each phone conversation between mother and daughter adds to the child's confusion and resentment. "The worst thing about these conversations," Margaret recalls, "was that when they began I could hear her missing me, but by the time they were over I could feel her almost hating me. What did she want from me? Why couldn't I ask her what I needed to know?" (158). The longer Ruth extends her vacation, the further she deviates from the conventional role of mother as young Margaret has learned to define it. "Was it comme il faut," she observes angrily after learning of Ruth's plan for Christmas, "to cook a Christmas turkey for a rude old man [Madelyn's father] way off somewhere, when you had a husband and daughter and presents waiting for you under your own tree at home? Was *that* behaving decently and properly?" (124). From her point of view, Ruth's behavior is unnatural, constituting an act of betrayal, a cruel relinquishment of responsibilities she has learned to associate with the social role of mother.

With Ruth's accidental death, questions about her motives for leaving and possible intentions to return become eternal mysteries. Growing up motherless, Margaret copes with her half-orphaned status by becoming an avid collector of stories of absent or runaway mothers. As close as within her own neighborhood, as far as across the ocean (Lady Diana Spencer), she finds in real life abundant examples of departed mothers. Books, too, keep her replenished with vivid stories of mothers' defection. From the childhood antics of the Nancy Drew stories to classics like *Jane Eyre,* books with absent mothers become her favorite adolescent reading. Fascinated with each individual story, real or imagined, she broods over the circumstances and consequences of the desertion, seeking revelations of motivation and character, trying to make sense of the baffling behavior of mothers running away from their children. More than an emotional outlet for her own frustration, Margaret's collection serves as her survival kit. Anything that might suggest that an orphaned daughter survives—and even thrives—after her mother's de-

8. Gail Forman, "A Motherless Child," *Belles Lettres,* VI (Summer, 1991), 16.

sertion or death stimulates her imagination. If her collection fails to resolve the enigma of her own mother's behavior, it at least sustains her sense of belonging to a wider world of motherless daughters—women who may succeed in living complete lives, despite the deprivation of orphanhood.

As she outgrows her self-definition as a motherless child and assumes the role of her father's caretaker and emotional mainstay, Margaret gradually comes to understand her mother's frustration as the rector's wife. The female figure most entrapped in the patriarchal version of Protestantism is the rector's wife. Her community, her husband, and—not the least—her daughter all expect her to conform to traditional, nineteenth-century womanly norms of companionship, subservience, domesticity, and to nurture both her own family *and* the parish community her husband leads. This understanding will eventually allow Margaret to accept Ruth's absence as a form of rebellion against the femininity that defines her life; it will also enable her to accept Madelyn, whose feminism calls that femininity into question, whose artistic calling represents truer avenues of self-expression, and whose friendship "offers an alternative form of intimacy grounded in gender identification."[9]

Remembering and reconstructing her mother's life assists Margaret in shaping and reshaping her perceptions of her mother and her proper place in the social universe. At the beginning of her narrative, for example, Margaret includes a detail about Ruth's hair in her description of Madelyn's visit. "Lately," she observes, Ruth "had taken to wearing her hair pulled back severely with a tortoiseshell clip, ever since one of our parish ladies had told her she looked more like a college girl than a rector's wife" (9). In one of her many subsequent memory sequences, Margaret relates another episode that points back to the first. As Lent approaches, she remembers Ruth's preparation for the annual Easter egg hunt. Ruth, she recollects, comments to Walter about how each year, as the rector's wife, she is expected to make the best possible egg. "No sooner am I putting away the Christmas decorations than I start to worry about my Golden Egg," Margaret remembers her mother complaining. Clearly, the best Easter egg and propriety in clothing and posture equally define a good rector's wife. "Or I'll be in church," Margaret can hear Ruth lamenting, "aware that I am undergoing my weekly inspection by our ever-watchful flock. Are my heels run-down? Is my skirt too short?

9. Felski, *Beyond Feminist Aesthetics*, 132.

Is my hair flying around too much . . . ? Should I let my arms hang down naturally at my sides, or clasp them demurely over my stomach?" (157).

In both cases, Margaret tells essentially the same story about her mother—how her life is defined by her social role as the rector's wife—respectively with the disarming sincerity of a six-year-old child reporting the whims of church ladies and the seeming detachment of a young woman describing Ruth's passionate outpourings. Yet the very juxtaposition of these two points of view communicates a conscious assessment on the part of the narrator. As the narrating agent, Margaret does more than tell the story as it is; she is reconstructing her mother's personal history by piecing together a subtext lost on her when she was a six-year-old child. Moving from the child's innocent impressions to the young woman's detached observations, subjecting both to interpretation and analysis, Margaret articulates a telling commentary on the social demands and expectations that constrain the freedom of an individual. As the rector's wife, Ruth is expected to stay within the moral confines of her husband's church. Further, she has internalized the script that defines her, constantly presenting herself as the parish ladies expect. By establishing a dichotomy of Ruth as an individual and the church ladies as the collective consciousness, Margaret achieves a growing understanding of her mother's frustration over the conflicting demands of her social role and her individual aspirations, which Margaret only begins to comprehend as she remembers and narrates.

The conflict between social demands and individual impulses also bears on Margaret's understanding of her mother as a thwarted artist. Did Ruth's role as the rector's wife set limits on her artistic aspiration? Could she have done better if she had avenues of artistic expression other than church holidays and domestic decoration? Was she maturing artistically by working with stage sets and teaching life drawing in New York? Alternately through direct reporting and subjective interpretation, Margaret returns time and again to the subject of her mother's artistic talent, trying to understand how it affected the choices Ruth had made. In her description of Madelyn's visit, for example, Margaret faithfully relates several exchanges between Ruth, Walter, and Madelyn about art: Walter's genuine admiration for and well-meaning defense of Ruth's talent, Ruth's quick dismissal of his compliments and any reminder of her potential as an artist, Madelyn's ardent

declaration of art as her chosen profession, and Ruth's passionate outburst of envy for Madelyn's "hot wand" of creativity. Unknowable to the six-year-old, these exchanges conceal an explosive subtext, with its dominant theme of female self-definition and subthemes of marital discord and female friendship.

Each time he compliments his wife's creativity, Walter expresses his guilt for having deprived her of an artistic vocation, which serves only to reinforce Ruth's sense of being trapped in the role of the rector's wife. He appreciates Ruth's creative energy, yet he does not share Ruth's definition of art; what he perceives to be genuine talent on Ruth's part is precisely what agitates Ruth's frustration—"flower arranging and playing piano for Sunday school" (24). Walter shows no understanding of how constrained and traditionally feminine flower arranging and playing piano are, how his remark cuttingly reminds Ruth of her abandonment of art. His innocent comment on Ruth's two watercolors as being "lovely" is ruthlessly challenged by Madelyn: "Everything she does is *lovely*, but I hardly think that's the point. *Lovely* is the art of pleasing others. Art is about pleasing yourself" (24). The agent provocateur's slashing comments may have sounded cruel to the defensive husband and child, but the essence of her remark would have won Ruth's full approval. For Ruth, the line separating a rector's wife (master of the art of pleasing others) from a true artist (master of the art of pleasing oneself) could not have been more sharply etched.

Ruth's artistic development becomes a key theme in Margaret's narrative, serving both as an excuse and a justification for Ruth's extended vacation. With days stretching into weeks and months, Walter's defense of his wife's absence begins to strike a different note. First, it is a little pleasure trip for a wife, overburdened by her husband's depression, to recover her lost girlhood. As Ruth becomes involved with Madelyn's stage set, the pleasure trip becomes a "*creative* excursion" (117) to invigorate Ruth through artistic stimulation. Finally it becomes an indefinitely extended working vacation, with Ruth presumably taking up a part-time job teaching life drawing at Madelyn's father's school.

When Ruth's Golden Egg—her "most amazing" (165) production, with painted "little white doves flying around with strawberries in their beaks" (163) on the outside and an exquisite little painting of "Mary Magdalene

facing the angels at the empty tomb" (164) inside—arrives in the mail, it provides the most forceful justification for Ruth's prolonged absence. Walter raves about the egg to his parishioners, launching into "an eloquent defense of the egg's absentee maker," claiming that Ruth is "at last coming into her own, . . . in a manner that would allow her to use her talents for the glory of God" (165).

After Ruth's death, her alleged artistic achievement continues to serve as a source of consolation for the melancholy father and deprived daughter. Yet with her more mature, critical perceptions of art, Margaret begins to suspect the unchallenged family verdict on her mother as an artist. In contrast to Walter's unwavering praise of Ruth's watercolors, she admits their defects to herself with candid skepticism: "At what age had I first realized with a sinking heart that the tiered steeple of her St. Philip's tilted precariously to the right and that all the columns on St. Michael's portico were the same size, even the ones in the background?" (275). Then Margaret recalls Madelyn's feisty defense of art as being a matter of pleasing oneself, replaying in her mind the taut exchange between a blindly admiring husband, an artistically thwarted wife, and an assertively critical artist. The act of remembering thus connects the past with the narrative present and illuminates the perceptual growth of the narrator-protagonist.

As Margaret grows into a young woman, close to the age at which Ruth left home, she encounters in her own life the inner conflicts that Ruth must have encountered. She willingly, and lovingly, takes up the nurturing role her mother relinquished, but she cannot escape feelings of resentment. She does not love Ben, her childhood friend, yet she allows a messy sexual relationship to develop and continue. Often she is unsure of what is right and what is wrong, whether something should make her feel disgusted or pleased. Caught between the traditional role of caretaker and modern feminist self-examination, Margaret feels all the more the pressing need to sort out the various strands of her mother's life, to understand what goes into each of her identities—mother, wife, artist.

Groping for direction and yearning for a mother to guide her through the ambiguities of modern young womanhood, Margaret begins more and more to imagine her mother's story from her mother's point of view, empathizing with her as a young woman pulled by opposing forces of desire and obliga-

tion, resentment and love, rebellion and conformity. She comes to see Ruth's "year away as a journey of some kind" (128), an inner journey similar to the one she herself is taking. She can feel her uncertain steps, her hesitant moves, her tentative gestures. She can identify with Ruth's frustration of being "The Rector's Wife," having herself acquired the title of "Father Melancholy's Daughter." She can feel her mother's unfulfilled yearnings, recognize her inner conflicts, and understand the dilemma that must have torn her apart. Having considered Ruth's identity as mother, wife, artist, she now can make room for contradictions, inconsistencies, and for revelations of her character and behavior:

> It was possible that she had been sitting exactly where I sat now, . . . when she had first called into question the whole life she was living: the things for which my father lived, having to worry about pleasing people . . . The Church itself. What if it all had been a wrong choice, not just her marriage, but the very way of life her husband worshipped? What if the Christ who had started all this had been after something else entirely . . . as she was now realizing *she* had been after something else? What did this routine that called itself religion, which could not cure her husband's sadness, which crimped and cramped her so, have to do with the brave, proud life she had dreamed of finding for herself? (189)

With frustration yet forceful determination, Margaret defends herself when her childhood friend Harriet accuses her of overdoing empathy and not getting on with her life: "But how can you finish with being a daughter when you don't know who your mother really was?" (130). Margaret's memory journey finally enables her to know her mother. Recursive, imaginative, and empathetic, it is her means of being a daughter again to a long-lost mother, of getting to understand her gendered identity. Through it, Margaret not only reconstructs her mother's personal history but, in the act of narrating that history, revises portions of the mother-daughter story she is telling. All discrete images—nurturer, runaway mother, frustrated wife, thwarted artist—with which she has associated her mother at various stages of her own development finally become integrated into a complex whole, neither flattering

nor disappointing, but convincingly real, accepted with loving forgiveness and all the ambiguities swirling around modern womanhood.

The early fondness for a loving, mischievous parent and companion, the angry half-silence of a lonely child resenting a mother's desertion, the negative labeling of a confused adolescent, the empathetic imagining of a maturing young woman—all of these are part of the mother-daughter dialogue Margaret has kept alive through years of grieving and yearning. She has yet to confront more revelations about Ruth—from Madelyn, the person she calls "a gloating witch" (149), but her memory journey has yielded a fuller understanding of her mother and of herself. She can see her mother as a woman of many faces; she can accept the double message of separation and togetherness; and she can both forgive and embrace. Through another "peephole into the past" (237), she resurrects a vision that she has wanted to believe to have been true: a "treasured view-from-behind" of mother and daughter "wrapped up in each other," having "real tête-à-têtes" (237). With this vision, Margaret validates her memory journey and the internal dialogue she has kept alive with Ruth, as a child, as a teenager, and finally as a young woman talking to another young woman, each confronted with conflicting impulses and ambivalent choices.

Her Father's Daughter: The Grace of Daily Obligations

"Where was *Mrs.* Stratemeyer when the daughters had been growing up? What part had that absent mother played in the creation of the Nancy Drew household?" (59), Margaret asks herself as a college student, intrigued by an encyclopedia entry she chanced upon. Edward L. Stratemeyer, who, with the syndicate of ghost writers he assembled, wrote the Nancy Drew stories that became a mainstay of her adolescent reading, left the syndicate to his two daughters, primarily to Harriet Stratemeyer Adams. "Had Harriet Stratemeyer, like myself and Nancy Drew," Margaret wonders, "been her father's mainstay, his intellectual and spiritual companion, his 'little wife' in social obligations?" (59).

As a small child, Margaret enjoyed a close relationship with both of her

parents. Ruth nurtured her creative talent and taught her social skills; Walter encouraged her intellectual development. Each parent shared special moments with her: mother and daughter reveled in their mischievous game of impersonation; father and daughter enjoyed bedtime reading and library trips. Ruth's departure and death, however, profoundly changed the domestic structure, leaving Margaret to develop a full, sympathetic relationship with her father.

While she narrates her intensely psychological search for Ruth, Margaret weaves in the story of her daily living with Walter, of the warm yet complex relationship father and daughter each depend upon for their own emotional well-being. In part, their relationship revolves around the story of Ruth's life. Not only do father and daughter both feed the "obsessive fervor" (21) with which they continue their "reconstructive marathons" (22), but the new, smaller household of Walter and Margaret forced upon them by Ruth's absence shapes Margaret's life. In part, the father-daughter story evolves against the backdrop of Walter's ministry, with its recurring crusades, occasional triumphs, and searing defeats.

Growing up in a motherless household, Margaret has a place carved out for her, an identity as "woman" ready made, and her break from traditional womanhood is especially difficult because she becomes her mother's stand-in as caretaker of her father. Loving her father, she willingly takes up this role and fulfills it with the utmost devotion. Yet as nurturing becomes central to her sense of self, she realizes the difficulty of overcoming its potential entrapment, so that her role as caretaker does not prevent her from searching for an independent identity.

Margaret remains close to her father, both geographically and emotionally, choosing to attend the University of Virginia so that she can be within commuting distance to the rectory, to "get [her] education in peace and keep an eye on Daddy" (97–98). Even when she contemplates graduate work, Walter's desires and needs come foremost to her mind. She assumes all household responsibilities, cleaning the house, cooking meals, washing clothes, and cutting her father's hair. She feels guilty over the slightest negligence on her part, for "being away so long without leaving a note," for leaving him to a "lunch of cheese and ice cream" (294).

The most challenging of all her responsibilities is the emotional nurturing

she provides during Walter's throttling bouts of depression. Once begun, the household battle against depression becomes a ritual, with father and daughter each playing their assigned roles. As soon as Walter begins to slip into melancholy, Margaret starts her rescuing mission, trying to console him by praising his eloquent sermons or admirable demeanor, to lift his spirits by catching a glimmer of light in what he paints as total darkness. Frustrated by her father's "joy in negative interpretations" (91), she would try to emulate Ruth by either shaming him or teasing him out of his fierce self-deprecation. Days, weeks, even months can go by with Walter mired in melancholic "unlust" and Margaret attempting to rescue him from his own worst enemies. As the ritual repeats itself, Margaret begins to suspect that her father's "chronic and deep-rooted disparagement of himself" (91) was what finally drove Ruth away from him. Yet as a caring daughter, she is determined that it is "still [her] job to try to save him from himself, even if [her] style was less potent or amusing than [Ruth's] would have been" (91).

She *has* become Walter's rescuer in his battle against depression, fulfilling, she realizes, a script she innocently concocted as a small child. Joining the household struggle to lift Walter's veil of melancholy, young Margaret fantasized a rescue scene in which she was the main heroine: "I would fling open the Black Curtain and descend into the chambers of my father's depression and walk alongside him naming each of its demons and confronting their dreadful visages until he would allow me to lead him back into the light, there would be no guide, no companion other than myself" (42–43). In the next sixteen years, Margaret faithfully fulfills the role of solitary rescuer, trying assiduously to dispel the darkness that assaults her father for no obvious reason, only to see it engulf him, with equal ferocity, once again. Even in her rich and vivid dream life, Margaret casts herself in the role of rescuer. Typically, her father would be "in trouble and needed [her]," and she would "travel home in sleep and get there just in time to rescue him" (150–51). She can effortlessly drive home in sleep, attuning herself to every turn and curve without thinking, just as she has attuned herself to the rise and fall of her father's "Black Curtain," to the "sorrowful but animating spirit who dwells within" and, in its vilest assault, reduces Walter to chilling despair.

Margaret's nurturing companionship with her father, distinctly different from the relationship most middle-class daughters and fathers shared in

the 1980s, gives her a purpose in life, an identity traditionally designated for women but targeted by feminists in the 1960s and 1970s as detrimental to female development. Godwin, too, has reflected this aspect of feminist thought in her previous work, depicting a dichotomy of traditional mothers and rebellious daughters. Nearly all heroines in her previous fiction, whatever their age in the novel, have shared Godwin's historical experience of a southern heritage—a conflicted relationship with an ambivalent mother figure, rebellious adolescence in the repressed and conformist 1950s, and an awakening in a time of feminist ferment. Typically, mothers are trapped in the role of caretaker and nurturer; daughters seek an identity outside the cultural script that compromised their mothers' lives.

Father Melancholy's Daughter, however, reverses that dichotomy to write a new version of the old script. The mother rebels against her traditional role of caretaker and, in leaving her husband and child, takes an uncertain first step toward self-definition. The daughter, born in Godwin's mountain South in the 1960s, reaps the benefits of feminism but cannot escape from the conflicts feminism provokes. If feminists abound—even in the 1980s South—so do antifeminist women who want to thrust women back into the home as nurturers rather than advocate female equality and independence. Margaret knows from her childhood that women have a strong role in the workplace, that they deserve the equality the women's movement has demanded; yet she experiences the differences between women—obliged to nurture children and men like her father—and men, dependent upon that nurturing. Left by circumstances to fill the traditional role of caretaker yet surrounded by feminist ideas of self-fulfillment, she must find ways to inject new meaning into the traditional role and make nurturing a source of spiritual renewal rather than an act of self-denial.

Margaret's heavy domestic responsibilities, especially the constant emotional nurturing her father demands, can be repressive and debilitating. Having missed a normal childhood, Margaret now questions "how much of a life of [her] own [she] could actually lay claim to" (170) as an adult, pulled by the conflicting demands of caretaking and her own emerging sexuality. She is insulted by her father's "cavalier command" that she start to live her young life by attending a college away from home: "I had never been young, what made him think I could suddenly start now?" (98). She resents her fa-

ther's deliberate obliviousness to her role as caretaker, contesting his way of looking at her childhood as "a daily rope of duty, something he could cling to, swinging back and forth over his pit of despair these past sixteen years" (88). She becomes enraged when Ben, her younger friend and sometime-lover, tells her that she sounds "like Father Melancholy's *mother*" (153), yet she can embrace with loving willingness her father's "whimsical image of himself as [her] child" (98). Although Ben's remarks about father and daughter making religious pilgrimages together infuriate her, she can fondly imagine a joyful trip to England the two of them plan to take. In many ways, she candidly admits, she and her father are "like an old married couple" (299), with tacit, subtle communication patterns through words, gestures, and silences. But she always becomes defensive when friends accuse her of undue obsession with her father's problems, claiming passionately, sometimes exasperatingly, that her father's problems and concerns come foremost in her life.

Looking around her, Margaret feels perturbed by the discrepancies between her own life and that of an average college student. None of the twenty-two-year-olds in a movie she watched "seemed to have any relationships with their parents, much less ever to think about them" (301). Born in the 1960s, most of her peers, women as well as men, seem to take an independent career for granted. Whereas Margaret has no idea what she will be doing this time next year, her friends have already mapped out their career paths. But instead of contemplating a fulfilling career, Margaret continues to focus on her father's well-being. Instead of "bicycling through Europe, or backpacking through Nepal with her lover" with the "requisite dope and lubricated colored condoms," like a "modern girl" (302), she resolves to renounce sex unless she is in love and makes arrangements to go to England with her father—decisions she believes no woman of her age in this era would make. Rather than be normal, a status she does not quite know whether one should aspire to or despise, she chooses to continue the nurturing script she learned when but a small child and "to behave according to the beliefs that were really [hers]" (302).

The nurturing relationship between Margaret and her father reflects, in Betty Friedan's felicitous phrase, the "second stage" of feminism, one that emphasizes family, community, and difference within a world of individuals pursuing economic equality. Women ought to be free and equal, but liber-

ating women from oppression does not mean freeing them from family responsibilities. To "deny the part of one's being as woman"—nurturing, for example—is "to deny part of one's personhood as woman." Feminism, Friedan argues, must confront and reembrace the family in new terms. Only when women integrate family and career, selfless nurturing and the search for identity, can they possibly become full human beings.[10] Friedan's ideas illuminate Godwin's own changing views of southern gentility and domesticity, her search for new images of traditional southern womanhood, for new ways women nurture other human beings.

Godwin's positive—if ambiguous—vision of Margaret and her father diverges greatly from both the "problem that has no name"[11] that preoccupied 1960s housewives *and* the negative vision of nurturing found in her first two novels. Her sympathetic characterization of Walter, a man in dire need of nurturance but at the same time a heroic, if ineffectual, fighter against his bouts of melancholy, differs markedly from her portraits of John Empson in *The Perfectionists* and Cameron Bolt in *Glass People,* domineering and exploitative men who stifle their wives' individuality. Through Margaret and Walter, Godwin builds a new kind of nurturing woman and a reciprocal nurturing relationship between father and daughter, one imbued with religious and spiritual power far beyond the secular workaday world. Margaret's nurturing grows out of the church community that her father heads and cannot be separated from it. She acts as her father's caretaker and emotional mainstay; he acts as her spiritual teacher and guide, sharing deeply religious experiences with her. In the tradition of the high church Anglo-Catholic Episcopal theology her father espouses, salvation comes from faith *and* works, liturgy *and* piety, pastoral care *and* the good works of daily life. Steeped in her father's religious values, Margaret finds her nurturing role a means of achieving redemption through the "grace of daily obligations," through the day-to-day task of attending to her father's well-being while staying alert to her own possibilities.

The relationship that Margaret and Walter slowly develop is embedded in the culture of the traditional Episcopal Church. Unlike either the modern church, steeped in rational discourse, psychological health, and social ac-

10. Betty Friedan, *The Second Stage* (New York, 1981), 84–86.
11. Betty Friedan, *The Feminine Mystique* (New York, 1963), Chap. 1.

tion, or the resurgent evangelicals, with their emphasis upon spontaneous prayer and individual salvation, the Anglo-Catholic parish places community before individual. Just as the vestry governs the church, the liturgy, with its repeated cycle of weekly and annual ceremonies and prayers, sustains the religious community and the spiritual identity of all its members. With her baptism, Margaret has become a part of that community, and she spends much of her childhood within its precincts, attending weekly services, reveling in the annual religious cycle of birth, death, and resurrection that stretches from Christmas to Easter. Later, Walter shares his sermons with Margaret, along with the self-criticism his melancholy presses upon him. Wherever she is (even at school), Margaret drops everything to assure him that the sermon strikes just the right note and will sustain the religious community for another week.

Walter Gower is profoundly alienated from newer reforms in the Episcopal Church, from the development of the church as a locus for individual and group therapy rather than religious communion. He upholds a traditional Protestant faith in which personal identity flows from ceremony and liturgy, in which the wisdom of the ancients and those who interpreted them can illuminate the present. He finds solace, for instance, in reading and preaching from Victorian Anglo-Catholic tracts. He—and Margaret, who comes to share that vision—abhor the therapeutic feel-good theology of Romulus's most popular Episcopal priest, not because it is new or comforting to the individual but because it explicitly downplays the significance of liturgy and implicitly rejects the supremacy of the parish community over the individual. The Gowers do not reject modernity but seek to make the contemporary world spiritual by conserving the symbols, ceremonies, and liturgies of the traditional church.

Father Gower's conservative communalism is perhaps best seen in his enthusiastic celebration of the Christian year, from the birth of the Christ child to the crucifixion and the resurrection. The perpetual round of ceremony entails, for him, the grand symbolism of the struggle of Jesus Christ to make men—even modern men—free. He believes that only by understanding the drama of the life and death of Christ can human beings truly understand themselves. Explicitly drawing "parallels between Christ's drama and the stages in our own lives" (241), he explicates how "the story of Christ's pas-

sion and suffering contained the key capable of unlocking the final secret room at the heart of [an individual's] own personality and allowing him to step inside and at last understand the meaning and purpose of his particular destiny" (240–41).

Margaret's status as the rector's daughter places her at the center of the parish community, giving her both advantages and responsibilities: she knows, for instance, the intimate details of the making of the golden Easter egg; at the same time she has to comport herself on Sundays with more dignity than other children. She has learned to respect the ceremonies of the harvest festival, Christmas, Lent, Palm Sunday, Good Friday, and Easter. But, as she grows older, she comes to "understand and share [her] father's secret preference for the whole of Passion Week, with its ever-darkening events, over the big Easter triumph" (212). For her, Passion Week depicts a way of life with which she becomes personally familiar: the remembering, the restructuring, "the different versions; the contradictions; the guesswork and the interpretations; the setting up of rituals and traditions to console and inspirit the survivors" (212).

Christ's passion is central in Margaret's search for a centered identity. His life and his message of communal service and salvation sustain her nurturing of her father, and the promise of redemption reminds her of the equality of all humankind before God. The Anglo-Catholic religion Margaret shares with her father, then, mediates between the poles of difference and equality of contemporary feminist belief, justifying both feminine difference *and* individual female equality, a fact that Margaret comes to see through taking care of her father and reconnecting with her mother.

The cross, for both Margaret and her father, symbolizes the story of Christ's life, death, and resurrection, a symbol directly connected to communal membership and individual identity. "Psychologically understood," Walter explains to an audience, "the cross of Passion Week can be seen as Christ's destiny, his unique life to be fulfilled." But *that* cross is also ours to bear; "to take up my own cross," he continues, "would mean to accept and *consciously* realize my own particular pattern of wholeness" (543). Personhood, then, flows from identification with Christ and his way. Not surprisingly, a statue of Christ, located on a corner at the foot of the parsonage and sculpted by a skilled Italian artisan in the nineteenth century, serves as a potent

daily reminder of Christ's message to his flock, especially to both Gowers. But the cross stands in the way of modern, material progress, obstructing traffic entering a new wealthy suburban subdivision. The builder, lacking the Gowers' sense of history, offers to pay $30,000 to the church for the land on which the cross stands.

Father Gower is defeated in his attempt to save the corner Christ when, during Passion Week, vandals mutilate it. The corner cross represents stability in a changing world, renewal of life in death; its demolition metaphorically presages both the crucifixion of Jesus and the destruction of a vital, changing tradition by the empty shell of modernity. The vandalism galvanizes the religious community into action, leading Walter to set up an ecumenical service for Good Friday. And it is at that service, as the remains of the cross are carried forward, that Walter Gower suffers a stroke and dies, repeating in his own life and death what Christ suffered.

The story of the destruction of the statue during the Easter season forms the central drama of *Father Melancholy's Daughter*. The Easter story is rich in metaphor but simple in structure—in Christ's death comes redemption from sin and salvation. Walter Gower's story clearly parallels the story of Christ: he upholds virtue and tradition (the ritual of the church and the symbolism of the corner Christ statue) against the latter-day money changers and sacrifices his own life to preserve the spirit of Christ's story.[12] Walter's death devastates Margaret, yet, like the Easter story, it is ultimately redemptive and liberating. Only with Walter's death can Margaret truly begin to find her own faith and her identity as a human being in the larger drama of humanity. Her memories of Walter's life and death will not only sustain her personal and psychological development but will also guide her spiritual quest for knowledge, conviction, and commitment.

12. Godwin describes Walter Gower as "a contemporary Christ figure who must confront challenges parallel to those in the life of Christ: abandonment, dejection, enemies to his ministry. Like Christ, he also has loyal and loving supporters whom he inspires." See Pearlman and Henderson, eds., "Gail Godwin," 40.

Beyond Memory, Beyond the Ending

Rereading the letters Ruth wrote to Walter many years ago, Margaret feels she has completed something: "The letters occupied me until midnight. Slipping the rubber bands back around them in their envelopes, I felt I was finished with something. . . . I felt compassion for the two people concerned, but it was their story" (350). Through much of her life, she has thought of herself as a character in the story of her two parents, searching for one and caring for the other, vicariously fulfilling both of their roles for each other. Now, through spiritual reunion with her mother and the martyred death of her father, both the mother-daughter and the father-daughter story come to an end. Watching once again the tape of her father's last religious performance, Margaret examines her own image captured by the camera: "A pleasant-enough looking girl, small in stature, low-key, in an unmemorable cotton-knit dress. Her attention was clearly on the speaker, where it properly should be. A well-behaved, low-profile daughter, most probably a clergyman's daughter. One's *ideal* of a clergyman's daughter" (352). These wry, self-mocking comments reveal a profound uncertainty about her own identity, as she stands at the outset of a different journey.

A twenty-two-year-old college graduate, completely free from any obligations and responsibilities, Margaret is at a loss about what she is and will become without her parents' story. "Where was my story?" she asks herself, "When was it going to begin? What would I have to go through to get to the beginning of it, or far enough into it to realize it *was* mine?" (351). Soon she will have to move out of the rectory and begin a new life. With standing invitations from several old family friends, she withholds herself from making any promise or commitment. She contemplates graduate work but makes no decision whether and where to do it. In love with Adrian Bonner, an older priest who commands her admiration and respect but seems to share her father's low self-esteem and melancholy, she keeps a safe distance from him, conscious of the similarities between her mother's love for Walter and her own for Adrian. Looking at the packed boxes piled up in the hall of the rectory, Margaret is seized by a revelation: "I had been working from the inside out," she observes. "Now, as of tonight, the 'out' had made its first appearance. I was getting ready to go. But where?" (351).

The "inside" and the "out" are physical as well as metaphorical. Margaret has completed an interior journey and is moving out of the place whose rhythm she knows as intimately as she does the feel of her mother's touch and the rise and fall of her father's Black Curtain. Leaving the rectory represents both a loss and a form of resurrection, which, as her father explained, "means coming up through what you were born into, then understanding objectively the people your parents were and how they influenced you." Only then can you begin to discover "who you yourself are, in terms of how you carry forward what they put in you, and how your circumstances have shaped you." Then "you have to go on to find out *what* you are in the human drama, or body of God. The what *beyond* the who" (276). Having gained an understanding of who she is—what she was born into, who her parents were, who she is in terms of parental heritage and social circumstances—Margaret is ready to embark on a journey to find what she is.

To begin her new journey, Margaret must exorcise the demons that have followed her since childhood: the closet witch—personification of Madelyn and the darkness she associates with her. By leaving Madelyn an animated phone message, breaking the silence and asserting for the first time her role as agent rather than victim, Margaret releases the witch from the closet. Then, when Madelyn shows up unexpectedly at the rectory, she invites her to be a house guest, despite repulsion and trepidation, ready to resume the long-dead dialogue that had a dubious beginning and a tragic ending, to meet the challenge she shunned sixteen years ago. With effort and time, repugnance gradually gives way to tolerance, even genuine appreciation. In the same woman in whom she saw nothing but arrogance, insensitivity, and blasphemy, she now senses a fierce creative energy, an imagination that, though lying fallow at the moment, still possesses the verve to get her going again. She journeys to England with Madelyn to visit the site where her mother was killed and the religious shrines that her father fondly remembered. The visit to the scene of the accident ties Margaret more closely to both Madelyn and her mother; the pilgrimage to religious sites rekindles her relationship with her father but at the same time binds her more completely to the church and to a vocation within it.

Far outside of the rectory, Margaret begins to prepare herself for new discoveries while continuing to fulfill her obligations as Father Gower's daugh-

ter. Just as Christ frees men and women to be good Christians, so Walter's death frees Margaret to nurture others as she nurtured him, and the release of her closet witch frees her to nurture her own creativity. She willingly attends a sick Madelyn, just as Ruth would have done; she keeps the door open to a love relationship with Adrian, though she is quite happy to have him as a trusting friend for the time being; and she writes to divinity schools to inquire about their graduate programs, contemplating the pastoral calling of the parish priest, to nurture a religious community as her father did. Yet she is not simply repeating her parents' stories; she is beginning to write her own, through journal entries that record her love, passion, and yearning. In contemplating a dual career of priest and writer, she is charting out a way of life for herself that affirms her own personality while integrating the best legacy Ruth and Walter left her—creative individuality and religious conviction, ardor for self-expression and passion for service. Still Ruth and Walter's daughter, she has emerged from the difficult memory journey and outgrown the ambivalent nurturing role, able to embrace nurturing, religion, and creativity all at the same time.

Using the final pages of her journal book, the heroine of *Father Melancholy's Daughter* brings her story to an end. Yet the narrative ending is also her first step on a spiritual journey. Fully awake and intensely aware, Margaret hears her father's voice reading Vaughan against the beautiful, spacious darkness that envelops everything outside her window. The darkness, no longer the Black Curtain that threw her father into an abyss of despair, embodies both challenge and promise: "It is a big and spacious night, with room for everything in it: me and all my great desires, an infinity of other things as well" (403). Reading "Prayer and Desire," a chapter in a book about prayer, contemplating, absorbing herself in the infinite possibilities of a spiritual life, Margaret ends her narrative with a dialogue with God, "the ultimate interlocutor, the final narrative goal"[13]: "Oh, You. What are you? What do You want of me? What will I be doing on this day next year? Don't tell me. . . . Do You know, Yourself, or is it left partly to me? Are you withholding my life from me, or unfolding it with me? Are You an eternal parent or are we eternal partners? Are You there for me now? I choose to think so. Oth-

13. Hawkins, Review of Godwin's *Father Melancholy's Daughter*, 1039.

erwise it would just be too lonely" (404). Fate, free will, original sin—the classic problems of Christianity—thus engage Margaret at the threshold of her journey. And her new journey of Christian discovery may be the beginning of a potentially liberating and feminist Christianity, one that weds the traditional issues of faith to female individuality and self-actualization.

Epilogue

From *The Perfectionists*, a novel of psychic isolation set on a secluded resort island, to *Father Melancholy's Daughter*, a novel that links a heroine's personal search for identity and humanity's spiritual quest for redemption, Godwin's eight published novels form an impressive body of work that contributes significantly to contemporary feminist transformation and revitalization of the traditional Bildungsroman. Responding on the one hand to the humanist belief in a centered, coherent self and on the other hand to the modernist abandonment as well as the postmodern deconstruction of that self, Godwin has conducted, over nearly two decades, in-depth novelistic explorations of the concept of the self, a central issue in the Western intellectual tradition, in the development of the Bildungsroman as a genre, and in feminist rethinking of existing ideological, cultural, and literary discourses. What emerges from her pursuit is a concept of self as process—complex, fluid, and evolving; resisting a rigid, fixed, or single identity; seeking cohesion, continuity, and centeredness through a dialogic, decentering process of becoming. Internally, such a process centers on memory and reconstruction of the self; externally, it revolves around interpersonal and social interactions of diverse voices and consciousnesses. Thus the self learns, grows, and coheres through constant self-redefinition. Each end generates a new beginning; each achieved identity opens up for renewed self-examination and leads to the next level of growth.

Such a dynamic concept of self has evolved in the course of Godwin's

novelistic endeavor, becoming increasingly more complex and multiple as the author continues to broaden her vision and develop her craft. *The Perfectionists* and *Glass People*, we recall, exhibit a narrative tension in their representations of the concept of self, granting the female protagonists an emerging sense of self yet endowing the male characters with an articulate vision of a self posited on the existential idea of becoming. In developing the dual theme of female victimization and feminist self-search, Godwin emphasizes the text of patriarchal oppression to such a degree that it overwhelms the text of feminist resistance and obstructs the possibilities of creating positive, compelling heroines-in-progress.

Transcending the ideology of patriarchal oppression and searching for narrative patterns to render images of a "fully human heroine," Godwin begins to develop the dimensions of feminist self-definition. In *The Odd Woman*, *Violet Clay*, and *The Finishing School*, she portrays single academic or artist heroines seeking identity outside the cultural text of marriage and motherhood. She explores such potent themes of female growth as family, place, memory, female networks, and the mother-daughter relationship, and delineates feminist self-definition as a process of contesting various norms that family, region, and culture impose on female development. Perceiving such a process as intensely solitary and interior, Godwin makes memory and internal dialogue the crucial means of self-understanding. By dramatizing the interplay of multiple versions of the self and granting her protagonist the active role of restructuring, interpreting, and claiming her different selves, she fully stretches the single point of view, making it increasingly more capacious, giving a dialogic dimension to solitary quest, individual consciousness, and the internal means of self-definition.

With multiple characters and points of view, *A Mother and Two Daughters* and *A Southern Family* open up new narrative possibilities for Godwin's representation of evolving selfhood. In these two novels, Godwin accentuates the concept of the self as complex and multiple by embedding solitary quest, individual consciousness, and the psychological process of memory in the strata of society. She explores in extraordinary depth and breadth the dialogic nature of human life by showing how diverse individuals—each in his or her distinct voice—engage, shape, and define each other in continual dialogue. Growth and self-definition now encompass both aspects of the dia-

logic process—the internal, solitary, retrospective process of memory and re-structuring, and the interactive, ongoing, social process of coming to know another's language.

Father Melancholy's Daughter builds upon earlier themes but extends the search for self into the spiritual realm of the Episcopal Church, bringing a theological dimension to the concept of self-becoming. Weaving into the narrative both a mother-daughter story and a father-daughter story, Godwin depicts a young woman's psychological growth as well as her religious coming of age. The ceremonies of the church, the liturgical calendar, and the church community play a central role in the novel, and the symbolism of the Christ story unites father and daughter in a holy search for salvation and identity.

Godwin's eight novels exhibit not only an extraordinary range of characters, themes, and narrative patterns but also continuous thematic and narrative development. Beginning with young heroines in search of self, she has reached backward to adolescence, forward to middle age and into old age, finally returning to childhood, adolescence, and beyond, to dramatize the continuity of self-becoming. She has increasingly embedded her exploration of female growth in the South as a region and added blacks and poor whites to her gallery of middle-class heroines. Although her fictive world is predominantly female, she has moved from a largely female-centered plot to a more balanced approach that considers men and women equally. Focusing on the daughter's perspective in earlier novels, she has come to emphasize the maternal voice and, in her latest work, writes a compelling father-daughter story. With such thematic and narrative expansion, Godwin brings into her novelistic world the language of social heteroglossia, presenting a multicentered world—across borders of class, gender, region, race, and generation—where men and women, whites and blacks, mothers (and fathers) and daughters, career women and housewives, aspiring middle-class professionals and self-sufficient poor mountain hillbillies, laity and priests—all have equal status, articulating their uniquely individual languages of truth in their own voices.

Godwin's contemporary Bildungsromane constitute a most articulate and forceful response to those who claim that "there is no *self*" and that a concept of a "unique," "consistent," "continuous," and coherent self is an

1. Godwin, "How to Be the Heroine of Your Own Life," 197.

anachronism in an age of increasing confusion and fragmentation.[1] Contesting the modernist abandonment and the postmodern deconstruction of the self, Godwin constructs an evolving self that grows by means of various dialogic activities, thus transforming presumptions of coherence into a dynamic process of becoming. Her conception of the self as a sense-making process expresses at once a profound understanding of the fragmentariness of contemporary life and an informed insistence on the desirability, and possibility, of the spirit of the humanist ideal. Through a collage of characters, Godwin asserts, against the blaring, collective voice of the "fashionable cynics" who proclaim the death of the self, the "unfashionable hope" for meaning, pattern, growth, and mature self-definition.

Margaret's spiritual beseeching at the end of *Father Melancholy's Daughter* echoes the self-probing inquiry of Clare Campion in *A Southern Family*. Although these two heroines speak out of very different experiences, they are united in the ongoing struggle for self-becoming, embedded in discrete psychological, social, and spiritual reality. With desire and passion, both of them take us beyond the ending of their own stories to the larger, open-ended stage of humanity's becoming, with each person "cutting her unique swath through the landscape of her times, adding her particular style and contribution to the great myth of humanity."[2]

2. *Ibid.*, 227.

Bibliography

Gail Godwin's Works

Novels
The Perfectionists. New York, 1970.
Glass People. New York, 1972.
The Odd Woman. New York, 1974.
Violet Clay. New York, 1978.
A Mother and Two Daughters. New York, 1982.
The Finishing School. New York, 1984.
A Southern Family. New York, 1987.
Father Melancholy's Daughter. New York, 1991.

Other Works
"Becoming the Characters in Your Novel." *Writer,* XCV (June, 1982), 11–14.
"How to Be the Heroine of Your Own Life." *Cosmopolitan,* March, 1988, pp. 194, 196–97, 227.
[Interview with Gail Godwin]. *Contemporary Authors,* n.s., XV (1985), 157–59.
"Journals: 1982–1987." In *Our Private Lives,* edited by Daniel Halpern. New York, 1990.
"The Many Masks of Kathleen Godwin and Charlotte Ashe." In *Family Portraits: Remembrances by Twenty Distinguished Writers,* edited by Carolyn Anthony. New York, 1989.
"The Southern Belle." *Ms,* July, 1975, pp. 49, 51–52, 84–85.
"Towards a Fully Human Heroine: Some Worknotes." *Harvard Advocate,* CVI (Winter, 1973), 26–28.

Secondary Works

Abel, Elizabeth, Marianne Hirsch, and Elizabeth Langland, eds. *The Voyage In: Fictions of Female Development.* Hanover, N.H., 1983.

Althusser, Louis. *Lenin and Philosophy and Other Essays.* Translated by B. N. Brewster. New York, 1971.

Bakhtin, Mikhail M. *The Dialogic Imagination: Four Essays.* Translated by Caryl Emerson and Michael Holquist. Edited by Michael Holquist. Austin, 1981.

———. *Problems of Dostoevsky's Poetics.* Translated and edited by Caryl Emerson. Minneapolis, 1984.

Barth, John. "The Literature of Exhaustion." *Atlantic Monthly,* CCXX (August 1967), 29–34.

Barthes, Roland. "The Death of the Author." In *Image, Music, Text,* translated and edited by Stephen Heath. New York, 1977.

Baruch, Elaine Hoffman. "The Feminine *Bildungsroman:* Education Through Marriage." *Massachusetts Review,* XXII (1981), 335–57.

Bauer, Dale M. *Feminist Dialogics: A Theory of Failed Community.* New York, 1988.

Belsey, Catherine. "Constructing the Subject: Deconstructing the Text." In *Feminist Criticism and Social Change: Sex, Class, and Race in Literature and Culture,* edited by Judith Newton and Deborah Rosenfelt. New York, 1985.

Benveniste, Emile. *Problems in General Linguistics.* Miami, 1971.

Braendlin, Bonnie Hoover. "Alther, Atwood, Ballantyne, and Gray: Secular Salvation in the Contemporary Feminist Bildungsroman." *Frontiers,* IV (Spring, 1979), 18–22.

———. "Bildung in Ethnic Women Writers." *Denver Quarterly,* XVII (Winter, 1983), 75–87.

———. "New Directions in the Contemporary Bildungsroman: Lisa Alther's *Kinflicks.*" In *Gender and Literary Voice,* edited by Janet Todd. New York, 1980.

Brownstein, Rachel M. "*The Odd Woman* and Literary Feminism." In *American Women Writing Fiction: Memory, Identity, Family, Space,* edited by Mickey Pearlman. Lexington, 1989.

Buckley, Jerome Hamilton. *Season of Youth: The Bildungsroman from Dickens to Golding.* Cambridge, Mass., 1974.

Christ, Carol. "Margaret Atwood: The Surfacing of Women's Spiritual Quest and Vision." *Signs,* II (1976), 316–30.

Cocalis, Susan L. "The Transformation of *Bildung* from an Image to an Ideal." *Monatshefte,* LXX (1978), 399–414.

Cornillon, Susan Koppelman, ed. *Images of Women in Fiction: Feminist Perspectives.* Bowling Green, 1973.

Donovan, Josephine. *Feminist Theory: The Intellectual Traditions of American Feminism.* New York, 1985.

DuPlessis, Rachel Blau. *Writing Beyond the Ending: Narrative Strategies of Twentieth-Century Women Writers.* Bloomington, Ind., 1985.

Ellman, Mary. *Thinking About Women.* New York, 1968.

Erikson, Erik H. *Identity: Youth and Crisis.* New York, 1968.

Felski, Rita. *Beyond Feminist Aesthetics: Feminist Literature and Social Change.* Cambridge, Mass., 1989.

Ferguson, Ann. "A Feminist Aspect Theory of the Self." In *Women, Knowledge, and Reality: Explorations in Feminist Philosophy,* edited by Ann Garry and Marilyn Pearsall. Boston, 1989.

Flax, Jane. "Postmodernism and Gender Relations in Feminist Theory." In *Feminist Theory in Practice and Process,* edited by Micheline R. Malson *et al.* Chicago, 1989.

Forman, Gail. "A Motherless Child." *Belles Lettres,* VI (1991), 16.

Fox-Genovese, Elizabeth. "The New Female Literary Culture." *Antioch Review,* XXXVIII (1980), 193–217.

Friedan, Betty. *The Feminine Mystique.* New York, 1963.

———. *The Second Stage.* New York, 1981.

Frye, Joanne S. *Living Stories, Telling Lives: Women and the Novel in Contemporary Experience.* Ann Arbor, 1986.

Gallop, Jane. *The Daughter's Seduction.* Ithaca, 1982.

Gardiner, Judith Kegan. "Gail Godwin and Feminist Fiction." *North American Review,* CCLX (Summer, 1975), 83–86.

———. "Mind Mother: Psychoanalysis and Feminism." In *Making a Difference: Feminist Literary Criticism,* edited by Gayle Greene and Coppelia Kahn. London, 1985.

232   Bibliography

————. *Rhys, Stead, Lessing, and the Politics of Empathy.* Bloomington, Ind., 1989.

Gaston, Karen C. "'Beauty and the Beast' in Gail Godwin's *Glass People.*" *Critique: Studies in Modern Fiction,* XXI (1980), 94–102.

————. "The Themes of Female Self–Discovery in the Novels of Judith Rossner, Gail Godwin, Alice Walker, and Toni Morrison." Ph.D. dissertation, Auburn University, 1980.

Gilbert, Sandra M., and Susan Gubar. *The Madwoman in the Attic: The Woman Writer and the Nineteenth-Century Imagination.* New Haven, 1979.

Goodman, Charlotte. "The Lost Brother, the Twin: Women Novelists and the Male-Female Double Bildungsroman." *Novel,* XVII (Fall, 1983), 28–43.

Gray, Francine du Plessix. "The Literary View: Nature as the Nunnery." *New York Times Book Review,* July 17, 1977, pp. 3, 29.

Grimshaw, Jean. "Autonomy and Identity in Feminist Thinking." In *Feminist Perspectives in Philosophy,* edited by Morwenna Griffiths and Margaret Whitford. Bloomington, Ind., 1988.

Grosz, Elizabeth. *Sexual Subversions: Three French Feminists.* Sydney, 1989.

Hassan, Ihab. "Prometheus as Performer: Toward a Posthumanist Culture?" *Georgia Review,* XXXI (1977), 830–50.

Hawkins, Peter S. Review of Gail Godwin's *Father Melancholy's Daughter. Christian Century,* CVIII (1991), 1037–39.

Heilbrun, Carolyn G. "Marriage and Contemporary Fiction." *Critical Inquiry,* V (1978), 309–22.

Hill, Jane. *Gail Godwin.* New York, 1992.

Hirsch, Marianne. *The Mother/Daughter Plot: Narrative, Psychoanalysis, Feminism.* Bloomington, Ind., 1989.

————. "Mothers and Daughters." *Signs,* VII (1981), 200–22.

————. "The Novel of Formation as Genre: Between Great Expectations and Lost Illusions." *Genre,* XII (1979), 293–311.

Holquist, Michael. Glossary to Mikhail Bakhtin's *The Dialogic Imagination: Four Essays.* Austin, 1981.

Labovitz, Esther Kleinbord. *The Myth of the Heroine: The Female Bildungsroman in the Twentieth Century.* New York, 1986.

Lacan, Jacques. *Écrits, A Selection.* Translated by Alan Sheridan. New York, 1977.

Lazzaro-Weis, Carol. "The Female *Bildungsroman:* Calling It into Question."
 NWSA Journal, II (Winter, 1990), 16–34.

Lieberman, Marcia R. "'Some Day My Prince Will Come': Female Acculturation Through the Fairy Tale." *College English,* XXXIV (1972), 383–95.

Lorsch, Susan E. "Gail Godwin's *The Odd Woman:* Literature and the Retreat from Life." *Critique,* XX (Winter, 1978), 21–32.

Marini, Marcelle. "Feminism and Literary Criticism: Reflections on the Disciplinary Approach." In *Women in Culture and Politics: A Century of
 Change,* edited by Judith Friedlander *et al.* Bloomington, Ind., 1986.

Meese, Elizabeth A. *Crossing the Double-Cross: The Practice of Feminist
 Criticism.* Chapel Hill, 1986.

Mickelson, Anne Z. "Gail Godwin: Order and Accommodation." In *Reaching Out: Sensitivity and Order in Recent American Fiction by Women.*
 Metuchen, 1979.

Miles, David H. "The Picaro's Journey to the Confessional: The Changing
 Image of the Hero in the German Bildungsroman." *PMLA,* LXXXIX
 (1974), 980–92.

Miller, J. Hillis. *Poets of Reality: Six Twentieth-Century Writers.* Cambridge,
 Mass., 1965.

Mulvey, Laura. "Visual Pleasure and Narrative Cinema." *Screen,* XVI (Autumn, 1975), 6–18.

Pearlman, Mickey, and Katherine Usher Henderson, eds. "Gail Godwin." In
 A Voice of One's Own: Conversations with America's Writing Women.
 Boston, 1990.

Pratt, Annis. "Women and Nature in Modern Fiction." *Contemporary Literature,* XIII (1972), 476–90.

Pratt, Annis, with Barbara White *et al. Archetypal Patterns in Women's Fiction.* Bloomington, Ind., 1981.

Press, Nancy. "Private Faces, Public Lives: The Women of the Downtown
 Group of Charleston, South Carolina." In *Women in the South: An Anthropological Perspective,* edited by Holly F. Mathews. Athens, Ga., 1989.

Rabuzzi, Kathryn Allen. *The Sacred and the Feminine: Toward a Theology
 of Housework.* New York, 1982.

Rhodes, Carolyn. "Gail Godwin and the Ideal of Southern Womanhood."
 Southern Quarterly, XXI (Winter, 1983), 55–66.

Rice, Philip, and Patricia Waugh, eds. *Modern Literary Theory: A Reader.* London, 1989.

Rich, Adrienne. *Of Woman Born: Motherhood as Experience and Institution.* New York, 1976.

Rubenstein, Roberta. *Boundaries of the Self: Gender, Culture, Fiction.* Urbana, 1987.

Sammons, Jeffrey L. "The Mystery of the Missing *Bildungsroman;* or, What Happened to Wilhelm Meister's Legacy?" *Genre,* XIV (1981), 229–46.

Scott, Anne Firor. *The Southern Lady: From Pedestal to Politics 1830–1930.* Chicago, 1970.

Showalter, Elaine. "Feminist Criticism in the Wilderness." In *The New Feminist Criticism: Essays on Women, Literature, and Theory,* edited by Elaine Showalter. New York, 1985.

Smith, Paul. *Discerning the Subject.* Minneapolis, 1988.

Stewart, Grace. *A New Mythos: The Novel of the Artist as Heroine 1877–1977.* Montreal, 1981.

Swales, Martin. *The German Bildungsroman from Wieland to Hesse.* Princeton, 1978.

Sypher, Wylie. *Loss of the Self in Modern Literature and Art.* New York, 1962.

Theriot, Nancy M. *The Biosocial Construction of Femininity: Mothers and Daughters in Nineteenth-Century America.* New York, 1988.

Thrall, William Flint, and Addison Hibbard. Revised by C. Hugh Holman. *A Handbook to Literature.* New York, 1960.

Westerlund, Kerstin. *Escaping the Castle of Patriarchy: Patterns of Development in the Novels of Gail Godwin.* Uppsala, 1990.

White, Barbara A. *Growing Up Female: Adolescent Girlhood in American Fiction.* Westport, 1985.

Woodward, Kathleen. "May Sarton and Fictions of Old Age." In *Gender and Literary Voice,* edited by Janet Todd. New York, 1980.

Xie, Lihong, and Allan Kulikoff. "A Dialogue with Gail Godwin." *Mississippi Quarterly,* XLVI (1993), 167–84.

Index

Dialogic, xiv, 3, 12, 14–15, 106, 107–109, 122, 126–27, 146–58, 162, 168, 171, 193–94; and multiple voices, 134–35. *See also* Bakhtin, Mikhail

DuPlessis, Rachel Blau, 97, 123

Eliot, George, 67, 68–69; and George Henry Lewes, 86

Ellmann, Mary, 97

Empson, Dane. *See* Heroines; *The Perfectionists*

Empson, John. See *The Perfectionists*

Erikson, Erik, 201

Evolving self. *See* Self, search for centered

Fairy tales, 40–41

Family drama: in nuclear families, 146; and interplay of voices, 149–51, 158; daughter's duty in, 191, 209; and search for self, 221

Farley, Madelyn. See *Father Melancholy's Daughter*

Father Melancholy's Daughter, 13, 29–30, 198–223, 224–27; male characters in, 26, 216; Margaret Gower's search for self in, 198, 209–10; mother–daughter relationship in, 198–99, 211; father–daughter relationship in, 200, 212–17; child nurturing in, 201–203; Margaret Gower's

search to understand her absent mother Ruth in, 201, 205–206, 210–11; Ruth Gower's inner conflicts as rector's wife in, 202–10; Margaret Gower's relationships with Madelyn Farley in, 203–204, 221; Ruth Gower's absence and death in, 204–205, 208; and Nancy Drew mysteries with absent mother, 205, 211; Ruth Gower's artistry in, 207–209; Walter and Ruth Gower's marriage in, 207–208; Margaret Gower as her father's caretaker in, 212–17; Walter Gower's depression in, 213, 216; religion in, 216–19; Walter Gower's death in, 219, 221–22; Margaret Gower's love for Adrian Bonner in, 220; Margaret Gower's spiritual journey beyond nurturing in, 220–23

Father–daughter relationship, 200, 212–17, 220–23

Felski, Rita, 23–24

Female Bildungsroman. *See* Bildungsroman

Female Künstlerroman, 97–98, 111, 123

Female networks, 25, 71, 85, 189–93

Female victimization, 53–55

Feminism: in 1970s, 60–61, 66, 72; in *The Odd Woman,* 68; in South, 140–41; versus nurturing in 1980s, 213–16

(*Violet Clay*), 2, 28; in Gail God-
win's novels, 12–13, 15, 29, 47,
61–62, 64–65, 87, 93–94,
98–99, 109, 145, 224–27; Dane
Empson (*The Perfectionists*),
37–43; artists as, 97–98; in *A
Southern Family,* 191–92
Hill, Jane, 32, 60, 85, 122, 162
Hirsch, Marianne, 19, 20–21, 25,
75–76, 154
Holquist, Michael, 98–99
Humanism, xiii, 4–5, 6–7, 39

Identity. *See* Self, search for centered
Individualism, 4–5

Künstlerroman. *See* Bildungsroman

Lacan, Jacques, 6
Langland, Elizabeth, 19, 20–21, 25
Language, theories of, 5–6
Lazzaro-Weis, Carol, 23
Lee, Wickie. See *A Mother and Two
Daughters*
Lieberman, Marcia R., 41
Lorsch, Susan E., 69
"Love Story." *See* Sexuality

"Major-key" novels, 13, 28–29,
129, 132, 136, 154, 165–66
Male gaze, 49–54, 57–58
Marriage, xiii; and identity in Gail
Godwin's novels, 12, 27, 31,
139, 143–44; patriarchal or

egalitarian, 39, 78; and romantic
love, 40–42; as an oppressive institution, 44, 49, 53–54; and
madness, 55; as escape,
102–103; in *A Southern Family,*
180–81
Memory: and the evolving self, 71,
122–26; in *The Odd Woman,*
73, 83–93; in *Violet Clay,*
106–107; in *The Finishing
School,* 111, 118; suppression of,
in *The Finishing School,* 126–27;
and artistic energy in *The Finishing School,* 128; in *A Mother
and Two Daughters,* 134, 158; in
A Southern Family, 185; in *Father Melancholy's Daughter,* 199,
202–204, 209–10
Miles, David H., 18–19, 83–84
"Minor-key" novels, 12–13
Modernism, xiii, 4
Morgan, Ellen, 22
A Mother and Two Daughters, 13,
28–29, 132–66, 225; as family
drama, 133, 134; South in, 134;
Cate Strickland's existential self-
search in, 136–37; heroines in,
136; aging in, 137–38; Cate
Strickland's love affair with
Roger Jernigan, 137–38, 157;
Cate Strickland as rebellious
southern daughter in, 138–39;
Lydia Strickland as traditional
southern daughter in, 139; Lydia
Strickland's self-search as ac-

37–38; passivity as ideal in, 38–39; female victimization in, 43–46; sexuality in, 44–47; relationship between Dane and Robin Empson (stepson) in, 45–46, 47; Dane Empson's retreat into isolation and self–degradation in, 46–47; narrative strategies in, 47
Postmodern thought, 5
Pratt, Annis, 20, 23, 142–43

Quick, Theo. See *A Southern Family;* Suicide
Quick family. See *A Southern Family*

Religion in *Father Melancholy's Daughter,* 199–200; and church ladies' social role, 206–207; and golden Easter egg, 206, 208–209; and search for self, 210; and nurturing and spiritual quest, 216; and Walter Gower's Anglo-Catholicism, 216–18; and Passion Week, Easter, and the Christian year, 217–19; and corner statue of Christ, 218–19; and Walter Gower as Christ figure, 219
Rhodes, Carolyn, 77, 82, 139, 156
Russ, Joanna, 65

Self, search for centered, xiii–xiv; in Gail Godwin's novels, 1–3, 10,

13–15, 26–30, 32–36, 60–62, 95–96, 224–27; debates about, 3–10, 17; in *The Perfectionists,* 33–36; in *Glass People,* 55–56; in *The Odd Woman,* 67–71; in *Violet Clay,* 102–103, 106; in *The Finishing School,* 110–11, 114–15, 117, 125; in *A Mother and Two Daughters,* 135–45; and nuclear family, 146; and multiplicity of female identity, 154, 190–93; embedded in class conflict, 179, 189; among southern mountain people, 184–87; as socially determined, 198; in *Father Melancholy's Daughter,* 199–200, 209–10, 220–23
Separate spheres, 50
Sexuality: and idea of intercourse as violence or filth, 44–47; and male gaze, 58; and plot of "Love Story," 70, 86, 88, 92; and repressed southern womanhood, 78; physical, in *Violet Clay,* 104; in *The Finishing School,* 120; in *A Mother and Two Daughters,* 137, 140–41, 157; in *Father Melancholy's Daughter,* 209; and love in 1980s, 215
Showalter, Elaine, 30
Social networks, 162–66, 189–93
South as region, 100; in *The Finishing School,* 112–13; in *A Mother and Two Daughters,* 138, 148; social change in, 140–41; social

DATE DUE

MAY 19 1998			
GAYLORD			PRINTED IN U.S.A.